THOMAS H. BRIGGS

# *POETRY*

## *And Its Enjoyment*

**BUREAU OF PUBLICATIONS**

Teachers College, Columbia University, New York

## PREFACE

Retirement has given me leisure to present ideas on the enjoyment of poetry that have been accumulating through the years. As a student in secondary school and college I was often puzzled by conflicts between the judgment of "authorities" and my own honest opinions, conflicts that continued later as I became familiar with music and pictorial art.

All this eventually led to a novel definition of art, a definition which has helped me not only to greater enjoyment but also to a preservation and development of my own aesthetic integrity. I hope that it will likewise help others.

The definition that I present may on first reading seem too simple, but, as I try to show in the book, it has tremendous implications, not only for one's own appreciation but also for leading to an intelligent and confident enjoyment of all the arts. The same principles apply to understanding and enjoyment of music and painting.

> But strings, brass, drums are not music, nor a page,
> The piano lives when hands strike music forth,
> But is not music, nor theater voices on a stage,
> Nor a command an action, nor a compass north.
> There is no word unless a listener to the word
> Hears it, and with all his branching blood hears,
> And makes happen in space the thing he heard.*

\* John Holmes, "The Eleventh Commandment," Phi Beta Kappa Poem, Harvard University, 1956.

I am deeply indebted to authors and publishers who have granted me permission to use quotations, and I regret that because of limited space it is impossible to include a number of poems that would have been highly illuminating as further illustrations of points made.

T.H.B.

*Meredith, New Hampshire*

# ACKNOWLEDGMENTS

APPLETON-CENTURY-CROFTS, INC., publishers, for an excerpt from "Pullman Portraits" from *Narratives in Verse*, by Rose Comfort Mitchell, copyright, 1923, D. Appleton and Company, reprinted by permission of the publishers Appleton-Century-Crofts, Inc.; and for the poem "To Helen—Middle-Aged" from *Many Devices*, by Roselle Mercier Montgomery, copyright, 1929, D. Appleton and Company, reprinted by permission of the publishers, Appleton-Century-Crofts, Inc.

THE ATLANTIC MONTHLY for permission to quote from the article "From a Symphony Program" in *The Atlantic Monthly*, September, 1930.

MRS. MARJORIE FLACK BENÉT for permission to use an excerpt from "Skater of Ghost Lake," by William Rose Benét.

THE BOBBS-MERRILL COMPANY, INC., publishers, for permission to use "Bereaved" from *Poems Here at Home*, by J. W. Riley, published by The Bobbs-Merrill Company, Inc.

MRS. MADELEINE BOYD for permission to quote from "If Literary Critics Wrote Like Music Critics," by Ernest Boyd, published in *Harper's Magazine*, September, 1932.

WITTER BYNNER for permission to use "The Single Song" from *A Book of Love*, translated by Witter Bynner from the French of Charles Vildrac, published by E. P. Dutton and Company, Inc.; WITTER BYNNER and ALFRED A. KNOPF, INC., publishers, for "A Tent Song" from *Book of Lyrics*, by Witter Bynner, published by Alfred A. Knopf, Inc.

THE CHRISTIAN SCIENCE MONITOR and MARY BILLINGS for permission to use "Cabin in the Snow," by Mary Billings.

THE CLARENDON PRESS, publishers, for permission to use the poem "On a Dead Child," by Robert Bridges; and for permission to use selections from *Keats' Craftsmanship*, by M. R. Ridley.

COWARD-MCCANN, INC., publishers, for permission to use "Counters," reprinted from *Compass Rose*, by Elizabeth Coatsworth, copyright,

1929, by Coward-McCann, Inc., and excerpts from "A Lady Comes to an Inn" from *The Creaking Stair*, by Elizabeth Coatsworth, copyright, 1949, by Coward-McCann, Inc.

CURTIS BROWN, LTD., agents, for an excerpt from "I Do, I Will, I Have," by Ogden Nash, published in *The Saturday Evening Post* of May 8, 1948 and in *Versus;* copyright, 1948, by the Curtis Publishing Company; reprinted by permission of the author.

DODD, MEAD AND COMPANY, publishers, for excerpts from "Symbols," by John Drinkwater, and from "Wanderer's Song" and "Memory," by Arthur Symons; reprinted by permission of Dodd, Mead and Company, Inc.

DOUBLEDAY AND COMPANY, INC., publishers, for permission to use an excerpt from "Martin" from *Poems, Essays and Letters*, by Joyce Kilmer, copyright, 1914, 1917, 1918, by Doubleday and Company, Inc.; and for an excerpt from "Sestina of the Tramp Royal" from *The Seven Seas*, by Rudyard Kipling, reprinted by permission of Mrs. George Bambridge and Doubleday and Company, Inc.

GERALD DUCKWORTH AND COMPANY, LTD., publishers, for permission to use "Sea Love" from *Collected Poems*, by Charlotte Mew, published by Gerald Duckworth and Company, Ltd., in London, and The Macmillan Company in New York, 1953.

E. P. DUTTON AND COMPANY, INC., publishers, for permission to use an excerpt from "The Donkey" from the book *The Wild Knight and Other Poems*, by Gilbert K. Chesterton; published by E. P. Dutton and Company, Inc.

MRS. GLADYS FICKE for permission to use a sonnet from "The Middle Years" from *Selected Poems*, by Arthur Davison Ficke.

MRS. CHARLIE MAY FLETCHER for permission to quote from the Preface to *Japanese Prints*, by John Gould Fletcher.

HARCOURT, BRACE AND COMPANY, INC., publishers, for permission to use selections from *The Theory of Poetry*, by Lascelles Abercrombie, and from *Poets at Work*, by D. A. Stauffer; also, for four "Preludes" from *Collected Poems, 1909–1935*, by T. S. Eliot, copyright, 1936, by Harcourt, Brace and Company, Inc., and reprinted with their permission; for an excerpt from "The Swimmers" from *Selected Poems and Parodies of Louis Untermeyer*, copyright, 1935, by Harcourt, Brace and Company, Inc., and reprinted with their permission; and for "The Masters" from *Collected Poems of Margaret Widdemer*, copyright, 1928, by Harcourt, Brace and Company, Inc., and reprinted with their permission.

HARPER AND BROTHERS, publishers, for permission to quote the poem "The Day Will Bring Some Lovely Thing" from *Songs of Courage*, by Grace Noll Crowell.

GEORGE G. HARRAP AND COMPANY LTD., publishers, for quotations from *The Poems of Sir William Watson, 1878–1935*, published by George G. Harrap and Company Ltd., and reprinted by their permission.

HOGARTH PRESS, publishers, for permission to use selections from *The Medium of Poetry*, by James Sutherland.

JOHN HOLMES for the first stanza of Part III of "The Eleventh Commandment," by John Holmes, Phi Beta Kappa poem, Harvard University, 1956.

HENRY HOLT AND COMPANY, INC., publishers, for permission to use selections from *English Verse*, by Raymond M. Alden, published by Henry Holt and Company, Inc.; for permission to use a selection from the Introduction, by Robert Frost, to *Complete Poems of Robert Frost;* and for "Cool Tombs" from *Cornhuskers*, by Carl Sandburg, copyright, 1918, by Henry Holt and Company, copyright, 1946, by Carl Sandburg, by permission of the publishers.

HOUGHTON MIFFLIN COMPANY, publishers, for permission to use the following: an excerpt from "Appreciation," by Thomas B. Aldrich, originally appearing in *Poems;* an excerpt from "Songs for My Mother: Her Words," by Anna Hempstead Branch; the poem "How the Helpmate of Blue-Beard Made Free with a Door," by Guy Wetmore Carryl; an excerpt from "A Lady," by Amy Lowell; excerpts from "Gloucester Moors" and "The Menagerie," by William Vaughn Moody; and for the poem "May," by Frank Dempster Sherman. All of the foregoing were published by Houghton Mifflin Company.

ALFRED A. KNOPF, INC., publishers, for "The Guarded Wound," "Triad," and "Dirge," reprinted from *Verse*, by Adelaide Crapsey, by permission of Alfred A. Knopf, Inc., copyright, 1915, by Algernon S. Crapsey, copyright, 1934, by Adelaide Crapsey; and for prose selections reprinted from *Music for the Man Who Enjoys Hamlet*, by B. H. Haggin, and from *A Musical Motley*, by Ernest Newman, by permission of Alfred A. Knopf, Inc.

JOHN LANE THE BODLEY HEAD LIMITED, publishers, and STEPHEN PHILLIPS for permission to use excerpts from "Marpessa" and "Marsyas," by Stephen Phillips, published by John Lane The Bodley Head Limited.

N. R. LEAVITT, Trustee of the Estate of Theodosia P. Faulks, for permission to use "Love Song" from *The Dreamers and Other Poems* and "The Tears of Harlequin" from *Joy o' Life*, by Theodosia Garrison.

LITTLE, BROWN AND COMPANY, publishers, for permission to use poems by Emily Dickinson; and for "Very Like a Whale," by Ogden Nash, by permission of Little, Brown and Company, copyright, 1935, by Ogden Nash.

HUGH MacDIARMID for permission to use an excerpt from his poem "Cattle Show."

THE MACMILLAN COMPANY, publishers, for permission to use the following: an excerpt from "Crystal Moment" from *Collected Poems*, by Robert P. Tristram Coffin; a quotation from the Preface by T. S. Eliot to *Selected Poems*, by Marianne Moore; an excerpt from *Kallyope Yell*, by Vachel Lindsay; an excerpt from "Spanish Waters" from *Collected Poems*, by John Masefield; and for selections from *Collected Poems*, by Sara Teasdale.

VIRGIL MARKHAM for "Lincoln, the Man of the People," by Edwin Markham, reprinted by permission of Virgil Markham.

MRS. ELLEN C. MASTERS for permission to use excerpts from *The Great Valley* and from *The Spoon River Anthology*, by Edgar Lee Masters, published by The Macmillan Company.

HUGHES MEARNS for permission to use "The Door Stands Open," by Wynne Fairchild, reprinted from *Creative Youth*, by Hughes Mearns, Doubleday and Company, New York; and for permission to use "Youth," by Aline Wechsler Liebman, from *Creative Power*, by Hughes Mearns, Doubleday and Company, New York.

G. AND C. MERRIAM COMPANY, publishers, and STEPHEN L. MOONEY for selections from "New Devices in Sound Repetition," by Stephen L. Mooney, and comment from *Word Study*, copyright, 1949, by G. and C. Merriam Company, publishers of the Merriam-Webster Dictionaries. Reprinted by permission.

MRS. ALIDA MONRO and GERALD DUCKWORTH AND COMPANY, LTD., publishers, for permission to use the poem "Solitude" from *Collected Poems*, by Harold Monro.

DAVID MORTON and G. P. PUTNAM'S SONS, publishers, for permission to use the poem "Lover to Lover," by David Morton.

NEW DIRECTIONS, publishers, for permission to use "The Raid" from *The Residual Years*, by William Everson.

OXFORD UNIVERSITY PRESS, publishers, for permission to use the poem "Pied Beauty," by Gerard Manley Hopkins; for permission to summarize a section on Keats in *The Poetic Image*, by C. Day Lewis, published by Oxford University Press, 1947; and for permission to use a selection from *Studies in Keats*, by John Middleton Murry.

NORMAN HOLMES PEARSON for the poems "Night" and "Storm" from the *Collected Poems of H(ilda) D(oolittle)*. By permission of Norman Holmes Pearson and the author.

LEROY P. PERCY for permission to use the poem "Overtones" and an excerpt from "The Unloved to His Beloved," by William Alexander Percy.

A. D. PETERS, author's representative, for permission to use a short quotation from C. Day Lewis.

RANDOM HOUSE, INC., publishers, for permission to use excerpts from the poems of W. H. Auden and a passage from the Introduction, by W. H. Auden, to his *Collected Poems*.

HENRY REGNERY COMPANY, publishers, for permission to use a selection from *Achievement in American Poetry*, by Louise Bogan, published by Henry Regnery Company, 1951.

RINEHART AND COMPANY, publishers, for permission to use an excerpt from "The General Public" from *Ballads and Poems, 1915–1930,* by Stephen Vincent Benét, published by Rinehart and Company, Inc.; and for "Exit" and "The Windmills" from *Selected Poems,* by John Gould Fletcher, copyright, 1938, by John Gould Fletcher, reprinted by permission of Rinehart and Company, Inc., New York, Publishers.

ALICE HENDERSON ROSSIN, trustee for Alice Corbin Henderson, for permission to use an excerpt from "Una Anciana Mexicana" from *Red Earth,* by Alice Corbin, published 1920.

SAINT MARTIN'S PRESS, INC., publishers, for permission to use an excerpt from "Horses," by Dorothy Wellesley; Saint Martin's Press and The Society of Authors for an excerpt from "Introit," by Katherine Tynan, reprinted by permission of The Society of Authors and Miss Pamela Hinkson.

CHARLES SCRIBNER'S SONS, publishers, for permission to use an excerpt from "Richard Cory" from *The Town Down the River,* by Edwin Arlington Robinson, published by Charles Scribner's Sons.

MARTHA HALE SHACKFORD and THE ATLANTIC MONTHLY for permission to use the poem "In Memoriam—Leo: A Yellow Cat," by Margaret Sherwood, originally published by *The Atlantic Monthly,* February, 1913.

THE SOCIETY OF AUTHORS for an excerpt from *Epigrams of Art, Life and Nature,* by William Watson, reprinted by permission of The Society of Authors as the Literary Representative of the late Sir William Watson.

TEACHERS COLLEGE BUREAU OF PUBLICATIONS, publishers, for permission to use exercises from the test *Appreciation of Poetry,* by Allan Abbott and M. R. Trabue.

UNIVERSITY OF GEORGIA PRESS, publishers, for permission to use a selection from *Music and Literature,* by Calvin S. Brown.

JOHN HALL WHEELOCK and CHARLES SCRIBNER'S SONS, publishers, for permission to quote the poem "I do not love to see your beauty fire" from *Dust and Light,* by John Hall Wheelock, copyright, 1919, by Charles Scribner's Sons.

MARGARET WIDDEMER for permission to quote the poem "De Senectute," by Margaret Widdemer.

DENYS WORTMAN for permission to use his cartoon "Every Day Movies," which appeared through the United Feature Syndicate, September 14, 1933.

# CONTENTS

# PART ONE

## *Poetry: What It Is and What It Does*

## Chapter One

# THE PUZZLED AMATEUR

THERE is a vein of sentiment in everybody. However stolid a person may seem or at times feel, he has his moments of radiant joy, of exaltation, of poignant grief that often lies too deep for tears, of crushing tragedy that frees the perfume of personality, and of yearning for beauty or comfort. But for the most, these moments are evanescent, becoming more and more rare as maturity freezes life into conventional confines. As Coventry Patmore wrote in "The Angel in the House,"

> Love wakes men, once a lifetime each;
> They raise their heavy lids and look;
> And, lo, what one sweet page can teach
> They read with joy, then shut the book.

After that moment, however often repeated for the sensitive, man is likely to go through the commonplace world with a yearning, by many only dimly felt, for beauty of sight or sound, for the inexpressible, for a glimpse of the light that never was on land or sea, for the echo of the inaudible, for the faint sweet perfume from the garden of some never-realized Juliet, or for a caress from the white hand of an imagined Isolt. Some are sensitive and expectant, senses alert for possibilities of beauty, of joy, of romance. They keep

3

the strings of the heart attuned for the chord that some experience may strike. Though often disappointed, they never
despair. As H. G. Wells wrote of his hero in *The Research
Magnificent*, ". . . he never faltered in his persuasion that
behind the dingy face of this world, the earthly stubbornness,
the baseness and drabness of himself and all of us, lurked the
living jewel of heaven, the light of glory, of things unspeak-
able."

Grace Noll Crowell has expressed the optimism of the seeking heart.

> "The day will bring some lovely thing,"
> I say it over each new dawn;
> "Some gay adventurous thing to hold
> Against my heart when it is gone."
> And so I rise and go to meet
> The day, with wings upon my feet.
>
> I come upon it unawares,
> Some sudden beauty without name,
> A snatch of song, a breath of pine—
> A poem lit with golden flame;
> High tangled bird notes keenly thinned
> Like flying colors on the wind.
>
> No day has ever failed me quite.
> Before the grayest day is done
> I find some misty purple bloom
> Or a late line of crimson sun.
> Each night I pause, remembering
> Some gay, adventurous, lovely thing.

And Sara Teasdale has told how small a thing can bring
loveliness to the one who seeks it.

> Stars over snow,
>     And in the west a planet
> Swinging below a star—
>     Look for the lovely thing and you will find it.
> It is not far—
>     It never will be far.

The feelings of all people are fundamentally alike; their sorrows and their joys and their yearnings are the same. And for that reason art in its various forms can stir all if they open their minds and their hearts and if they learn to interpret and respond to its varied language. In his translation from the French poem by Charles Vildrac, Witter Bynner, long eminent in American letters, has emphasized the communality of feeling and its response to song.

## THE SINGLE SONG

Tonight in the lumbering emptiness of his cart,
A waggoner is quiet again;

A hundred leagues away, a great lord
Roams his great park all alone;

And I know a shopkeeper in town
Crouched at the rear of his gloomy shop.

This is the moment when they take advantage, all three,
Of being alone, and of the evening,
To cringe with twisted lips
And to feel the tears roll down their faces,
Each of them thinking of his dead child.

From lights on the way
And from other vehicles and passers-by,
The waggoner hides under his hat
Amid the hubbub . . .

The great lord, turning aside from the lawns
Where remnants of light
Gather and stare and startle him,
Chooses the blackest paths . . .

And the shopkeeper puts off a little longer
The moment for lighting his window and his eyes.
Yet, if they were here this evening, these three men
Who do not wear the same clothes,
Nor eat the same food,

Nor talk in the same fashion,
Who do not know the same houses
Nor the same women,

If they were here, all three, this evening,
Seated on a bench behind you in the shadow,
And you should sing to them
That song, say, of the man who walks gently,
Who goes with his feet in the water and his shoulders bare,
Through the bitter-blowing night-air,
But who blessedly shelters the eyes
Of his little child,
Whom he carries cradled from the storm,
Rolled in his great coat,
Asleep and warm,

If you sang that song for these three men,
O you who know the language
Which finds and reaches in their nakedness
The men and the women with whom you are
Upon the earth,

If you sang that song without turning your head
—Because of eyes and of shyness—
Might you not hear
The stifled sound of only one sob?

If an actual experience does not come to stir emotions or
to satisfy yearnings, we are pleased by vicarious release from
the monotony of life. We read of old unhappy far-off things
and battles long ago; we catch awakening suggestions from
the lyrics of Burns, Heine, or maybe Edgar Guest; for an
hour we live a different life in a drama by Shakespeare or
Euripides, in a novel by George Eliot or Thackeray or a more
recent teller of tales; we see beauty in the paintings of Monet
and Sisley or strength in the statues of Michelangelo and
Rodin; and we feel that somehow Beethoven and Wagner
and Verdi are expressing for us what we have felt and could
not say. Sometimes an exact word, a perfect phrase, a theme
in music, a harmony of line and color will free us from the

accustomed and launch us imaginatively into the beauty for which we all have a longing and a hope.

However dormant sentiment may become, it responds to experiences, actual or presented vicariously through art. But unless constantly exercised, sentiment becomes dulled and when occasion calls it out it comes sluggishly and has disappointing means of expression. That is one reason why we need to make a wide acquaintance with the arts—music and poetry especially—for they can often express for us what we feel and have no skill to say.

There is a natural, though often not conscious, desire, even a yearning, for emotional experiences—experiences that call forth the better part of human nature. As they are infrequent in the humdrum routine of life, we turn to art for the vicarious stirring of the emotions. And of all the arts, poetry better than any other performs this service. It is more moving than painting or sculpture or architecture, and more definitely satisfying than music.

Probably the majority of our young people come out of school with a feeling that in order to become "cultured" they should listen to great music, become familiar with great paintings, and read great literature. Some continue to cultivate these acquaintances, with a continued growth in richness of life; but many drop their ambitions, and with a suddenness that should disturb their former instructors. Why do they turn from the road that has led many to a fullness of appreciation and enjoyment of life? The causes are no doubt varied, but one is fairly common; they have never learned what art is, or have developed no means of understanding and enjoying it. Consequently their tastes are uncertain and their reactions lacking in satisfactions that impel them forward in a search for the grail.

When we find that after school compulsions cease, the "classics" of music, painting, and literature are abandoned for the superficial tunes that merely move the feet to rhythm, humorous cartoons more eagerly looked at than the wonderful colored reproductions of Rembrandt, Corot, and Constable, and magazines read and forgotten while Keats, Poe, and Hawthorne accumulate undisturbed dust, we are rightly disturbed because so many people are limiting their possibilities of sharing in the larger life of understanding and beauty. It may be argued that the reading of great literature is forwarded most by developed interests that come in maturity. Certainly many have learned as adults to love it, and a not inconsiderable number of young people continue to follow the gleam that awakened them to infinite possibilities.

There is objective evidence that teaching of the arts has been less effective than is desirable. Drought has reported that when nine sets of five drawings prepared by experts to illustrate variables in perfection of unity, proportion, congruity, and harmony were presented to educated adults, they selected the best in only one half of their judgments, and that there was a wide range in their rankings. Another study, in a junior high school, showed that of five designs the pupils ranked as best the one that a group of experts judged mediocre, and that the one considered best by the experts, the pupils ranked third.

An experiment with poetry showed similarly disappointing results. Professor Allan Abbott wrote for twenty-six selected poems or passages from classics, three parodies.[2] In lowering the quality of each poem he attempted "in one version (called 'sentimental') to falsify the emotion by introducing silly, gushy, affected, or otherwise insincere feelings; in another version (the 'prosaic') to reduce the poet's imagery to a more pedestrian and commonplace level; in a third (the 'metrical') to render the movement either entirely awkward or less fine and subtle than the original."

Following is the set of four versions, the original and the three parodies, of a poem by Leigh Hunt. In parentheses are the per cents of high school seniors, of college juniors and seniors, and of graduate students in English who judged each version best.

## A (49.3; 35.1; 23.8)

Jenny kissed me when we met,
  She was very glad to meet me;
And I never could regret
  Such a pleasant way to greet me.
Sometimes when I'm feeling blue
  And think that all good things have missed me,
I can say, still it is true
  Jenny kissed me.

## B (13.7; 5.0; 5.4)

Jenny kissed me on the cheek
  With her lips as soft as satin;
In my diary for the week
  You just bet that I'll put that in!
I am getting old and fat,
  Kisses,—ah, how I have missed them!
But my cheeks remember that
  Jenny kissed me.

## C (27.1; 55.4; 64.0)

Jenny kissed me when we met,
  Jumping from the chair she sat in;
Time, you thief, who love to get
  Sweets into your list, put that in!
Say I'm weary, say I'm sad,
  Say that health and wealth have missed me,
Say I'm growing old, but add,
  Jenny kissed me.

## D (9.9; 4.5; 6.9)

Jenny kissed me as I sat,
  Rising from the chair in which she sat.
Time, you robber, who like to get
  Tidbits down in your book, put in that!
Say that I'm weary and sad,
  Say that health and wealth have missed me,
Say I'm an old man, but add
  Jenny kissed me.

These sets of versions were presented to some 3500 judges, ranging from the fifth grade in the elementary school to and including university graduate students in English. The resulting evidence of a lack of unanimity and of sound taste in judging poetry is appalling, as can be seen by examining the figures given in parentheses. Even the elevated passage from Milton's "Paradise Lost" beginning

> Let there be light, said God, and forthwith Light
> Ethereal, first of things, quintessence pure,
> Sprung from the Deep. . . .

was judged superior to the parodies by only 19.3 per cent of high school seniors, by 29.2 per cent of senior students in college, and by 44.8 per cent of graduate students. For the entire set used in the test, it is not until college classes are reached that half of the judgments of a class are right as to which version is best.

Such studies and common observation as well show that there is need of a better conception of what art is and of a pattern that can be used in coming to sincere and sound judgments, which alone are a firm foundation on which to build an aesthetic appreciation that will continue, grow, and contribute pleasure as long as life lasts. This book will attempt to give a practical definition of art and to show how it can be used to develop sound judgments and increased pleasure from the reading of poetry.

In our schools there are brilliant successes in teaching young people to understand and to enjoy poetry of this and all previous ages. However, there is also much pedestrian instruction which not only fails to achieve a continuing interest but even sets up hostilities that prevent later independent exploration, discovery, and growth. A genuine love for poetry is inculcated best probably by the contagious passion that inspires a real teacher. It takes fire to kindle fire. And probably nothing else sets young people against poetry so much as a meticulous emphasis on details without appreciation of how each one contributes to the whole effect. As will be emphasized later, each work of art is a unit, all the parts of which articulate to build up a pleasing whole. It not infrequently happens that poems assigned for study contain so many unusual words and constructions, so many references and allusions, that they require literally a translation before appreciation is possible. This exercise undoubtedly does something to build up a vocabulary and to prepare a background for the understanding of future references; but often it fails to create enthusiasm for the poem under consideration. It may safely be asserted that it fails to result in appreciation unless the details are related to the whole, with unremitting emphasis on the central thought and the central emotion that the artist has attempted to convey. Some details, but not all, must be accurately and exactly known, of course; but all are effective only if they are seen to contribute, directly or indirectly, to the total effect. Translation into simple language may be essential as a beginning, but it is not sufficient. Pupils will

> See the sun, the cloud
> But not the spring.

Appreciation is also inhibited by overemphasis on technical details, such as meter, stanza form, and figures of speech, without a realization of how essential each is to the conveyance of the poet's feeling. Teaching them apart from their contribution to the total effect is like examining the bricks and the structure of a house to appreciate architecture, concentrating on the sharps and flats and the modulations from key to key to enjoy music, or examining brush strokes and the thickness of pigment to understand a painting.

Overemphasis is frequently given to biographies and to social background. The biographies of many poets are dramatically interesting and in some cases highly contributory to appreciation of their works. It is true that Chatterton died tragically by his own hand, that Keats had consumption, that

Byron led a profligate life, that Shakespeare married Anne Hathaway, that Wordsworth at one period was intrigued by the French Revolution, and that Pope proposed marriage to Lady Mary Wortley Montague, who introduced into England inoculation against smallpox. But in learning to love poetry, how is one inspired by such isolated facts? In themselves they make no contribution, however important they may be in general cultural education. Some biographical facts are important for appreciation, but only if they are related to the poems studied. The bitter venom in Pope's poems is understood if one knows certain facts of his life and the background against which he wrote; and Keats's last sonnet, "Would I were steadfast as thou art," gains pathos if one knows that it was written as he set out on the voyage that ended in his death. Lyly, Peele, Greene, Nash, and other frequenters of the Mermaid Tavern could not have written their lovely lyrics during the Puritan period, nor could the naughty Cavalier dramatists have published them; and one must know something of New England, where Whittier wrote, to appreciate his "Snow-Bound" and his anti-slavery poems. "Comus" is likely to bore a reader who does not know what a masque was and its place in aristocratic entertainment during the mid-seventeenth century. Much of Aristophanes is meaningless to one who does not know the political and social Athens of his day, and likewise most of the humor of Will Rogers has no point now that the incidents which he satirized are forgotten. Biography and social background, then, must be related to poems if they are to add to understanding and appreciation.

A. E. Housman asserted that "most readers, when they think that they are admiring poetry, are deceived by inability to analyze their sensations; they are really admiring not the poetry of the passage before them but something else in it, which they like better than poetry." This "something else," often overemphasized in school teaching, is usually an idea—religious, moral, or philosophic—that a poet has chosen to present artistically. It may be interesting and important, whether expressed in verse or in prose. But it would not have been expressed in verse unless the poet had felt that he could contribute by his art some emotional effect that prose could not achieve. It would be perfectly proper to present a certain group of Browning's poems—"Caliban on Setebos," "Saul," "Cleon," "Rabbi Ben Ezra," "A Death in the Desert," and "Christmas-Eve and Easter-Day"—as evidencing ways in which men have sought or found God. But if the artistic means that are used in the presentation and the results that are peculiarly achieved are not emphasized, the reading might almost as well be of Sunday school leaflets; there will be no addition to the foundation for building appreciation of poetry. Not all the riches of thought will atone for a poverty of style, nor will any beauties of style atone for a paucity of thought. There may be no meaning added to a thought by the way it is put, but there certainly can be more power added to it. As Swift wrote,

Truth shines the brighter clad in verse,
And all the fictions they pursue
Do but insinuate what is true.

It is a difficult task that a teacher of poetry has. Day after day he presents poems that inevitably vary in content, in style, in background, in pertinence to young people's immediate interests, and also in the values that the teacher himself sets upon them. His challenge is to get each poem understood and enjoyed. Every student will bring to it a different background, a different mood, and a different attitude; and in consequence each one will have a different initial reaction. To admit that the poem of the day is inferior to the one considered yesterday is to set up an obstacle to getting such enjoyment as it may give; and yet it is absurd to assume that all poems are equally good—in general or especially in the situation in which they are considered. Responses will be infinitely varied. If honest responses are not respected and if sincerity of expression is not encouraged, the result will inevitably be bad and will cumulatively become worse. A teacher who professes to like equally well every assigned poem, who attempts the same enthusiasm day after day, will fail, as he should fail, because perspicacious youth will detect the sham and discredit expressions of praise. Sincerity is demanded of teacher as well as of students. And appreciative enjoyment will most assuredly come from concentration on merits rather than on defects.

It is all very well for amateurs to consider, and to consider hospitably, what "authorities" have written about poems. But to accept their judgments uncritically is the worst possible habit that a person can develop. He will be confused when he finds that "authorities" differ, and then he will be, or he should be, forced to a judgment of his own—or he will abandon the poem as not worth more of his time. One of the best things that an amateur can learn is that he has as much right to his own judgment as any other person has, and that respect for his own judgment is the only sound foundation for the development of taste and enjoyment. In appreciating the arts there is no substitute for sincerity. Of course one should respect the opinions of critics of long experience, and he should seek their reasons and consider their cogency. Likewise he should attempt to give definite reasons, which is not always easy, for his own judgments.

As he has presented to him a series of poems from the earliest times to the present, a person is often puzzled by changes in the style of expression. Naturally one style will appeal to him more than another, but his challenge is to learn to appreciate each against a background of the time in which it was used. He should understand that some "classics" are important today chiefly in a historical sense because they made possible later achievements. He will agree with Addison, who wrote of Spenser

But now the mystic tale that pleased of yore
Can charm our understanding age no more.

He may not read with any genuine pleasure much of the "Faerie Queene," but he can be made appreciative of it if he realizes how it made possible later poetic "tales" that he will enjoy. Great harm is done to amateurs when they are told that they should thrill to Beowulf or Spenser or be enthralled by "The Spectator Papers" or by "Comus" when teachers themselves seldom, if ever, reread them for their own pleasure. A cynic remarked, "If I found a friend reading Dryden, I'd be confident that he was boning up to help his daughter who is in high school." The "classics" do have superiorities to much that young people naturally enjoy, but appreciation is more likely to come after wide reading in literature has developed canons of taste and after maturity has brought a new sense of values. A measuring rod of growth is furnished by the pleasure that one ultimately gets from the poetry that has won the accolade of the ages.

Styles change and tastes change, often slowly and reluctantly. Music by Wagner was hissed when first performed, and that of Shostakovich is by many ridiculed today; the paintings by Fra Lippo Lippi amused and then aroused to protest in the early sixteenth century as those by Dali do in our generation. Some innovations prove their worth and persist; many are abortions that soon perish.

Artists in words, like those in sound, color, and form, climb on the shoulders of those who have gone before them, and always there are "praisers of the past" who attempt to pull down the adventurous. To get pleasure from the art of the past one must understand and accept its conventions—the stiff profiles of ancient Egyptian paintings, the wood-shaving curls and blank eyes of Greek statues, the gold backgrounds and unnaturally mature infants in Italian primitive Madonna pictures. Listen to the Decca records in "Two Thousand Years of Music," to the music of Monteverdi and the other early contrapuntalists, to that of Gluck, Mozart, Beethoven, Wagner, Debussy, and the moderns, and you will realize something of the shock that each innovator brought to listeners and to music lovers of the past. Giotto was not generally praised when he introduced natural scenery into religious paintings, a novelty that found beautiful culmination in the landscape seen beyond the Crucifixion, by Perugino. Fra Lippo Lippi was all but excommunicated because he made his saints real people, but he prepared the way for the lovely human Virgins of Mainardi and Raphael. Follow the development of landscape painting from decorative background to presentation for its own moving loveliness by the Barbizon painters and you will learn something of how each generation moves forward, adapting and improving on the good that adventurers invented and discarding that which did not prove its worth. Styles change, and each work of art should be judged by the canons of its own period as well as by the effects that it had on later productions.

In poetry we have passed from style to style, in subject matter as well as in methods of expression. Reading an anthology with historical arrangements, we find courtly elegance, pretty artificiality, religious sentiment (simple and elevated), cold intellectual brilliance, homely incidents and characters presented in professedly "natural" diction, romance, imaginative treatment of science, and elaborate playing with language—each type adding something to the moving stream of literary art. But each novelty has met opposition, gibes, and at least temporary rejection. The ridicule of Wordsworth is a notable illustration, and one famous critic wrote of Kipling's verses, "clever rhymes, . . . for the most part comic, often grotesque, sometimes terrible, but poetry? Pooh!" Yet there are many people who accept "The Barrack Room Ballads" as poetry, and few would omit the "Recessional" from a golden treasury.

Recognizing the habit of critics to condemn every novelty in art, Kipling wrote his scathing verses that begin

> When the flush of a new-born sun fell first on Eden's green
>    and gold,

Our father Adam sat under a tree and scratched with a stick in
  the mould
And the first rude sketch the world had seen was joy to his
  mighty heart
Till the Devil whispered behind the leaves, "It's pretty, but is
  it Art?"

The amateur is puzzled, too, when without prejudice and
without awe of famous names he reads extensively in the
works of famous authors. For inevitably he finds much that
falls far short of the samples that he has been taught to revere.
Schools select *Macbeth* and *The Merchant of Venice* and
Shelley's "Ode to the West Wind" to teach, and then young
people are disappointed when independently they attempt
*Timon of Athens* and "Queen Mab." Every painter uses
his brush to present what he feels when he perceives beauty,
but the tedious process of developing a picture apparently
discourages him from completing, or at most exhibiting, the
least worthy of his canvases. That is peculiarly true of the
great painters of the past. Vermeer did only his thirty pictures of jeweled light, and even in the multitudinous pictures
by Rembrandt there is none that is contemptible. The self-
critical faculty of the painter is fairly high; that of the poet
is often sadly low.

A poet is constantly alert to the world about him, to what
he sees and hears, to the thoughts that pop up in his mind,
to the feelings that move him, deeply or feebly, "always
roaming with a hungry heart" searching for the beautiful and
the true. And, being an artist, he has "an itch, a tang" to
write. Sometimes what seems to him beautiful and worthy
is not really so to others; sometimes he fails to penetrate to
real significance; and sometimes he fails to find the technical
means of conveying his feelings convincingly. Leaf through
the complete works of even our great poets and you are likely
to find verses that are commonplace or worse, even fragments
which paternal pride could not consent to destroy. By and

large, poets are poor critics of their own work. Many a reputation would be higher if from all composition there were preserved only, as Matthew Arnold said of the poems of Keats, what is worthy of being bound in pure gold.

One can understand how in his attempts to present the beautiful and the noble a poet writes much that fails to convey his feelings to others, but it is difficult to understand how the author of "Paradise Lost" could retain

> A while discourse they hold,
> No fear lest dinner cool,

or the poet who wrote "Tintern Abbey" and "Intimations of Immortality" could consent to publish

> A Household Tub, like one of those
> Which women use to wash their clothes.

Wordsworth is often quoted in ridicule for sounding the depths of bathos and for using language that is far from evoking tender feelings, but other poets who have written enduring masterpieces can be cited as having poor judgment of what is aesthetically successful. Byron, one of the most caustic critics in the history of literature, was also one of the most erratic in his production. In the "Hebrew Melodies" we find "She walks in beauty like the night" and "The Assyrian came down like a wolf on the fold," once popular as a "reading" because of its powerful rhythm and its exotic figures of speech; but we also find the weak "The harp the monarch minstrel swept."

Preceding two justly famous passages in "Childe Harold's Pilgrimage"—"There is a pleasure in the pathless woods" and "Roll on, thou deep and dark blue ocean, roll!"—Byron wrote the awkward

> Ye elements!—in whose ennobling stir
> I feel myself exalted—Can ye not
> Accord me such a being? Do I err
> In deeming such inhabit many a spot,
> Though with them to converse can rarely be our lot?

And in "Oscar of Alna" we find

> Yes, on some desert rocky shore
> My Oscar's whitened bones must lie;
> Then grant, thou God! I ask no more,
> With him his frantic sire may die!

These quotations of doggerel from Byron are presented partly because they are examples of the depths to which a great poet can descend and partly because he was so vicious, and oftentimes devastating, in his criticism of others. After having personally met Southey, who had been the object of some of his bitterest barbs in "English Bards and Scotch Reviewers," in "Hints from Horace," and in "A Vision of Judgment," he reversed himself and declared the laureate's "Don Roderick" "the finest poem of our time," a judgment that posterity has been far from confirming.

From an examination of the works of almost any poet one could cull a collection of verses that would justly deserve an F in English A, verses such as

> And Jennie was large for fifteen years

> Princely offspring of Braganza,
> Erin greets thee with a stanza.

> Of Nebuchadnezzar it was said that he
> Sighed as he munched the unaccustomed food,
> "It may be wholesome, but it is not good."

The fact that poets have been such poor judges of the worth of their own verses, that they have often regarded their poorest production with the fondness which parents are said to feel for their least favored offspring is one compelling reason why amateurs should rid themselves of awe of great names, learn a pattern of appreciation, and develop a fearless independence based upon sincerity which will lead to aesthetic integrity and growth. Without this they are likely to achieve vague pleasure which is too lacking in satisfaction to stimulate continued excursions into the realms of richness.

Taught to rely on "authorities" instead of their own judgments and confused by changes in style and by variations in merit in the product of revered poets, young people—all people, for that matter—need a conception of what is essential in art, a simple, convincing definition that will give them a pattern for reading poetry and will permit intelligent enjoyment of what they like and rejection of what they do not like, with preservation of sincerity and self-respect. Such a definition and such patterns will be presented in this book.

## Chapter Two

# A HELPFUL CONCEPT OF ART

WHEN a person really begins to think for himself about art, he is confronted by a number of confusing facts. First of all, he realizes that what is generally called art is expressed in several different media—in music, painting, sculpture, architecture, artifacts, and literature, both prose and poetry; and he realizes further that expressions in each of these media range from great art down to a point at which they are approved only by the lowest taste. There must be some common element in all art, he is assured; but what is it?

In each medium there is, as everyone knows, great variety. In music one hears the solemn funeral march in "Die Götterdämmerung" and the Brahms "Wiegenlied," the lovely melodies of Rossini, Verdi, and Puccini, and the technically complex contrapuntal compositions of Palestrina, Lassus, Byrd, and Bach, the tunefulness of Mozart and the cacophonies of Prokofief. The paintings by Cimabue, Duccio, and Lorenzetti, which moved the early Italians to public celebration and to worship, are today interesting historically, later admiration turning to the canvases of Titian, Raphael, Rembrandt, Corot, and Monet. Sculpture ranges from Michelangelo's massive "Moses" to Bernini's delicate "Daphne," Houdon's smiling children, Rude's stirring "Marseillaise," and the horrible Imp

21

on the Lincoln Cathedral. Architecture is Byzantine, Greek, Gothic, Colonial, and Frank Lloyd Wright. And in poetry critics praise "the organ voice of Milton," the lyrics of Lyly, the biting intellectualism of Pope, the mysticism of Blake, the philosophy of Browning, the elegance of Tennyson, the music of Swinburne, and the rough strength of Whitman. It is no wonder that the question "What is art?" continues to be asked.

The answer is not made easier by the changes in style from nation to nation and from time to time. The plain song gave way to the horizontal music of melody and the vertical music of harmony, and then architectonic structure, increasingly complex, became the dominant element. Oriental pentatonic music sounds as strange to our ears as our music sounds to the Chinese. The gold background and halos for holy characters disappeared from ecclesiastical paintings, and the Christ child became a human infant interested in ball or bird or fruit.

In poetry, fashion has approved mediaeval romances with their affected praise of Dulcineas, the cosmopolitan products of the Elizabethans, the wit and artificiality of the unmoral Carlovingians, the reverence of lowly folk by the Romanticists, and so on. In style we find similar changes: the strong, direct verse of Chaucer, the varied verse forms of Marlowe, Peele, Nash, Herrick, Donne, and Suckling, the acrostics and anagrams and verses printed in the form of altars and wings, blank verse, rhymed couplets, and free verse. Today we read experiments in "polyphonic prose," in verses printed with no punctuation, no capital letters at the beginning of lines, no indicated stanzas, and, at least to some readers, with no sense or sentiment. What, then, is the essential characteristic of art, enduring from age to age and persisting through every change of style?

It is confusing to realize how reactions, even by critics of the highest reputation, differ. Novelty always brings a chorus of condemnation. On being shown Cezanne's portrait of his sister, Whistler, who had not escaped criticism for his own novelties, remarked, "If a child of ten had drawn this upon his slate, his mother—if she were a good mother—would have spanked him." Beethoven was soundly rated when he substituted a scherzo for a minuet as the third movement of a symphony and also when he introduced the melodic drum. The award by a jury of contemporary poets of the Bollingen prize to Ezra Pound's *Pisan Cantos* created a nationwide uproar. There is, of course, disagreement about the works of all artists.

> One man loves what I hate,
> Hates what I love.

The old saying that there can be no disputing of tastes may be comforting in a way, but it gives no direction to one's seeking to know what art is.

Memory, enforced by marked passages in books, testifies that our tastes change. In childhood we chanted with keen delight the Mother Goose rhymes; in adolescence we thrilled to

> Tell me not in mournful numbers
> Life is but an empty dream,

which in maturity we recall with an apologetic smile. "Some poems," said Drew, "we outlive very quickly; some we grow to slowly; some step along life with us and are emotionally and intellectually inexhaustible like life itself." Can it be that there is an art for childhood and an art for maturity, as there are different arts for the several nations and ages?

Even more disturbing to one who attempts to get a valid concept of art is the fact that in one mood or environment we crave and enjoy something to which in another mood or environment we respond quite differently. This morning my mood is for Edward Lear's limericks and I pull down from the shelf Gilbert's libretti for Sullivan's rollicking tunes; this afternoon I relax with Wordsworth and Beethoven's Pastoral symphony; and in the evening I turn to the religious

poems of Keble and Herbert and play the records from a
Handel oratorio. The first time I saw Bernard Shaw's *Fanny's
First Play* I was struck in the opening scenes by the tragedy
of misunderstanding between father and son, and until the
final curtain, being a father, I could scarcely smile at the
author's brilliant witticisms. Seeing the play again a fortnight
later in a different mood, I chuckled from beginning to end.
In one situation a story by Mark Twain—for example the
account of the funeral in *Roughing It*—may be hilariously
funny; in another, it will seem uncouth and in execrable taste.

Interpreters differ in what they try to make a drama, a
poem, a painting, or a musical composition mean. Consider
the Hamlets that Booth, Irving, Sothern, and Maurice Evans,
among many actors, have portrayed on the stage. What did
Shakespeare mean Shylock to be? And Lear? And Julius
Caesar, for that matter? In a powerful story Gouverneur
Morris told of an actor who at his last performance played
Oedipus Rex as a farce!

One Sunday afternoon at the Harvard Club in New York
I heard Percy Grainger play a Shadow Dance. His skillful
fingers brought forth music that made me imaginatively a
Sybarite sitting luxuriously in an overstuffed chair in an elegant library, its walls paneled in rich mahogany, its books
bound in varicolored morocco; and over all this elegance the
shadows from a log fire played softly. That evening at a settle-
ment house I heard Leo Ornstein, a strange young genius,
play the same composition. He too moved me. As he played,
I thought of myself on the front seat of an antiquated car at
night bumping with a deflated tire over a corduroy road, a
cracked headlight casting delirious shadows over steep banks
and broken tree trunks along the roadside. Both Grainger
and Ornstein were developed musicians and skilled per-
formers, and they had the same notes before them. But their
understanding of the music, their interpretation of it, and their
intentions were different. Involved were the composer, the
performer, and one listener, who responded imaginatively as

perhaps no one else in either audience did. Again the question "What is art?"

Certainly there can be no pictorial art to the blind, and what they might make of a piece of sculpture is suggested by John Godfrey Saxe's familiar verses "The Blind Man and the Elephant." Equally obvious is the fact that no music, however much it is enjoyed by others, can be art to the congenitally deaf. Does it not follow, then, that there can be no art of any kind to the aesthetically blind and deaf? Or at least that something in the person who looks at a painting, hears music, or reads a poem determines whether or not in it art exists for him?

> Like stars in the deep of the sky,
> Which arise on the glass of the sage,
> But are lost when their watcher is gone.

## What Is Poetry?

An analogy from physics is pertinent and clarifying. All of us were taught that when a tree falls in a forest with no animal nearby there is no sound. A falling tree sets up air vibrations, which become sound only when, for man, they stimulate through the ear nerves that carry to the brain, and in the brain sound is registered. Likewise the artist sends out his vibrations in music or painting or poetry, and they die ineffectually if they cause no response in a human being. They become art only if there is a response, and this response must be not only emotional but also satisfying. All agree that emotion is an essential in art; and if the appeal is not effective, the response is one of disapprobation, rejection, and subsequent neglect. Obviously response, being personal, is highly variable. This explains why something is art to one person and not to another, to an individual at one maturity, in one mood, or in one environment and not when he experiences it under different conditions.

*Poetry may be defined, then, as the beautiful or forceful expression, usually in metrical and certainly in rhythmical form, of a satisfying emotion, more or less universal and eternal, felt by a sensitive human being and so modified for effective expression by his good taste that it arouses a similar feeling in others.*

Once long ago, puzzling over the meaning of art, I walked by the former home of John Greenleaf Whittier, in Amesbury, Massachusetts. On the roof of the house was a radio antenna erected by a young man who was experimenting with the recent invention. Realizing that I had never received any of the signals, I asked myself why. The answer was easy: First, I had no receiving set; and, second, possessing one, to get signals I should have to tune it to sympathetic wave lengths. At once I realized that like the young experimenter, Whittier had broadcast his messages from the same house. Some people failed to get them because they had no receivers; many were not tuned to his wave lengths; and others who did receive the messages, for several reasons responded with different emotions. "Snow-Bound" could awaken few if any thrills in the tropics, while it recalled pleasant nostalgic memories to the New Englander who enjoyed an emotional interpretation of experiences that he had stored in his memory. Whittier's anti-slavery poems stirred the emotions, but how differently in Boston and in South Carolina!

> The sun's light when he unfolds it
> Depends on the organ that beholds it.

For art to exist, then, requires a response. And this response must, first of all, be emotional; feelings must be aroused. Furthermore, these feelings must in some way be satisfying, a test of which is a resultant desire for a repetition of the same or of a similar stimulus. There is no sincere appreciation when a person after a single experience professes enjoyment, giving lip service to "authorities," and then never again seeks the same pleasure by recall or by renewing the experience, or when he never later seeks the same kind from stimuli by the same artist or by others who use the same media.

The enjoyment of any art is personal. It depends on sincerity and it puts responsibility on the individual to respond to and to supplement what the artist has created. Matthew Arnold gave one of the clearest definitions of poetry when he said that it has "the peculiar power of so dealing with things as to awaken in us a wonderfully full, new, and intimate sense of them and of our relation with them." Hawthorne wrote, "Nobody, I think, ought to read poetry or look at pictures or statues who can not find a great deal more in them than the poet or artist has actually expressed." Carlyle said, "We are all poets when we read a poem well." William Blake declared,

> I give you the end of a golden string:
> Only wind it into a ball,—
> It will lead you in at Heaven's gate,
> Built in Jerusalem's wall.

And Walt Whitman asserted,

> All architecture is what you do to it when you look upon it.
> All music is what awakes from you when you are reminded by
> the instruments.
> To have great poets, there must be great audiences, too.

Once years ago I was looking with intellectual curiosity at a series of paintings by Tissot of the life of Christ. Having recently learned something of pictorial composition, I was intent on seeing how the artist had put his details together— the balance, the contrast of figures and lines and masses and color, the harmony, the unity of the whole. Before the representations of the Crucifixion and the Resurrection, I became aware of a person standing by my side, a humble woman who had probably never heard of artistic techniques. Her hands were tense and tears were rolling down her cheeks as she contemplated the suffering and the victory of Christ. Who had got what the artist intended, she or I? What is appreciation anyway?

For a proper response to be probable, one must receive the

art stimulus with sympathy, trying to understand and to feel as the artist intended him to do. As Kenyon said in *The Marble Faun*, "I defy any painter to move and elevate me without my own consent and assistance."

The reader who sits down with an anthology of humor and says in effect "Now make me laugh if you can" is assured of disappointment. To get the feeling that the poets felt, one must read Burns's lyrics as a lover, the "Idylls of the King" as a romanticist, "Hyperion" with a Greek sensitiveness to beauty, and "Bishop Blougram's Apology" as a logician. Artists do much to put us in receptive moods, but they require sympathetic and imaginative help. As Goethe wrote in *Faust*, "Man sees what in his bosom lurks." Try reading the love scene from *Othello* or the passion of the mad Lear when you are not in the proper mood or when you are in an environment of bustling confusion, and you are likely to get little pleasurable feeling. Like every effective dramatist, Shakespeare does not begin his plays with high passion; he uses his first scenes to tune his audience, as it were, for a crescendo of feeling. The person who comes late to the theater seldom gets full pleasure from the play.

In all fields of art, particularly in literature, emotions are associated with a degree of intellectual response. "Reason may be the lever," said Dr. Holmes, "but sentiment gives you the fulcrum and the place to stand on if you want to move the world—or any person in it." In some cases the intellectual factor is small; one is moved emotionally by the beauty of color or shape or by ravishing music. In poetry we often find verbal music, as in some of Swinburne, that demands a minimum of intellectual concentration. And at the other extreme, as in Tennyson's "Flower in the Crannied Wall" or Browning's "Karshish," the intellect must be active before any emotion can be evoked.

In every human heart there is a great variety of latent emotions—emotions of joy and sorrow, hope and despair, resignation and resentment, admiration and disgust, ambition and complacency, love and hate. Obviously some emotions are more likely to be pleasurable when aroused than others, but there is human satisfaction in feeling of any kind. That is one reason why the arts have always been and always will be popular. There is a pleasure in sorrowing with Enoch Arden who, returning after a long absence, finds his wife wedded to another and happy, in sympathizing with the bereft lover in "The Blessed Damozel," in sharing the bitterness felt by the envious monk in Browning's "Soliloquy of the Spanish Cloister," and in hating cowardice, meanness, and revenge wherever presented. When the expression of such feelings is carried too far or is too personal, however, as in the sonnet that Browning wrote when he heard that Fitzgerald at the death of Elizabeth Barrett Browning had exclaimed "Thank God, there will be no more 'Aurora Leighs'!" a reader may understand and intellectually approve the indignant resentment and may appreciate the skill of the artist; but the bitterness is too severe for the feeling aroused to be pleasurable. No wonder the sonnet was suppressed.

I have argued that there is no such thing as art existing objectively apart from some human being. Rather, what is ordinarily called art is a stimulus, becoming art only when it moves someone to a satisfying emotional response. Therefore art is personal, resulting only when one responds sympathetically to the objective appeal, becoming real only when it draws out latent thoughts and feelings, all of which must be pleasurable. This concept demands sincerity and permits an independence not generally granted.

The concept that has been presented is in marked contrast to that traditionally held, a concept which assumes that only "authorities," whoever they may be, can decide whether or not something is art. "The genuineness of poetry," writes a self-recognized representative of the aristocracy, "is something which we have some warrant for believing that a small number, but only a small number, of contemporary readers can recognize." This is an arrogant assumption that the few, who have made many mistakes in the past and who will be contradicted again and again by the future, will decide what the rest of mankind should call art. The artist, in whatever medium, strives to please, and when his work gives satisfying pleasure, no matter to whom, it is art. If the pleasure is lasting and increases, so much better the art.

*"EVERY DAY MOVIES"*     *By Denys Wortman*

*"Julie dear, please come here and tell me what I think of this one."*

## WHY GREAT ART?

If art is, as has been argued, personal, becoming real only when there is an individual response that is emotional and satisfying, the question then naturally arises "Is there no great art, universal and persisting through the ages?" The answer is affirmative, of course, for there are paintings and music and sculpture and poems which gave general pleasure in the past and continue to do so in our time. As long as they do this, they are great art. If they cease to do so, they no longer are.

Do we owe no deference to the opinions of the past, to the "authorities" who from age to age have lauded Chaucer, Shakespeare, Milton, Spenser, Dryden, and Whitman? We certainly do, for they represent the best judgments of past experience. They have seen what was good in their time and they may point out what in carelessness or in ignorance we have not seen. But we can give deference without surrendering sincerity, without abandoning the assumption that a poem was written for us, and without surrendering the conviction that unless it produces in us a satisfying emotional response it is not art to us, whatever it may be to others.

If a reader is concerned to preserve his own aesthetic integrity and to lay a sound foundation for enjoyment and for assured growth in taste, he must respect his own responses. If he abnegates his own taste and depends on others to tell him what is art, he denies himself real pleasure and effectually inhibits a steady widening and deepening of appreciative enjoyment in the future. Depending on others, he is faced with alternatives: on the one hand, of confusion from guides who differ in their own tastes and judgments; and, on the other, of accepting one guide to whom he surrenders his own personality. "That way madness lies."

Although opinions of critics may differ, may be wrong, or may be invalidated by changes in taste or in approved style, they are worthy of open-minded consideration if for no other reason than that they come from perspicacious men who may lead us to appreciations which otherwise we might fail to achieve, and to refinements in taste. It requires a degree of courage and of self-confidence to take a stand in the face of generally expressed judgments of approval or disapproval, a

stand that to others may indicate incompetence or even im-
pudence. But one should take an honest stand nevertheless.
It is himself that he is concerned to satisfy, not others. It is
his own pleasure and growth that he wishes to assure.

> Recognize the drop's use, love the same,
> And loyally declare against mirage
> Though all the world asseverated dust
> Was good to drink.

Similarly, a reader should become acquainted with what
others have thought to be "the best that has been thought and
said in the world." For those poems that have persisted in
popularity have something that has enriched life in the past
and that is likely to do so in the future. But in reading the
"classics" one is looking, it should be remembered, for beauties that appeal to him, for beauties that will arouse in him
pleasurable and satisfying emotions, will so arouse them that
he will return again and again for renewed and increased
pleasure. It is most assuredly profitable to dig for gems in
fields that have been proved by others.

The distinguished French critic Charles Augustin Sainte-
Beuve presents what he considers the characteristics of a
classic author. "A classic author," he wrote in his *Causeries
du Lundi,* is "an author who has enriched the human mind,
who has really added to its treasure, who has got it to take a
step further, who has discovered some unequivocal moral
truth or penetrated to some eternal passion in the heart of
man where it seemed that all were known and explored, who
has produced his thought or his observation or his invention
under some form, no matter what, so it may be large, acute,
and reasonable, sane and beautiful in itself, who has spoken
to all in a style of everybody—in a style that is at once new
and antique and is a contemporary of all the ages."

Each detail of this definition should be thoughtfully considered, and one should ask himself in what great poems he
finds each characteristic manifested. It would be unreason-

able to expect that all are to be found in any one work, especially if it is brief, and it is possible that some poems that one approves as classic may not exemplify a single one of them. But the statement does represent what most expert critics, it is believed, would approve.

A poem, as I have defined it, must produce a satisfying emotional response in a reader. *A great poem is one that produces such a response in many readers and contiues to do so.* When for any reason it ceases to do this, it is no longer a great poem, whatever its successes have been in the past. What Apthorp wrote of opera is true of all forms of art. "The surest test of a work of art's having some of the eternal essence in it is its power of adapting itself, in its voyage down the centuries, to successive, ever-changing styles. . . . If a work of art reflect or embody nothing more than the special spirit of its own time, then its span of life is measured; for it is only by being ever fresh and new that it can hope to live."

Dante's "Divine Comedy" is generally accepted as one of the great classics of world literature. But, read in translation, it appeals today chiefly to those who can respond with pleasure to mediaeval religious mysticism. One who has read it carefully seeking to find what others have enjoyed and who fails to find great pleasure in it should feel no shame in acknowledging that it moves him little or not at all. "Comus" can no longer give the pleasure that it did when the masque was the popular entertainment in court circles.

To be consistent, we must admit as great a poem that has wide popular appeal—so long as that appeal is potent. But the history of literature has examples of poems or of poetic styles that flashed like meteors across the skies and then either disappeared or hung in the heavens as second- or third-class stars. Greatness is determined by general popularity that persists. When it ceases to persist, greatness is gone.

To continue to be great, a poem must be concerned with the eternal interests and passions of mankind. The "Iliad" and the "Odyssey" are still great poems because they tell movingly of courage, sacrifice, jealousy, bafflement, and other happenings that still are powerful in life. The translation may be that of Pope or of Lang, Leaf, and Myers, but the moving power remains in the characters and the story. The tragedy of Paolo and Francesca will arouse sympathy as long as love moves the heart. The exhilaration of spring, the beautiful sadness of autumn, the acceptance of duty, that "stern daughter of the voice of God," the courageous facing of death —these are universal subjects of art. In "Nuages" Debussy thought of "the unchanging aspects of the sky, with the slow and melancholy passing of clouds dissolving in a gray vague-ness tinged with white." This is a beauty perceived by seeing eyes since man first looked at the sky. Debussy makes us feel by his music more definitely and more pleasingly what every man has dimly felt and wished that he had the power to ex-press. The sonnets on Milton's blindness and on Toussaint L'Ouverture remain great poems not because of interest in the men but because the sentiments expressed are still noble to intelligent readers. Tennyson wrote "In Memoriam" after the death of his personal friend Arthur Henry Hallam, but what he said in his poem expresses much that one feels and should like to express at the loss of any dear companion. Uni-versal and continuing passions are essential to make any art great. Another illustration is the poem which follows.

### HERACLITUS

#### WILLIAM CORY

They told me, Heraclitus, they told me you were dead,
They brought me bitter news to hear and bitter tears to shed.
I wept as I remember'd how often you and I
Had tired the sun with talking and sent him down the sky.

And now that thou art lying, my dear old Carian guest,
A handul of grey ashes, long, long ago at rest,
Still are thy pleasant voices, thy nightingales, awake;
For death, he taketh all away, but them he cannot take.

A great poem gives more and more pleasure and calls out more and more from us the longer we know it and the oftener we return to it.

> A thing of beauty is a joy forever,
> Its loveliness increases.

The verses of James Whitcomb Riley and of thousands of other clever men give on first acquaintance a pleasure, but it soon wears out. We seldom go back to them; and when we do, we are likely to find that we get no more than we did at a first reading. That exhausted all that was in them. Popular music lasts for a day or for a season, but Mozart's "Divertissement in E♭ Major" gets better the oftener we hear it.

The cartoons in the daily paper or a magazine may give a temporary titillation, but who remembers them or goes back to them for renewed pleasure? On the other hand, the cartoons that Michelangelo drew for the Sistine Chapel are stronger and more moving every time they are seen.

Of course this means that, as one should reasonably expect, there are degrees of goodness in any art: one poem is good for a single reading, another is good for a short season or for a recurrent mood, and another still lasts for life—and grows better and better the longer we know it.

Finally, a work of art always depends for its greatness on what it makes one say back to it. If it does not bring out from one's experience and passion a supplementation that he is impelled to recall and feel, it is to him a dead thing. The little poem tells everything; the great poem demands—and gets— much in the way of an intellectual and emotional response. Because it stirs us to feel and to express the best that is in us— the most beautiful, the most profound, and, let us add, the liveliest—it is great, and it will continue to be great only so long as it does this. As Hawthorne once said, it requires a poet to read a poem, a thought that Thomas Bailey Aldrich repeated:

To the sea-shell's spiral round
'Tis your heart that brings the sound:
The soft sea-murmurs that you hear
Within, are captured from your ear.

You do poets and their song
A grievous wrong,
If your own soul does not bring
To their high imagining
As much beauty as they sing.

# Chapter Three

## THE VALUES OF POETRY

A PERSON is usually given respect because he has a habit of reading. But actually in some instances reading is merely a mild anesthetic, used when there is nothing better at hand to rid oneself of boredom and to kill time. It does kill time, and even though it may be pleasant, it is murder nonetheless. I still remember the shock that I had hearing a young man say that when he had nothing worth while to do he took a walk or read a book.

But there are many kinds of reading. At the one extreme there is the almost passive running of the eyes over a page, with little attention to meaning, which, if got, quickly passes from consciousness; and at the other extreme there is responsive reading that sets up feeling as well as broadens ideas. This kind demands quite as much from the reader as it does from the author. In it one's eyes are on the pages less than one's reflection is directed to suggested meaning. When one brilliant student was asked why his room was dark in the evening when his fellows were poring over their books, he replied that then he was thinking of what the authors whom he had read meant and of how what they wrote might affect him and his future life.

This reflective reading, whether done with book in hand

37

or after it is laid aside, is of course the kind that yields most, not only of practical profit but also of pleasure. It is the cultivation of viable ideas so that they will bear fruit even after the author and his words are forgotten.

The reading of poetry especially demands more than casual attention. A reader must find not only what the poem means but also what it implies, and, what is even more important, he must supplement it with his imagination and make the expressed feeling his own. Many a person has failed to appreciate poetry because he expected it to be clear and straightforward like good prose, demanding nothing but intelligent understanding. Poetry should be clear, of course, for the ordinary reader has "no truce with . . . that obscurity which on a third reading deepens to opacity." But simple clarity is not enough. Real poetry is rich in suggestiveness. It stimulates a reader to cooperate with the poet to arouse in himself feelings that give pleasure.

If successful, poetry is entertaining, is one means of "harmless enjoyment." It soothes the ear with music, it sets forth beautiful and vivid pictures, it often tells an interesting story or presents a person with emphasis on some unusual facet of character. But it has other and far more important values.

In the first place, poetry brings variety to life, which constantly tends even in the best of us to monotonous repetition of the commonplace. We get up in the morning, greet the family usually in the accustomed manner, and throughout the day think, say, and do mostly accustomed things. It is like playing one-finger exercises on the middle register of a piano keyboard, which has all but infinite possibilities. There are

> Five-and-thirty black slaves,
>   Half-a-hundred white,
> All their duty but to sing
>   To their Queen's delight,
> Now with throats of thunder,
>   Now with dulcet lips,
> While she rules them royally
>   With her finger tips.

Poetry can call for music from seldom-used keys, can keep them sounding, while disuse tends to powerlessness to respond when unusual feeling demands expression. Without the vicarious experiences that poetry can bring more intensely than any other form of literature, one may lose the power to respond at all satisfactorily to the stimulus of love, sorrow, beauty, or noble thoughts. That the extremes of the emotional keyboard may be kept alive, they must be exercised. The infrequent demands of life can be supplemented at will by poetry which creates a mood that craves such expression as gives satisfaction. It is no minor tragedy if when joy or grief, exultation or unusual depression fills the heart there is in one no means of expression.

One morning, glancing through the door of a schoolroom in which "expression" was taught, I saw students making what seemed to be grimaces. "What on earth," I later asked the teacher, "were you trying to do with those young people?" She replied, "Did you ever notice the expression on the countenances of the boys?" I had: the faces were habitually almost as expressionless as the palm of my hand. The teacher continued, "They have lost, if they ever had, power to express their feelings. Something funny happens and they merely grin; a sorrow comes, and they merely don't grin. I am trying to break up the fountains of the deep, to teach them how to laugh out loud, to express physically the feelings that they have. Expression deepens feelings." It is something like that which poetry can do for all of us.

It is a great loss if the sensitiveness, the exuberance of youth, the ability to respond unabashed to the beauties and novelties of the world so surely fade as maturity comes to the majority of people. Poetry can keep the spirit and the power alive. It was an anonymous high-school girl who wrote

### YOUTH

I must laugh and dance and sing,
Youth is such a lovely thing.

Soon I shall be old and stately;
I shall promenade sedately

Down a narrow pavement street,
And the people that I meet

Will be stiff and narrow too,
Careful what they say and do;

It will be quite plain to see
They were never young like me.

When I walk where flowers grow
I shall have to stoop down low

If I want one for a prize;
Now I'm just the proper size.

Let me laugh and dance and sing,
Youth is such a lovely thing.

With this expression of alive sensitiveness contrast Ruth
Comfort Mitchell's pathetic picture in her "Pullman Portraits."

Down the green plush lane, at the forward end of the car,
There are seven Iowa farmers' tired old wives
With their faces set toward the perfumed orange groves
For a lyrical end to their prosy, cumbered lives;
And all day long with their red, work-twisted hands
On their black silk laps they idle, they rest, they play;
They badger the grime-gray brakeman, make new friends,—
"Say, Pa, this gentleman here's from Ioway!"

And contrast also Rosabelle Houston's "A Woman of the
Soil."

To her a sunset is only a thing of color—a symbol of fair or
    foul weather.
She does not know the calm and peace found in a quiet chapel—
Yet she knows God; her every waking moment is an unconscious
    prayer.
Beauty, to her, lies in the form of a geranium slip, potted in a
    tin tomato can.

Once there was a dream in her eyes—a dream of what lay
  beyond her prison hills;
But as the years rolled on, the dream died—
Until now she wonders about the potato crop on the other side
  of her chicken fence.

She has felt the cruel sting of many winters,
And the blistering heat of summer suns—
And before them all she has bent a little farther down.
To her the word, Love, is a mocking sound.

She of all the world's wives knows what it is to be a man's slave,
  to wrest life-sustaining food from the soil, and to bear dream-
  less-eyed, sluggish-brained children.
She does not fear death—her life she did not fashion;
And sometimes she dimly wonders if he who did create her
  and her uneventful life,
Will not soon clear her burdened mind of visions of swine and
  cockleburs and dirty little hands.

And as she wonders, for a moment her hardened hand
Reaches out and caresses the sickly geranium slip—
And something clear and sparkling glimmers on her cheek.

By beautiful recall of the best things in life, poetry may
help to keep us young, for poets, as Emerson said, are

> Olympian bards who sung
> Divine Ideas below,
> Which always find us young
> And always keep us so.

Browning wrote

> Grow old along with me!
> The best is yet to be.

But old age may be the emptiest, dreariest, most tragic period
in man's life. It may reveal "wearisome old souls who have
gathered nothing worth preservation from their experience
in life." Old age is likely to be barren if experience has not
been contributory to richness of understanding and appreciation. Whatever actual experiences have been, old age will be

broader and deeper, more exciting as well as more placid through understanding, if it has been prepared for by much traveling in the realms of gold of poetry. It is only for persons who have steadily grown through vicarious as well as actual experiences that

> The best is yet to be,
> The last of life, for which the first was made.

Compare the person who has been taught by art to seek what each event means, what it implies, what it may contribute of beauty or of joy to his life and to the lives of others with his fellow, who, though in the moving stream of human events, perceives what passes as incidents in a tedious day.

## SONNET

### ARTHUR DAVISON FICKE

> This is the burden of the middle years:
> To know what things can be, or not be, known;
> To find no sunset lovely unto tears;
> To pass not with the swallow southward-flown
> Toward far Hesperides where gold seas break
> Beyond the last horizon round strange isles;
> To have forgot Prometheus on his peak;
> To know that pilgrim-miles are only miles.
> Then death seems not so dreadful with its night
> That keeps unstirred a veil of mystery.
> Then no acclaimed disaster can affright
> Him who is wise in human history
> And finds no godhead there to earn his praise
> And dreads no horror save his empty days.

## IN TEMPORE SENECTUTIS

### ERNEST DOWSON

> When I am old,
>     And sadly steal apart,
> Into the dark and cold,
>     Friend of my heart!

Remember, if you can,
Not him who lingers, but that other man,
Who loved and sang, and had a beating heart,—
　　When I am old.

When I am old,
　And all Love's ancient fire
Be tremulous and cold:
　My soul's desire!
Remember, if you may,
Nothing of you and me but yesterday,
When heart on heart we bid the hours conspire
　To make us old.

When I am old,
　And every star above
Be pitiless and cold:
　My life's one love!
Forbid me not to go:
Remember nought of us but long ago,
And not at last, how love and pity strove
　When I grew old.

The poet, more sensitive to the beauty and to the significance of what happens in the world, says with skill what ordinary mortals sometimes feel and fain would say. He sings what we would sing in rapturous pleasure, in triumph, or defeat. He brings comfort in sorrow, and in depression he raises our spirits. He keeps alive the finer feelings,

　　The infinite passion, and the pain
　　Of finite hearts that yearn.

As Coventry Patmore says in "The Angel in the House,"

　　An idle poet, here and there,
　　　Looks round him, but, for all the rest,
　　The world, unfathomably fair,
　　　Is duller than a witling's jest.
　　Love wakes men, once a lifetime each;
　　　They lift their heavy lids, and look;
　　And, lo, what one sweet page can teach
　　　They read with joy, then shut the book.

And some give thanks, and some blaspheme,
And most forget; but, either way,
That and the Child's unheeded dream
Is all the light of all their day.

When feeling strives for expression an ordinary mortal is rich indeed if he knows where to find in poetry the exact words that he himself is helpless to call up. To have a reservoir of expression, one must read widely, respond sympathetically, and remember.

Poetry can do what Stevenson prayed the Lord to do.

### THE CELESTIAL SURGEON

#### ROBERT LOUIS STEVENSON

If I have faltered more or less
In my great task of happiness;
If I have moved among my race
And shown no glorious morning face;
If beams from happy human eyes
Have moved me not; if morning skies,
Books, and my food, and summer rain
Knocked on my sullen heart in vain:—
Lord, thy most pointed measure take
And stab my spirit broad awake;
Or, Lord, if too obdurate I,
Choose thou, before that spirit die,
A piercing pain, a killing sin,
And to my dead heart run them in!

And the verses of Sara Teasdale open our eyes to the miracle of spring and say perfectly what we have felt and been unable to say for ourselves.

### BLUE SQUILLS

#### SARA TEASDALE

How many million Aprils came
Before I ever knew
How white a cherry bough could be,
A bed of squills, how blue!

And many a dancing April
  When life is done with me,
Will lift the blue flame of the flower
  And the white flame of the tree.

Oh burn me with your beauty, then,
  Oh hurt me, tree and flower,
Lest in the end death try to take
  Even this glistening hour.

O shaken flower, O shimmering tree,
  O sunlit white and blue,
Wound me, that I, through endless sleep,
  May bear the scar of you.

Literature offers an infinite variety of vicarious experiences that anyone, whoever he may be, can share for the seeking.

Just as a drudging student trims his lamp,
Opens his Plutarch, puts him in the place
Of Roman, Grecian; draws the patched gown close,
Dreams, "Thus should I fight, save, or rule the world!"
Then smilingly, contentedly awakes
To the old solitary nothingness,

anyone can get from poetry all the variety that he wishes; but he will never return to "solitary nothingness," for the vicarious experiences will in some manner and in some degree have changed him forever. Neither Pippa nor the people who heard her songs were ever again the same after she had passed.

In a letter to Vettori more than four hundred years ago the statesman Niccolo Machiavelli wrote of his pleasures in his library.

The evening being come, I return home and go to my study; at the entrance I pull off my peasant clothes, covered with dust and dirt, and put on my noble court dress, and thus becomingly reclothed I pass into the ancient courts of the men of old where, being lovingly received by them, I am fed with that food which is mine alone; where I do not hesitate to speak with them and to ask the reason of their actions, and feel no weariness, I forget every trouble, poverty does not dismay, death does not terrify me; I am entirely possessed by those great men.

And more in detail John Kendrick Bangs tells of the multifarious world opened by books. Only one paragraph is quoted.

At any time of the day or night I can follow the fortunes of Ulysses with no less a person than Homer himself for my guide. I can touch hands with all the gods of high Olympus on the cachet of his guidance, and all the splendors of the court of Zeus I am privileged to look upon, not through my purely mortal eyes alone, but with the vision of one who is himself immortal. If I desire to consort with men of power and purpose in ancient times, I have only to walk a foot or two from my desk to find in Plutarch a guide, who will introduce me to as many of the Caesars as I care to know, will present me at the court of Pericles, where I may have revealed to me the glory that was Greece; who will gossip to me engagingly of Solon and Themistocles, take me to dine with Lucullus, and give me the pleasing sense of having set no limit upon my associations, and though I dwell in a hemisphere they never knew, and in an age to theirs remote, Plato and Socrates through my books speak to me and pour their wisdom into my ears, while cynical old Diogenes with surprising agility leaps over seas and centuries to make me laugh. If I have need for song, Horace responds to my call, day or night. Omar Khayyam leaves his vine, drops his jug, and deserts his "thou" for a moment to charm me with verses, while if I be depressed in spirit a mere tap at the door of their books will bring Epictetus, or the Emperor Marcus himself to minister to my need of cheer.

After vicarious experiences the world is wider; things that we have never seen belong to us because they have been revealed by poets. John Greenleaf Whittier said of the Scotch heather of which Robert Burns sang,

> No more these simple flowers belong
> To Scottish maid or lover;
> Down in the common soil of song
> They bloom the wide world over.

Life holds much loveliness, sensuous and intellectual, that is ours if we supplement our own vision with that of the poets.

## BARTER

SARA TEASDALE

Life has loveliness to sell,
  All beautiful and splendid things,
Blue waves whitened on a cliff,
  Soaring fire that sways and sings,
And children's faces looking up
Holding wonder like a cup.

Life has loveliness to sell,
  Music like a cup of gold,
Scent of pine trees in the rain,
  Eyes that love you, arms that hold,
And for your spirit's still delight
Holy thoughts that star the night.

Spend all you have for loveliness,
  Buy it and never count the cost;
For one white singing hour of peace
  Count many a year of strife well lost,
And for a breath of ecstasy
Give all you have been, or could be.

## THE ENCHANTER

RALPH WALDO EMERSON

In the deep heart of man a poet dwells
Who all the days of life his summer story tells;
Scatters on every eye dust of his spells,
Scent, form, and color; to the flowers and shells
Wins the believing child with wondrous tales;
Touches a cheek with colors of romance,
And crowds a history into a glance;
Gives beauty to the lake and fountain;
Spies oversea the fires of the mountain;
When thrushes open their throats, 'tis he that sings,
And he that paints the oriole's fiery wings.
The little Shakespeare in the maiden's heart
Makes Romeo of the plough-boy on his cart;
Opens the eye to Virtue's starlike need
And gives persuasion to a gentle deed.

Besides giving vicarious experiences, poetry brings to consciousness beauty of all kinds, which without its help we might fail to see and to enjoy. It presents beauty so charmingly that ever afterward our eyes are open to find it, wherever it may be, and to interweave it into the fabric of our lives. Moreover, by the beauty or emphasis of expression, poetry gives a reality to "things we have passed a hundred times nor cared to see." Holmes wrote in *The Autocrat*, "As the monk said about the pictures in the convent, . . . he sometimes thought the living tenants were the shadows, and the painted figures the realities."

The poet sees beauty and points it out to us; but, more than that, he perceives other beauties that it leads to, similarities and significances, and he points them out too. In writing the following verses Browning probably began with the pleasure that spring brought to the barren earth; that suggested the analogy of the star breaking through "a scowl of cloud," then the beauty of the vernal earth and the clearing sky brought him the beauty of his "lyric love, half angel and half bird."

> Such a starved bank of moss
> Till, that May-morn,
> Blue ran the flash across;
>     Violets were born!
>
> Sky—what a scowl of cloud
>     Till, near and far,
> Ray on ray split the shroud:
>     Splendid, a star!
>
> World—how it walled about
>     Life with disgrace
> Till God's own smile came out:
>     That was thy face.

In his *Study of Poetry* Bliss Perry said that the potentialities of poetry are

. . . its power to seize upon a physical image like that of a woman planting bulbs, and transmute it into a symbol of the resurrection of the dead; its capacity for turning fact into truth and brown earth into beauty; for remoulding the broken syllables of human speech into sheer music; for lifting the mind, bowed down by wearying thought and haunting fear, into a brooding ecstasy wherein weeping is changed into laughter and autumnal premonitions of death into assurance of life, and the narrow paths of individual experience are widened into those illimitable spaces where the imagination rules.

Poetry directs our attention to

> The beauty and the wonder and the power,
> The shapes of things, their colors, lights, and shades,
> Changes, surprises.

And ever afterward we are alert to find these pleasures for ourselves, for

> There's a world of capability
> For joy spread round us, meant for us,
> Inviting us.

The Psalmist well said, "Let not my heart forget the many things mine eyes have seen."

It is the poet who helps us see the beauty of the world, to see it so that it is memorable and stimulating to alertness for whatever else is good and true and beautiful. William Watson wrote

> The poet gathers fruit from every tree,
> Yea, grapes from thorns and figs from thistles he.
> Plucked by his hand, the basest weed that grows
> Towers to a lily, reddens to a rose.

Once I was bored by bird enthusiasts who daily reported seeing a yellow goldfinch on a purple thistle, a bittern with neck outstretched like a dead reed, or of a pileated woodpecker tearing and scattering huge chips from a dead tree. None of their reports stirred my interest. But one day, reading William Vaughn Moody's marvelous "Gloucester Moors," one of the greatest poems written in America, I was caught by the lines:

That green-gold flash was a vireo,
And yonder flame where the marsh-flags grow
Was a scarlet tanager.

Instantly I thought, "The poet has seen beauty and is trying to share it with me. I must make myself capable of enjoying what up to now I have been blind to." That was the stimulus I needed, a stimulus that had not come from my prosaic friends who were chiefly interested in identification and in increasing their annual list. I too became an enthusiast, and now every spring, birds bring their color and grace and music to enlarge and beautify my world. "The more good things one is interested in, the more ardently does one live."

A youth once complained to a sage that where he lived there was nothing worth while, only the ugly commonplace of mud and common rocks. While he continued his jeremiad the sage stooped and picked up pebbles from the muck and the mire at his feet. Then he held out to the youth his hands filled with diamonds, amethysts, and rubies. That is what the poet does. It was a poet who made us see in the colored pebbles on the beach in Sicily the Pentelic marble of which the Greeks carved the statues which still, even though in fragments, awe us by their beauty. It is the poet who finds beauty and shows "good in everything."

## THE POET

RALPH WALDO EMERSON

But in the darkest, meanest things
There's alway, alway something sings.
'Tis not in the high stars alone,
Nor in the cups of budding flowers,
Nor in the redbreast's mellow tone,
Nor in the bow that smiles in showers,
But in the mud and scum of things
There's alway, alway something sings.

What do we choose from a world that offers ineffable riches?

## DAYS

RALPH WALDO EMERSON

Damsels of Time, the hypocritic Days,
Muffled and dumb, like barefoot dervishes,
And marching single in an endless file,
Bring diadems and fagots in their hands.
To each they offer gifts after his will,
Bread, kingdom, stars, and sky that holds them all.
I, in my pleached garden, watched the pomp,
Forgot my morning wishes, hastily
Took a few herbs and apples, and the Day
Turned and departed silent. I, too late,
Under her solemn fillet saw the scorn.*

## LOST DAYS

DANTE GABRIEL ROSSETTI

The lost days of my life until today,
What were they, could I see them on the street
Lie as they fell? Would they be ears of wheat
Sown once for food but trodden into clay?
Or golden coins squandered and still to pay?
Or drops of blood dabbling the guilty feet?
Or such spilt water as in dreams must cheat
The undying throats of Hell, athirst alway?
I do not see them here; but after death
God knows I know the faces I shall see,
Each one a murdered self, with low last breath.
"I am thyself,—what hast thou done to me?"
"And I—and I—thyself," (lo! each one saith,)
"And thou thyself to all eternity!"

* Oliver Wendell Holmes quotes from Emerson's *Works and Days* a prose
sentence from which this poem developed. "The days are ever divine as
to the first Aryans. They come and go like muffled and veiled figures, sent
from a distant friendly party; but they say nothing, and if we do not use
the gifts they bring, they carry them as silently away."

"Now," wrote Holmes, "we see in the poem this thought in full dress,
and then ask what is the difference between prose and poetry. . . . Cinderella at the fireside, and Cinderella at the prince's ball! In full dress version
the thought is glittering with new images. . . . Mark that now the poet
reveals himself as he could not in the prosaic form. . . . Self-revelation of
beauty embellished by ornaments of verse is the divine right of the poet."

One student was puzzled by his failure, as he expressed it, "to get anything out of Ben Jonson's 'Hymn to Diana,'" which his teacher had called one of the great poems of the ages. Being young and romantic, he had responded to other poems on the moon—Sir Philip Sidney's "With how sad steps, O Moon, thou climb'st the skies," Coleridge's

> The moving moon went up the sky.
> And nowhere did abide:
> Softly she was going up,
> And a star or two beside,

and, his favorite, Josephine Preston Peabody's lovely lyric in her drama "Marlowe." But the "Hymn to Diana" had found no response in his feelings.

Walking home one crisp autumn evening, he became conscious of the cold silver beauty of a full moon in the sky, and he found himself repeating what he had been compelled to learn in school:

> Queen and huntress, chaste and fair,
> Now the sun is laid to sleep,
> Seated in thy silver chair
> State in wonted manner keep.
> Hesperus entreats thy light,
> Goddess excellently bright!

"Yes," he thought, "this is different. No warm, friendly summer moon, but something regal—cold, aloof, and at the same time in its way beautiful." He found himself recalling what he had learned of Diana the huntress and queen of the skies, and he felt it entirely appropriate that she be seated on a silver throne, remote but worshipful. And, turning toward the western sky, he saw, as the poet had seen, Hesperus hanging low. The rest of the poem then took on meaning and made an appeal to which he had not before been able to respond.

> Earth, let not thy envious shade
> Dare itself to interpose;
> Cynthia's shining orb was made
> Heav'n to clear, when earth did close:

Bless us then with wished sight,
    Goddess excellently bright!

Lay thy bow of pearl apart,
    And thy crystal shining quiver;
Give unto the flying hart
    Space to breathe, how short soever:
Thou that mak'st a day of night,
    Goddess excellently bright!

It is such an experience, repeated time after time by other readers of poems on diverse themes, that warns us not quickly to turn aside from what has pleased, moved, and elevated others throughout the years. While preserving his own integrity of taste and judgment, one is likely to cheat himself if he does not try, sincerely and with reasonable persistence, to find what has inspired the poet and what has given pleasure to others who have made perhaps an instant response to the poem.

In revealing, poetry creates a desire for beauty and adventure that we may never have had before. In proportion as the poet selects and presents attractively what is most beautiful, most worth while, and most stirring, we expand our lives in anticipation, and not infrequently go on to actual fulfilment in the experience itself. Who has not thought after reading Browning's "Home Thoughts from Abroad" how wonderful it would be to live in England when spring burgeons? And who knowing William Vaughn Moody's "Gloucester Moors," from which the following two stanzas are quoted, would not like to see the coming of spring that he describes?

Jill-o'er-the-ground is purple blue,
Blue is the quaker-maid,
The wild geranium holds its dew
Long in the boulder's shade.
Wax-red hangs the cup
From the huckleberry boughs,
In barberry bells the grey moths sup,
Or where the choke-cherry lifts high up
Sweet bowls for their carouse.

Over the shelf of the sandy cove
Beach-peas blossom late.
By copse and cliff the swallows rove
Each calling to his mate.
Seaward the sea-gulls go,
And the land-birds all are here;
That green-gold flash was a vireo,
And yonder flame where the marsh-flags grow
Was a scarlet tanager.

## WANDERER'S SONG

### ARTHUR SYMONS

I have had enough of women, and enough of love,
But the land waits, and the sea waits, and day and night
        is enough;
Give me a long white road, and grey wide path of the sea,
And the wind's will and the bird's will, and the heart-
        ache still in me.

Why should I seek out sorrow, and give gold for strife?
I have loved much and wept much, but tears and love are
        not life;
The grass calls to my heart, and the foam to my blood
        cries up,
And the sun shines and the road shines, and the wine's
        in the cup.

I have had enough of wisdom, and enough of mirth,
For the way's one and the end's one, and it's soon to
        the ends of the earth;
And it's then good-night and to bed, and if heals or heart-ache,
Well, it's sound sleep and long sleep, and sleep too
        deep to wake.

Poetry lays up stores of beauty for later recall and enjoyment.

## THE DAFFODILS

WILLIAM WORDSWORTH

I wandered lonely as a cloud
That floats on high o'er vales and hills,
When all at once I saw a crowd,
A host of golden daffodils,
Beside the lake, beneath the trees
Fluttering and dancing in the breeze.

Continuous as the stars that shine
And twinkle on the milky way,
They stretched in never-ending line
Along the margin of a bay:
Ten thousand saw I at a glance
Tossing their heads in sprightly dance.

The waves beside them danced, but they
Out-did the sparkling waves in glee:
A poet could not but be gay
In such a jocund company!
I gazed—and gazed—but little thought
What wealth the show to me had brought:

For oft; when on my couch I lie,
In vacant or in pensive mood,
They flash upon that inward eye
Which is the bliss of solitude;
And then my heart with pleasure fills,
And dances with the daffodils.

Everyone has had experiences that bring pleasure afterward by imaginative repetition. But everyone is limited as to what he can see and do. The poets present experiences that others cannot achieve actually, but can enjoy vicariously, and they also suggest other experiences that we can achieve. We may never have actually seen a host of golden daffodils fluttering and dancing in a breeze; but, like Wordsworth, we can recall the imagined picture with a heart filled with dancing pleasure. Moreover, by the poem we are made more sensi-

tive to similar beauty, more alert to see it and to enjoy it,
actually and in retrospect. We may find similar beauty in a
bed of tulips, in Queen Anne's lace along the roadside, in a
field of wild mustard, or in ripening wheat as it waves in a
breeze. A recall of beauty may give the same pleasure that the
poet had.

### THE COIN

SARA TEASDALE

Into my heart's treasury
I slipped a coin
That time cannot take
Nor a thief purloin—
Oh better than the minting
Of a gold-crowned king
Is the safe-kept memory
Of a lovely thing.

Poetry not only points out truth and beauty that we otherwise might not see, but also interprets it and shows new rela-
tionships or applications that bring pleasure and enrichment.
Just as the Levites among the ancient Hebrew tribes had the
responsibility of living in close communion with God and
of interpreting His will to the people, so we may conceive
of poets, spending their genius in searching for and in contemplating whatsoever is true and good and beautiful, and
then by art presenting it to others for their understanding and
appreciation and direction. They are like guides through an
art gallery; they have seen the exhibits before, they understand, they discriminate, they respond emotionally to the best,
and they have the power to make us see, understand, discriminate, and appreciate. Through their poems they are
ready to conduct us through the galleries of life and to enable
us without leaving seated comfort to share, by merely opening
mind and heart, in feeling the best that has been seen, thought,
and said in the world. As D. A. Stauffer said, "Poets transmute the trivial into the significant, the accidental into the

essential, the vague into the clear, the dispirited into the inspiriting." They teach us

> To look with feelings of fraternal love
> Upon the unassuming things that hold
> A silent station in this beauteous world.

Of course we may not always agree with the interpretation that a poet gives. He may see what we cannot see or even what we do not care to see; but he reveals an insight for our consideration. Wordsworth declared that

> One impulse from the vernal wood
> May teach you more of man,
> Of moral evil and of good,
> Than all the sages can.

And in "Tintern Abbey" he wrote that he had learned, as few other men have done,

> To look on Nature, not as in the hour
> Of thoughtless youth; but hearing oftentimes
> The still, sad music of humanity,
> Nor harsh nor grating, though of ample power
> To chasten and subdue. And I have felt
> A presence that disturbs me with the joy
> Of elevated thoughts, a sense sublime
> Of something far more deeply interfused,
> Whose dwelling is the light of setting suns,
> And the round ocean and the living air,
> And the blue sky, and in the mind of man;
> A motion and a spirit, that impels
> All thinking things, all objects of all thought,
> And rolls through all things.

We may not sympathize with the poet's feeling, but the hard-headed economist John Stuart Mill said, "What made his [Wordsworth's] poems a medicine for my state of mind was that they expressed not mere outward beauty, but states of feeling and of thought colored by feeling under the excitement of beauty. I needed to be made to feel that there was real permanent happiness in tranquil contemplation."

Everyone has felt the beauty of quiet as evening closed the day, but only a poet can express the feeling, specify the beauty, and make a personal application, as George Sterling did.

### EVENING

Slowly she wanders up the evening sands,
  Faint on her brow the flush of lapsing day.
She comes with silence from the twilight lands,
  And smiles to think the dawn so far away.

Day's fragrance lingers round her. In her hair
  Are tiny lilies trembling lest they die;
And Sleep, her child, is near, who has in care
  The weariness of worlds. The ceaseless cry,

Of timid voices that the day had stilled,
  Comes to her wandering. Are those her eyes
That greaten with the dew, as if tear-filled,
  Or lovely stars awaking in the skies?

I shall not hear until mine evening come,
  And flower-shadows fall across my grave,
The gentler voices that the day made dumb,
  Nor hold the plenitude of peace I crave.

Poetry interprets nature, as we have indicated, and the most important nature is human nature. And this the poets from the earliest times onward have interpreted. They have made the personalities of Odysseus, Oedipus, Lear, Macbeth, and Guinevere almost as familiar to us as our most intimate acquaintances. They have made us understand the patient Job, and David, the shepherd, psalmist, and king, the Prioresse, the duke jealous of his last duchess, the Blessed Damozel grieving for her bereft lover, La Belle Dame Sans Merci, Richard Cory, and Mr. Flood. And since poets reveal themselves through what they write, we know the real Sidney, Pope, Byron, and Robinson perhaps better than if we had been personally acquainted with them. We know George Chapman when he wrote:

> Give me a spirit that on life's rough sea
> Loves to have his sails fill'd with a lusty wind
> Even till his sail-yards tremble, his masts crack,
> And his rapt ship run on her side so low
> That she drinks water and her keel ploughs air.

We might have passed old Martin day by day and pitied him that he had not achieved wealth and station in life. But Joyce Kilmer looked beneath the surface and interpreted him to us, who, understanding, change pity to envy.

> Martin? Why, he exhaled romance
>     And wore an overcoat of glory.
> A fleck of sunlight on the street,
>     A horse, a book, a girl who smiled,—
> Such visions made each moment sweet
>     For this receptive, ancient child.
>
> Because it was old Martin's lot
>     To be, not make, a decoration.
> Shall we then scorn him, having not
>     His genius of appreciation?
> Rich joy and love he got and gave;
>     His heart was merry as his dress.
> Pile laurel wreaths upon his grave
>     Who did not gain, but was, success.

One great national hero of our country is Abraham Lincoln. Everyone has studied in histories his life and works, and few men have been blessed with as able biographers. But it is to the poets that we go for such interpretation of the man that shakes us with emotion. From the many tributes we quote the characterization by Edwin Markham, who rose to his subject as he did in contemplation of the man with the hoe.

### LINCOLN, THE MAN OF THE PEOPLE

> When Norn Mother saw the Whirlwind Hour
> Greatening and darkening as it hurried on,

She left the Heaven of Heroes and came down
To make a man to meet the mortal need.
She took the tried clay of the common road—
Clay warm yet with the genial heat of Earth,
Dashed through it all a strain of prophecy;
Tempered the heap with thrill of human tears;
Then mixed a laughter with the serious stuff.
Into the shape she breathed a flame to light
That tender, tragic, ever-changing face;
And laid on him a sense of the Mystic Powers,
Moving—all hushed—behind the mortal veil.
Here was a man to hold against the world,
A man to match the mountains and the sea.

The color of the ground was in him, the red earth;
The smack and tang of elemental things;
The rectitude and patience of the cliff;
The good-will of the rain that loves all leaves;
The friendly welcome of the wayside well;
The courage of the bird that dares the sea;
The gladness of the wind that shakes the corn;
The pity of the snow that hides all scars;
The secrecy of streams that make their way
Under the mountain to the rifted rock;
The tolerance and equity of light
That gives as freely to the shrinking flower
As to the great oak flaring to the wind—

To the grave's lone hill as to the Matterhorn
That shoulders out the sky. Sprung from the West,
He drank the valorous youth of a new world.
The strength of virgin forests braced his mind,
The hush of spacious prairies stilled his soul.
His words were oaks in acorns; and his thoughts
Were roots that firmly gript the granite truth.

Up from log cabin to the Capitol,
One fire was on his spirit, one resolve—
To send the keen ax to the root of wrong,
Clearing a free way for the feet of God,
The eyes of conscience testing every stroke,
To make his deed the measure of a man.
With the fine gesture of a kingly soul,

He built the rail-pile and he built the State,
Pouring his splendid strength through every blow:
The grip that swung the ax in Illinois
Was on the pen that set a people free.

So came the Captain with the mighty heart;
And when the judgment thunders split the house,
Wrenching the rafters from their ancient rest,
He held the ridgepole up, and spikt again
The rafters of the Home. He held his place—
Held the long purpose like a growing tree—
Held on through flame and faltered not at praise.
And when he fell in whirlwind, he went down
As when a lordly cedar, green with boughs,
Goes down with a great shout upon the hills,
And leaves a lonesome place against the sky.

The following poem, written in the general sadness on
the day of Lincoln's funeral, is an interpretation of the man
as well as an expression of universal sorrow.*

## THE DEATH OF LINCOLN

### WILLIAM CULLEN BRYANT

Oh, slow to smite and swift to spare,
    Gentle and merciful and just!
Who, in the fear of God, didst bear
    The sword of power, a nation's trust!

In sorrow by thy bier we stand,
    Amid the awe that hushes all,
And speak the anguish of a land
    That shook with horror at thy fall.

Thy task is done; the bond are free:
    We bear thee to an honored grave,
Whose proudest monument shall be
    The broken fetters of the slave.

* In Granger's *Index to Poetry and Recitations* one can find listed numerous poems about Lincoln. Two of the less well known that are well worth looking up are Edward Arlington Robinson's "Lincoln: The Master" and John Gould Fletcher's "Lincoln."

> Pure was thy life; its bloody close
> Hath placed thee with the sons of light,
> Among the noble host of those
> Who perished in the cause of Right.

Even more revealing of human nature is what literature makes us know of ourselves. Filled with admiration for a character, we suddenly and sometimes with a shock realize that the hero is manifesting qualities which we think or hope we have, which we aspire to have, or which we try to make others think we have. Despising a villain, we recognize that he is what we know with a difference in environment or pressure we might be. Edward Arlington Robinson's "Miniver Cheevy" is amusing until, and perhaps even after, we perceive that some of his romantic uselessness is in ourselves as well.

It is especially the dramatic, in poetry or in prose, that interprets human nature most strikingly. However novel the characters and the experiences, they are made to seem as real as if they were happening in one's own life and they often give wholly new insights. The character of one's own emotions must inevitably be affected by the manner in which we share the emotions of others.

Many men have poetic feelings, "the vision and the faculty divine," but are "wanting in the accomplishment of verse." For them the poet speaks. On reading Wordsworth, George Eliot wrote "I have never before met with so many of my own feelings expressed just as I should like them," and Keats said in a letter that a poem "should strike a reader as the wording of his own highest thoughts and appear almost a remembrance." A true poem

> is nature to advantage dressed,
> What oft was thought, but ne'er so well expressed.

As Holmes said, a reader

> finds in them his lurking thought,
> And on their lips the words he sought.

Durant summarizes Emerson's expression of the idea in his essay on "The Poet."

When genius speaks to us we feel a ghostly reminiscence of having ourselves, in our distant youth, had vaguely this self-same thought which genius now speaks, but which we had not art or courage to clothe with form and utterance. And indeed, great men speak to us only so far as we have ears and souls to hear them; only so far as we have in us the roots, at least, of that which flowers out in them. We too have had the experiences they had, but we did not suck those experiences dry of their secret and subtle meanings: we were not sensitive to the overtones of the reality that hummed about us.

Poetry can also, like music, create moods. Either alone can bring about a mood that is pleasurable or can dispel one that drowns in gloom or despair. Together, as in lyric song, they are most effective, the words giving definiteness to the mystery of harmony. Who has not been lifted to exuberance by "Hark, hark, the lark at heaven's gate sings" set to Schubert's music, or filled with exalted, holy feeling by Handel's "Hallelujah Chorus"? The short lyric "Lilac Time," by James Oppenheim, quickly induces a mood that could be brought about only by pages of prose.

The old harper in the Fourth Canto of Byron's "Don Juan," when other means fail, tries by singing of ancient days and of love to arouse Haidee from her despondency at the loss of her lover. And David in Browning's "Saul" successfully uses song in a continuing and climactic effort to bring the great king back to life. Through song he became

Saul, ye remember in glory,—ere error had bent
The broad brow from the daily communion; and still, though
    much spent
Be the life and the bearing that front you, the same God did
    choose,
To receive what a man may waste, desecrate, never quite lose.

At times we are in moods from which we wish to be lifted. Poetry, and also music, in such a situation are potent, especially by carrying us into another mood that is stronger and more wholesome. They achieve the catharsis that Plato attributed to the drama—purging the bad and substituting the good. Certainly poetry can "take one out of oneself," as the saying is, and bring him into a mood in which he has satisfaction. Being itself a complete thing, a poem makes us happy because it presents us with "an image of complete desire." The catharsis of experience expressed in the following poem by Joan McKowen, a high-school girl, carries over and becomes vicariously a catharsis for one who understands what is told.

> I had a love once, sweet and pure
> As any Angel's dream;
> Fond fancy fanned my young heart's love
> Into ethereal flame.
>
> Then came a wind from out the sky,
> And with the wind came rain;
> My lovely fire lay ruined there,
> My young heart filled with pain.
>
> Today my fancy lightly dwells
> On kisses, words, and such;
> Perhaps my heart's not full, but, then,
> It does not hurt so much.

King David in Walter de la Mare's poem had his mood changed by the song of a bird, and so did Percy.

### OVERTONES

WILLIAM ALEXANDER PERCY

> I heard a bird at break of day
> Sing from the autumn trees
> A song so mystical and calm,
> So full of certainties,
>
> No man, I think, could listen long
> Except upon his knees.
> Yet this was but a simple bird,
> Alone, among dead trees.

A father in the depth of sorrow because of the death of his child reads Eugene Field's "Little Boy Blue" and purges some of his grief through the realization of expression; or he reads James Whitcomb Riley's "Bereaved" and has created in himself a mood of sympathy for one who has never had a child to lose.

> Let me come in where you sit weeping,—aye,
>   Let me, who have not any child to die,
> Weep with you for the little one whose love
>   I have known nothing of.
>
> The little arms that slowly, slowly loosened
>   Their pressure round your neck; the hands you used
> To kiss.—Such arms—such hands I never knew.
>   May I not weep with you?
>
> Fain would I be of service—say some thing,
>   Between the tears, that would be comforting,—
> But ah! so sadder than yourselves am I,
>   Who have no child to die.

Poetry interprets and broadens our understanding and appreciation of life, and it also prepares us to meet the future. As we have reacted in the past to situations, either actual or imagined, we tend to react to similar situations in the future, especially if the former reactions have given emotional satisfactions. Responding to the stimulus of the poet, we recognize and approve ideals which set up in us lasting attitudes. The sum of one's emotionalized attitudes may confidently be asserted to be one's character.

Everyone who has really read poetry and who is reflective can give illustrations of lines that have almost literally leapt out at him, lines that contain ideals which affected his whole life. Such lines may have been Edward Rowland Sill's "Opportunity," in which the hero in apparent defeat found a broken sword and led to victory; or Joaquin Miller's "Columbus," which supports a persisting courage; or Arthur Hugh Clough's "Say not the struggle naught availeth," which brings hope when skies are dark; or Burns's "A man's a man for a' that," which gives respect for one's own dignity and worth. Professor Fairchild appositely wrote: "Happily some innate nobility in man stirs him to seek chiefly ends that are worthy. . . . Something calls to him out of himself; it forces him to be other and usually more than he is. . . . One of the chief means of meeting this imperative need is poetry."

Poetry does what Carlyle says in his essay "On Heroes" books do, influences our actions by setting up ideals and attitudes.

Do not books still accomplish *miracles* as *Runes* were fabled to do? They persuade man. Not the wretchedest circulating-library novel, which foolish girls thumb and con in remote villages but will help to regulate the actual practical weddings and households of these girls. So "Celia" felt, so "Clifford" acted: the foolish Theorem of Life stamped into those young brains comes out as a solid Practice one day. Consider whether any Rune in the wildest imagination of Mythologist ever did such wonders as, on the actual firm earth, some Books have done!

Poetry, as all good literature, is an economical source of concepts and ideals. It enables one quickly and without dangers to experience the dreams, the aspirations, the struggles, and the achievements of the race as condensed and interpreted by the sensitive artist. It not only presents ideals but it clothes them with such emotion that they persist as an integral part of character. Vicarious experiences prepare the reader for impulsive action in moments of indecision; they are potentialities of the greatest importance. In recalling and reliving these experiences one intensifies and enforces them by intellectual approval, and thus makes more probable the influence of acquired concepts and ideals on action.

Who has not learned from the poets what true love is? And who has not had his natural feelings and his ideals purified and elevated by the sentiments in emotion-arousing poetry? The Elizabethan lyrists, Burns, Shelley, Coventry Patmore, and many others have sung of love of man for maid, presenting ideals that vary with the times and with the personality of the poet. One reader will be affected by the expressed unselfish devotion, another by the light-hearted raillery of the loved one, and another still by the celebration of untold worship. Poems of love may be gay, but they often are tinged with sadness; sincere they must be if they set up any ideal that finds a response in the heart of the reader.

Anthologies are full of love poems, and everyone has in school been acquainted with those that are famous in the history of literature. Three contemporary poems of unusual love themes follow.

## KNOWLEDGE

### JUANITA SMITH

I thought love came like a tempest,
Strong and sudden, in a blast of wind
Carrying all before it,
Lifting for one sweet, mad taste of ecstasy;
Then dropped, and passed,
With not a trace to show it had been there.

I know, now, love comes tiptoeing
On soft-sandaled feet,
And almost passes with just a breath of fragrance
Before one sees and knows that love is near.

But love cannot be held; it passes always.
Only one does not cry; it is too sweet for that.
But one does not forget.

## LOVER TO LOVER

### DAVID MORTON

Leave me awhile, for you have been too long
A nearness that is perilous and sweet:
Loose me a little from the tightening thong
That binds my spirit, eyes and hands and feet.
For there are old communions I would hold,
To mind my heart what field and sky may be:

Earth bears her fruit . . . November has a gold . . .
And stars are still high points in constancy.
Loose me a little, now. . . . I have a need
Of standing in an open, windy place,
Of saying names again, of giving heed
To these companions of man's lonely race . . .
Loose me to these, between one dusk and dawn;—
I shall have need of them when you are gone.

## I DO NOT LOVE TO SEE YOUR BEAUTY FIRE

JOHN HALL WHEELOCK

I do not love to see your beauty fire
The light of eager love in every eye,
Nor the unconscious ardor of desire
Mantle a cheek when you are passing by;
When in the loud world's giddy thoroughfare
Your holy loveliness is noised about—
Lips that my love has prayed to—the gold hair
Where I have babbled all my secrets out—
O then I would I had you in my arms,
Desolate, lonely, broken, and forlorn,
Stripped of your splendor, spoiled of all your charms;
So that my love might prove her haughty scorn—
So I might catch you in my heart, and prove
'Tis not your beauty only that I love!

Of course it is not of love only that poetry presents ideals. It celebrates ideals in every phase of life—ideals of courage, endurance, loyalty, patriotism, friendship, sacrifice, hope, and the meeting of death itself. And poets, varying as they do in their own ideals and attitudes, present to the reader many choices. Contemplating death, some will accept as ideal peaceful passing, as in Tennyson's "Crossing the Bar"; others will prefer bold and courageous facing of the dark angel, as expressed by Browning's "Prospice" or by his "Epilogue to Asolando."

That a reader may see several attitudes toward death as expressed by poets, the following are quoted.

## REQUIEM

ROBERT LOUIS STEVENSON

Under the wide and starry sky,
Dig the grave and let me lie.
Glad did I live and gladly die,
   And I laid me down with a will.

This be the verse you grave for me:
*Here he lies where he longed to be;*
*Home is the sailor, home from the sea,*
*And the hunter home from the hill.*

## MARGARITAE SORORI

W. E. HENLEY

A late lark twitters from the quiet skies;
And from the west,
Where the sun, his day's work ended,
Lingers as in content,
There falls on the old grey city
An influence luminous and serene,
A shining peace.

The smoke ascends
In a rosy-and-golden haze. The spires
Shine, and are changed. In the valley
Shadows rise. The lark sings on. The sun,
Closing his benediction,
Sinks, and the darkening air
Thrills with a sense of the triumphing night—
Night with her train of stars
And her great gift of sleep.

So be my passing!
My task accomplished and the long day done,
My wages taken, and in my heart
Some late lark singing,
Let me be gathered to the quiet west,
The sundown splendid and serene,
Death.

## EXIT

JOHN GOULD FLETCHER

Thus would I have it:
So should it be for me,
The scene of my departure.
Cliffs ringed with scarlet,
And the sea pounding.

The pale brown sand
Miles after miles;
And then, afar off,
White on the horizon,
One ship with sails full-set
Passing slowly and serenely,
Like a proud burst of music,
To fortunate islands.

The fear of death itself is for most people less than the dread of something after death

The undiscover'd country from whose bourn
No traveller returns.

The most helpful and persistent ideals that we derive from poetry often slip into the mind unsuspected at the time. A situation, an incident, a character, a short passage, perhaps so deep in the mind that it has not been recalled for a long period, pops into consciousness at need and influences thought and action. Or a poem admired and remembered for its sheer beauty or for its cogency of thought may without our being aware of it determine what we think or do.

The influence of poetry on conduct or character may be, and probably often is, consciously accepted. Evidence is in marked passages, especially in books read when we were young and most impressionable. Looking at such passages years afterward, we may smile at the immaturity of the ideals and congratulate ourselves that we have grown to accept something higher; but at the same time we recognize that

"when we were a child . . . we thought as a child" and that
the sentiments expressed in the marked and remembered
passages did express the ideals held then, ideals which doubtless to some extent contributed to the forming of character.

But it is not only in childhood that poetry—all literature,
for that matter—exerts its influence. Adolescence is probably
more susceptible to such influence than either childhood or
maturity. A young man at college who had refused to join
his friends in some escapade that they called fun, was later
asked by a fellow student why he abstained. Feeling that his
friend would appreciate and respect a sincere answer, he replied, "One rainy afternoon when I was reading 'The Idylls
of the King,' an assignment in English 2, I came upon a passage in 'Guinevere.' Arthur was recounting to his prostrate
sinful Queen how he had gathered his knights and organized
the Round Table. He said:

> I made them lay their hands in mine and swear
> To reverence the King, as if he were
> Their conscience, and their conscience as their King,
> To break the heathen and uphold the Christ,
> To ride abroad redressing human wrongs,
> To speak no slander, nay nor listen to it,
> To honour his own word as if his God's,
> To lead sweet lives in purest chastity,
> To love one maiden only, cleave to her,
> And worship her by years of noble deeds,
> Until they won her; for indeed I knew
> Of no more subtle master under heaven
> Than is the maiden passion for a maid,
> Not only to keep down the base in man,
> But teach high thought, and amiable words
> And courtliness, and the desire of fame,
> And love of truth, and all that makes a man.

"When I read that oath," the young man continued, "I
recognized that in substance it expressed the ideal that every
gentleman should accept. I want to be a gentleman."

Probably every reader of poetry can go back in his memory

and recall instances when he was consciously influenced by an ideal strikingly expressed.

> I could not love thee, dear, so much,
> Loved I not honor more.

> . . . . .

> Who has given to me this sweet,
> And given my brother dust to eat,
> And when will his wage come in?

> . . . . .

> Is there, for honest poverty,
>    That hings his head, an' a' that?
> The coward slave, we pass him by,
>    We dare be poor for a' that!
>       For a' that, an' a' that,
>          Our toils obscure, an' a' that;
>             The rank is but the guinea's stamp;
>             The man's the gowd for a' that!

Literature has been known to exercise a powerful influence even when a reader has stubbornly resisted it. Schoolboys often complain against requirement that they study a classic, especially when they are required to memorize some part of it. But despite the hostile attitude, the literature has not infrequently, at the time of study or later, had its effect. The presented ideal is accepted, the sentiment retained, the beauty remembered to enrich and even to ennoble life.

An extreme case was reported orally by the warden of a reformatory to which a supposedly incorrigible youth was committed. At first the boy wholly lived up to his bad reputation. One day, sitting in solitary confinement for some infraction of the rules, he determined to become the most wicked and the most feared man in the community. He realized that he might not have the ingenuity himself to invent adequate means of achieving his ambition; so, being intellectually superior, he hit upon the idea that he would read literature and find how genius had presented men of evil thought and deed. When he was released from solitary he spent all of his spare time reading, greatly pleasing his keepers, who thought that punishment had achieved a real reformation.

The boy read assiduously, but, as he related some time afterward, he focused his attention not on poor Silas Marner and his restoration through Eppie, but on Dunstan Cass. His interest was to ascertain how Dunstan made himself hated and feared and to think how he himself might have escaped punishment by man. When he read *Romola* he concentrated on Tito, trying to admire the deeds that marked the steps in degeneracy and then to contrive in his imagination means by which he in Tito's situation might have escaped the fate on the bank of the Arno or elsewhere. But try as he might, the influence of Romola and of other noble characters subtly but surely won his admiration, and at first against his will he finally found himself hopeful of emulating them. He became an exemplary prisoner and after his release an admired citizen, wholly, he asserted years later, because literature had revealed to him what is good, true, and of good repute.

All this potential enrichment of the world poetry can give, an enrichment suffused with feeling that quickens the blood. It is with reverence that we should hold poetry, blessing the opportunities that it gives vicariously to share in the pleasures that sensitive men have revealed to us.

## A POET'S BOOKCASE

LLOYD MIFFLIN

Oh, gently, gently near the bookcase tread;
  Speak only in hushed whispers, soft and low;
These are the urns that hold the deathless dead,
  The souls of those passed onward long ago.

At this still shrine your heartfelt homage give;
  With reverence touch each tome upon the shelves;
These are the Dreams of Genius,—hence they live—
  The fine quintessence of their finer selves.

## Chapter Four

## THE POET AND HOW HE WORKS

WHAT is a poet? Wordsworth said that he is a person who is "endowed with more lively sensibility, more enthusiasm and tenderness, who has a greater knowledge of human nature, and a more comprehensive soul than are supposed to be common among mankind, . . . who rejoices more than other men in the spirit of life that is within him."

In "Ulysses" Tennyson might have had in mind a poet instead of the fabled wanderer when he wrote

> I will drink
> Life to the lees; all times I have enjoyed
> Greatly, have suffered greatly, both with those
> That loved me, and alone; . . .
> For always roaming with a hungry heart
> Much have I seen and known: cities of men
> And manners, climates, councils, governments.
> I am a part of all that I have met. . . .
> Yearning in desire
> To follow knowledge like a sinking star,
> Beyond the utmost bounds of human thought.

Poets are endowed by nature to be sensitive to the world around them—to see more quickly, perhaps, and certainly to feel more acutely and more deeply than most people what

74

they see. They perceive, often without the exercise of conscious effort, the "significance which life has come to have for them, with perceptions and insights that you and I do not possess." As Newman said, "The subconscious is of much more importance in the artist than the conscious; and the subconscious proceeds by its own mysterious inner chemistry and obeys its own mysterious laws."

Tennyson declared that the poets are "dowered with the hate of hate, the scorn of scorn, the love of love." They "learn by suffering what they teach in song," wrote Shelley; and Rossetti expressed the same idea in "The Song-Thrush,"

> By thine own tears thy song must tears beget.

It is this power to see in the world what is beautiful and true and significant, to penetrate to its core, that enables a poet by his skill in expression to move others, to make them see and feel as they would like to do but cannot without his help. Rummaging in his store of rich experiences he creates images and stories, and presents the truths that ordinary men could not by themselves discover.

> Touched by his hand, the wayside weed
> Becomes a flower; the lowliest reed
> Beside the stream
> Is clothed with beauty; gorse and grass
> And heather, where his footsteps pass,
> The brighter seem.

Seeing at an Oklahoma automobile show a gray sports roadster bearing on the windshield a card inscribed "Bought by ——" (a well-known Osage Indian), Paul Eldridge's imagination was moved to wonder what would happen to it.

> I wonder what ditch in northeastern Oklahoma
> You will presently adorn, slim gray roadster.
> Will the slim young Osage who steers you
> Snuff you out some flaring night
> When the cars roar deep-throated
> Down the Bartlesville road?
> Or will he destroy you by day

In a flowering plum thicket,
Intoxicating in its perfume?
(There are plum trees at every curve of the road in his country.)

Is your steel more sturdy,
Are your fibres more felted
Than those of the eight Nashes and the Paige
Who have preceded you in the hands of the indefatigable de-
    stroyer
The slim young Osage?

Will he release you, too—
Leap lightly as a cat from your body
In the ever-present crisis?
Or will you kill him?
Perish together to the pulsations of a powerhouse,
The mutter of a gas torch,

The soft blows of a night wind;
You, wrenched and stoical,
He, twisted and cursing,
With the fumes of gasoline and whisky in the soft night air?

For I see menace in the lines of you; your beauty—
There is smooth insolence about your beauty—
Equal to his.
There should be written on your hood the name Nemesis—
Not Lincoln. . . .

I wonder what ditch in northeastern Oklahoma
You will presently adorn, slim gray roadster!

And William Everson was inspired by the air raids to
stimulate our imaginations as to what might happen to the
bombers who after their mission returned to find no waiting
mother ships. The contrast between the raid and the tragic
end is most effective.

### THE RAID

They came out of the sun undetected,
Who had lain in the thin ships
All night long on the cold ocean,

Watched Vega go down, the Wain hover,
Drank in the weakening dawn their brew,
And sent the lumbering death-laden birds
Level along the decks.

They came out of the sun with their guns geared,
Saw the soft and easy shape of that island
Laid on the sea,
An unawakening woman,
Its deep hollows and its flowing folds
Veiled in the garlands of its morning mists,
Each of them held in his aching eyes the erotic image,
And then tipped down,
In the target's trance,
In the ageless instant of the long descent,
And saw sweet chaos blossom below,
And felt in that flower the years release.

The perfect achievement.
They went back toward the sun crazy with joy
Like wild birds weaving,
Drunkenly stunting;
Passed out over the edge of that injured island,
Sought the rendezvous on the open sea
Where the ships would be waiting.

None were there.
Neither smoke nor smudge;
Neither spar nor splice nor rolling raft.
Only the wide waiting waste,
That each of them saw with intenser sight
Than he ever had spared it,
Who circled that spot,
The spent gauge caught in its final flutter,
And straggled down on their wavering wings
From the vast sky,
From the endless spaces,
Down at last for the low hover,
And the short quick quench of the sea.

A girl on the point of graduation from high school imagined
with uncanny and moving vividness what the experience of
taking the first step into an unsheltering world would be.

## THE DOOR STANDS OPEN

WYNNE FAIRFIELD

The ever-passing steps went by the door;
We did not listen then, nor did we look outside;
But now the door stands open.

Some hang back, afraid to join the crowd that passes;
Some gather in the doorway to watch eagerly.
I am not afraid;
I am not eager.

I stand by the window and look at the faces.
I would know what life is, what the world is,
Before I go.
Those who come back are often sad or tired;
The stories they tell are not always pleasant;
Yet all who go out are happy; and they hurry,
Looking ahead at something just beyond.

There goes one now. She almost runs.
And there come some who are returning;
Their faces are lined and ugly, but their eyes are wise.
Not all of them. I see one coming back
Whose face is smooth and happy,
But her eyes are empty—foolish.
Why?
I will find out.

There goes a face like mine that searched for an answer.
What has she learned? She may tell me—
But she has passed.

I see a youth whose eyes are fixed on something far away;
His is a face to follow and respect.
I lean out. "Where are you going?"
The vague, deep eyes turn slightly,
"Just over there."
"Where?"
But he is gone.

Here returns a man whose face must have been like that youth's;
His eyes are broken windows, and he babbles without sense;
What is this world that does such things to men?

There stands a man who watches those who start out;
He sees them drop unnoticed things of value
For which he stoops and searches in the dust;
He is one who went out and has returned
With nothing.

I leave the window and look about the empty room.
They all have gone! I cannot warn them. . . .
'Tis just as well.
Youth's saving gift, I think, is that it will not look,
And cannot see.

I take a last glance back and gently close the door behind me;
I catch a friendly hand that's half outstretched;
And I am part of the crowd.

The true poet is so sensitive that he is likely to project himself into what he sees and to identify himself with it. Keats
said that he could not refrain from imagining himself one of
the sparrows that he saw feeding in the yard; Wordsworth,
an extreme possessor of what the psychologists call "empathy," wrote "I communed with all that I saw as something
not apart from, but inherent in, my own immaterial nature";
and Byron declared

> I live not in myself, but I become
> A portion of that around me. . . .
> Are not the mountains, waves, and sky a part
> Of me and of my soul, as I of them?

The artist is compelled to create. "An itch I have, a tang
to write," said Browning, and Walter Savage Landor declared "There is delight in singing, tho' none hear." Andrea
del Sarto anticipated the sentiment that Keats expressed in
one of his letters:

> I, painting from myself and to myself,
> Know what I do, am unmoved by men's blame
> Or their praise either.

Much has been said about the right of an artist "to express himself." Assuredly he has that right, and sincerity requires that if he expresses anybody, it be himself. It is by so doing that he proposes new beauty and novel truth as he sees it. When successful, he has contributed to the richness of the world. But that self-expression is not the only motive for creation is evidenced by the offering of paintings or music or poems to the public. Just as an artist has a right to sincere self-expression, other people have a right to accept or to reject what he produces. Personal sincerity is also a right of "consumers" of art. A painter has a right to draw unconventionally and to use bizarre colors; a composer has a right to produce cacophonies previously unheard in music or to use a form that is lopsided; and a poet has a right to celebrate filth or to express himself in enigmatic verses printed in dislocated phrases without capital letters or punctuation. But they have no right to resent or to blame others for not applauding. Consumers too have a right—to admire and accept or to reject and ridicule. One may doodle to his heart's content, but he must not consider himself superior if nobody buys what he has done merely to please himself. There is no real enjoyment, in either creating or consuming, without sincerity.

In Browning's "Balaustion's Adventure" we find:

> Ah, that brave
> Bounty of poets, the one royal race
> That ever was, or will be, in this world!
> They give no gift that bounds itself and ends
> I' the giving and the taking: theirs so breeds
> I' the heart and soul o' the taker, so transmutes
> The man who was only a man before,
> That he grows godlike in his turn, can give—
> He also, share the poet's privilege,
> Bring forth new good, new beauty, from the old.

The word "inspired" has often been applied to artists. The important thing, however, is not that a poet be inspired, but rather that his work be inspiring. It is possible that some readers who are loyal in their faith that the Bible is inspired, get from it—or at least from some parts of it—little that is inspiring to better and more holy lives. If verses inspire a reader to appreciation of beauty and truth, they are poems. If they do not inspire, they remain—just verses.

Besides being sensitive to the multifarious natural world and to equally multifarious men and women, human situations, and ideas in them, the poet has perceptions and insights to see in them significances, refined and tenuous relations—elements that others are glad to have pointed out to them. There is poetry everywhere if we but had the genius to perceive it. Swinburne in "Ave atque Vale" wrote of the French poet Charles Baudelaire:

> Thou sawest, in thine old singing season, brother,
> Secrets and sorrows unbeheld of us:
> Fierce loves, and lovely leaf-buds poisonous,
> Bare to thy subtler eye, but for none other
> Blowing by night in some unbreathed-in clime;
> The hidden harvest of luxurious time,
> Sin without shape, and pleasure without speech;
> And where strange dreams in a tumultuous sleep
> Make the shut eyes of stricken spirits weep;
> And with each face thou sawest the shadow on each,
> Seeing as men sow men reap.

In "Aurora Leigh" Mrs. Browning declared that poets are

> The only truth-tellers now left to God—
> The only speakers of essential truth,
> Opposed to relative, comparative,
> And temporal truths.

And the philosopher John Dewey wrote that "artists have always been the only purveyors of news, for it is not the outward happening in itself which is new, but the kindling by it of emotion, perception, and appreciation." In this statement he echoes Aristotle, who asserted that art is more nearly true than history, for the latter records what was true only once, while the former presents truth everlasting. William Blake was convinced that "the world of imagination is the world of eternity."

The poet needs no assignment. The world that he has experienced is rich with subjects: beauty that he has seen, tastes and smells and sensations of touch that he has enjoyed, music of common things and of the spheres, ideas that have moved him—all are grist for his mill. What has stimulated one poet may be of no import to another. Shelley would never have written of machines and modern materialism, but they inspired Walt Whitman to "Miracles," Kipling to "The Secret of Machines," Harry Kemp to "Chant of the Box Cars," Macknight Black to "Express Trains," William Rose Benét to "The Roundhouse," Charles Malam to "Steam Shovel," Sandburg to "Prayers of Steel," and Edmund Leamy to "The Ticket Agent."

The quotations following tell what two poets have said stimulated them to composition.

## THE ARGUMENT OF HIS BOOK

### ROBERT HERRICK

I sing of Brooks, of Blossoms, Birds, and Bowers:
Of April, May, and June, and July-flowers.
I sing of May-poles, Hock-carts, Wassails, Wakes,
Of Bride-grooms, Brides, and of their Bridal-cakes.
I write of Youth, of Love, and have access
By these, to sing of cleanly-wantonness.
I sing of Dews, of Rains, and piece by piece
Of Balm, of Oil, of Spice, and Amber-Greece.
I sing of Times trans-shifting; and I write
How Roses first came red, and Lilies white.
I write of Groves, of Twilights, and I sing
The Court of Mab, and of the Faerie-King.
I write of Hell; I sing (and ever shall)
Of Heaven, and hope to have it after all.

## PIED BEAUTY

GERARD MANLEY HOPKINS

Glory be to God for dappled things—
   For skies of couple-color as a brindled cow;
     For rose-moles all in stipple upon trout that swim;
Fresh fire-coal chestnut-falls; finches' wings;
   Landscape plotted and pieced—fold, fallow, and plow;
   And all trades, their gear, tackle and trim.

All things counter, original, spare, and strange;
   Whatever is fickle, freckled (who knows how?)
    With swift, slow; sweet, sour; adazzle, dim;
He fathers forth whose beauty is past change:
   Praise him.

Although the poet is sensitive to what he experiences, in a way he is a summation of all that has been said by other poets before him, for it is the exception when he has not absorbed much from his predecessors. Lowell noted this fact in his "Franciscus de Verulamio Sic Cogitavit."

   While you thought 'twas You thinking as newly
    As Adam still wet with God's dew,
   You forgot in your self-pride that truly
    The whole Past was thinking through you.

      . . . . .

   And yet there's the half of a truth in it,
    And my Lord might his copyright sue;
   For a thought's his who kindles new youth in it,
    Or so puts it as makes it more true.

      . . . . .

   We call a thing his, in the long run,
    Who utters it clearest and best.

But in his "Sunthin' in the Pastoral Line" Lowell warns that the poet must be indigenous; it is a fatal defect for him merely to imitate what others have written and to attempt celebration of what is not real to him.

Jes' so with poets: wut they've airly read
Gits kind o' worked into their heart and head,
So 's 't they can't seem to write but jest on sheers
With furrin countries or played-out ideers,
Nor hev a feelin', ef it does n't smack
O' wut some critter chose to feel 'way back:
This makes 'em talk o' daisies, larks, an' things,
Ez though we'd nothin' here that blows and sings
(Why, I'd give more for one live bobolink
Than a square mile o' larks in printer's ink.)

The true poet's subjects are not "mistily seen, murmuringly heard, mistakenly felt." He has experienced the world in a variety of ways, but he selects for interpretative presentation only what has moved him and what in his judgment is most likely to contribute to the pleasure or the elevation of others. And knowing that a reader can receive only a little at one time, he discriminatingly chooses that on which he wishes to focus attention. He "paints the things that matter, the tints that all pass by."

One of the artist's chief difficulties is that of subordinating various materials to a unity of design. In his Dedication to *The Rival Ladies* Dryden spoke of a time when the prospective drama "was only a confus'd Mass of Thoughts, tumbling over one another in the Dark: When the Fancy was only in its first Work, moving the Sleeping Images, things toward the Light, there to be distinguish'd, and then either chosen or rejected by the Judgment."

Failure to omit or to subordinate is not infrequently seen in the works of even great pictorial artists and musicians. The grotesque animal in Dürer's "Virgin with a Monkey" certainly detracts from the holy intention. Someone has said that "Debussy is like a painter who looks at his canvas and asks himself what more he can take out; Strauss is like a painter who has covered every inch with paint and when there isn't another inch to cover takes the paint he has left and throws it at the canvas." A critic of Flaubert wrote, "The great mistake of the realists is that they profess to tell the truth because they tell everything. . . . The effect is a kind of dazzled confusion mingled with fatigue and disgust. . . . Truth is lost in its own excess." One resents being told too much unless the technique is unusually satisfying, or too little even if the technique is good. Longfellow fails often on the first count, and Browning on the second. Does the poet in the following verses tell too much or not enough?

> Today is best.
> Tomorrow will always be today.
> If there be no happiness now,
> It will not come—ever.

Truly, selection and arrangement are as important as the possession of a wealth of ideas and images.

Something seizes on the poet's attention. . . . It delights and kindles his mind with the sense of its significance, of its wide relationship with other experiences. . . . It brings with it a certain joy and excitement, to which is due the urgency it takes on in the poet's mind, driving him to express it in some appropriate form. But as he attends to it, it . . . collects feelings and associations round it; other experiences, remembered or imagined, come crowding in with their comment or illumination. . . . The image has become enriched and complicated; . . . its significance . . . has widened and deepened and become more peculiarly his own. . . . But imagination will never be satisfied until it has brought out all possible and appropriate enrichment . . . ; and, what is even more important, will never be satisfied until it can hold the whole complexity clearly before it in one single act of attention, organized into one inclusive experience, isolated into self-sufficing unity by its triumphal internal harmony of unique and presiding significance.[1]

Successful poetic choice results in a focus that intensifies realization. Possessing from his wealth of experience multitudinous images of beauty, the poet draws on them to enrich an idea that has flashed into his mind or an object that he has seen or a person that he has known. Sometimes the enrichment comes to him in a flash of inspiration; sometimes it is

[1] Lascelles Abercrombie, *The Theory of Poetry*, pp. 60–61. Harcourt, Brace and Co., New York.

a result of long reflection and meditation. He sees a spring gone dry and perceives the tragedy of the contrast with the bubbling freshness that has gone; he has an acquaintance, who becomes Flammonde, Richard Cory, or Mr. Flood; he reads of Helen of Troy and imagines her grown to middle age, as Roselle Mercier Montgomery did.

### I

The strife on Ilium's windy plain is still;
  Cool, now, the blood that in the veins of men
  So madly coursed to view your beauty when
The Greek and Trojan fates hung on your will;
Unkindling, eyes that could not look their fill
  Upon the wonder that was Helen then.
  They will not wake to burn for you again,
Those thirsting fires that drove mad men to kill.

Now ships and towers are ashes on the wind
  And Paris, dead, your springtime shepherd lover . . .
Here by your side your lawful liege leans over
  To smooth, mechanically, your graying hair
And say, in that calm voice, forever kind,
  "Please, dear, a stitch; my tunic has a tear!"

### II

You take the garment from his hand and smile . . .
  "That hand struck Paris!" you think suddenly,
  And all the facile floods of memory,
Unsealed, pour over you. Your hands, meanwhile,
Are dutifully busy, as your lord
  Relates to you the details of the chase;
  You listen, with a half-averted face,
And give him back an absent-minded word.

For far away a cool, clean wind is blowing
  High on a hill, and you are there again:
  Your Paris is beside you: green, the spring,
And warm the young blood in you, leaping, flowing:
  His lips are on your throat—*and then, and then
You are this Helen, here, remembering!*

### III

The tunic mended, with a "Thank you, dear!"
  Your Menelaus takes it from your hands
  That, snow and rose-leaf once, laid their commands
On kings and kingdoms in a long-gone year.
Transparent, fragile, but unwrinkled still,
  The small, domestic tasks engage them now. . . .
  Strange, that to-day you should remember how
Young Paris crushed and kissed them on a hill.

And yet, not strange. You are not first, ah, no!
  Of sister women, nor will you be the last,
  To summon spectres from the passioned past
While you sit quietly and listen so
  To your lord's tale—tasting the tempered joys
  Time leaves to Helens who outlive their Troys.

In this connection we like to recall the most famous celebration of Helen since Homer, Christopher Marlowe's lines from his drama, "The Tragical History of Doctor Faustus."

Was this the face that launched a thousand ships,
And burnt the topless towers of Ilium?—
Sweet Helen, make me immortal with a kiss.—
Her lips suck forth my soul: see, where it flies!—
Come, Helen, come, give me my soul again.
Here will I dwell, for heaven is in these lips,
And all is dross that is not Helena.
I will be Paris, and for love of thee,
Instead of Troy, shall Wittenberg be sacked;
And I will combat with weak Menelaus,
And wear thy colors on my plumed crest;
Yea, I will wound Achilles in the heel,
And then return to Helen for a kiss.
O, thou art fairer than the evening air
Clad in the beauty of a thousand stars;
Brighter art thou than flaming Jupiter
When he appear'd to hapless Semela;
More lovely than the monarch of the sky
In wanton Arethusa's azur'd arms;
And none but thou shall be my paramour!

The poet selects from his experience and from his ever-active imagination what he thinks is most likely to arouse in others the emotions that have stirred in him. He disciplines his own excitement by the requirements of his art to convey his feelings to readers. "On the first suspicion," however, "that a poet is being ingenious, his poetry shrivels up and dies. The poet is not to be ingenious; he is to be inevitable."

> When happiest Fancy has inspired the strains
> How oft the malice of one luckless word
> Pursues the Enthusiast.

The poet knows that he will be successful if he can induce the reader to put himself in the place of the poet or of a character made important in the poem. Everybody is egocentric, and when one can be made to identify himself with the presented situation or character, he will feel as the poet did. Although a poem may concern a very special occurrence, if successful it will seem a personal expression to others. Any elegy may become an expression of personal grief. A poet's love for Stella or Delia or Corinna is every person's love for his own sweetheart.

A poet may communicate an idea, but in itself that is not enough; prose does that. In addition, he must express emotion; that is the essence of poetry. Communication and expression may use almost identical words, but the purpose is different, and the effect is different. One may say, "The train is late again": that is a communication of fact. Or one may say, "Heavens! The train is late again!" That is expression of feeling because of a fact. Compare any plain statement of a contemplation of suicide, for example, with Hamlet's soliloquy. Hamlet was attempting to communicate no information; he was merely expressing the emotions that possessed him.

> O, that this too too solid flesh would melt,
> Thaw and resolve itself into a dew!
> Or that the Everlasting had not fix'd
> His canon 'gainst self-slaughter! O God! O God!
> How weary, stale, flat, and unprofitable

Seem to me all the uses of this world!
Fie on't! oh fie! 'tis an unweeded garden,
That grows to seed; things rank and gross in nature
Possess it merely. That it should come to this!

What a poet selects to present reveals himself just as his presentation does. We know more of the real Keats and of Burns from their poems than we can learn from factual biographies. "The verse is weak and shallow as its source" and also as strong and deep. It is interesting to run over a table of contents of the works of any poet and to consider from what he chose to write about what manner of man he was, and it is also illuminating to learn of his real inner self by considering his treatment of common themes, like death and duty, spring and autumn, birds and flowers, heroes and history. From their writings compare the several men who wrote of Pheidippides, the story of the glove, and the tragedy of Paolo and Francesca. Writing of a musical composition, Ernest Newman said, "The C Sharp Minor Prelude is simply a young-mannish attempt at profundity. 'What a vale of tears is this world,' it says; 'but see with what dignity I fold my arms, wrap my black cloak around me, pull my black hat over my eyes, contract my brows . . . , and gaze mournfully but still nobly into the abyss that yawns at my feet!' "

The poet draws from his own store of images those that build up for others an imaginary world more satisfying than ordinary mortals know. "Imitations," Dr. Johnson declared, "produce pain or pleasure, not because they are mistaken for realities, but because they bring realities to mind." The poet's "brains beat into rhythm to tell what we felt only" and were incompetent to express.

The poet's eye in a fine frenzy rolling,
Doth glance from heaven to earth, from earth to heaven;
And as imagination bodies forth
The form of things unknown, the poet's pen
Turns them to shapes and gives to airy nothing
A local habitation and a name.

In a sense, one must be a poet to enjoy poetry, having something of

> The vision and the faculty divine,
> Though wanting the accomplishment of verse.

Having "the vision and the faculty divine," the poet expresses for us what we may have dimly felt but had neither the constructive imagination to make definite nor the words to say it. The poet's

> Speech is as a thousand eyes
> Through which we see the earth.

As Hans Sachs says in *Die Meistersinger*, the dream and the poet's art are never far apart.

Poets also give immortality to places and to characters. Yarrow and Chillon are almost as real to lovers of poetry as their own countryside and like Keats's town in the "Ode to a Grecian Urn" they are unchangeable in our memories.

### HELEN

#### WALTER SAVAGE LANDOR

> Past ruined Ilium Helen lives;
>   Alcestis rises from the shades.
> Verse calls them forth; 'tis verse that gives
>   Immortal youth to mortal maids.
>
> Soon shall oblivion's deepening veil
>   Hide all the peopled hills you see,
> The gay, the proud, while lovers hail
>   These many summers you and me.

The true poet has an urge through artistic representation to clarify vagueness and to set in order the confusion of the world. To do this he must have not only perception but also discrimination in selection of the significant and skill in presentation. Tennyson said that when he had an idea for a poem the composition was easy, and Amy Lowell declared that planning is the most difficult part of composition. All the selected details must be so fitted together that there is an articulated unity, so that the whole is greater than the sum of the parts. This of course requires technical skill, but Coventry Patmore has called attention to "the careful luck of him who tries many words and has the wit to know when memory, or the necessary meter or rhyme, has supplied him unexpectedly with those which are perhaps even better than he knew how to desire."

Not every attempt of even the greatest artists will result in unvarying success. There are records of as many as eighty versions of one poem before the author was satisfied. W. H. Auden in the introduction to his collected poems writes:

> In the eyes of every author, I fancy, his own past work falls into four classes. First, the pure rubbish which he regrets ever having conceived; second—for him the most painful—the good ideas which his incompetence or impatience prevented from coming to much . . . ; third, the pieces he has nothing against except their lack of importance; these must inevitably form the bulk of any collection since, were he to limit it to the fourth class alone, to those poems for which he is honestly grateful, his volume would be too depressingly slim.

It is saddening to read through the collected works of almost any poet and to realize how often he fails to convey anything that makes an effective appeal. He may have felt his aesthetic temperature rise at some experience, but he was unable to convey his feelings to others. Perhaps the best known complete failure is Wordsworth's description of an infant's grave.

> I've measured it from side to side;
> 'Tis three feet long and two feet wide.

One can readily perceive the pathos of the tiny grave of the dead child and all that it connotes. But cold arithmetic is not a means to arouse emotions. We should not wonder so much that Wordsworth could thus fail as we should have admiration for his success in "Tintern Abbey" and "The Solitary Reaper." Many "poems" included in complete works are obviously exercises in composition: they are perfectly proper for practice in developing skills or they are experiments that did not come off. But before one becomes too critical he should remember that for success a poem requires an appreciative reader: there must be a good receiving set properly tuned as well as good transmission. The poet is not always a good judge of his own work, nor is the reader always a competent judge of powers of assimilation. Judgment of generations of readers ultimately decides what, in the words of Matthew Arnold, should be preserved and bound in pure gold.

I have recently read an anthology of verses selected and published for young people. Many of the selections are almost poems. The authors have attempted with facile rhythm to convey to others the mild emotions that they felt when contemplating a dog, a cat, a singing bird, three green parrots flying through the trees, apple blossoms, a petrified fern, and a post-office inkwell. The verses read easily and all of the subjects have possibilities, but many of them arouse little interest and less emotion, chiefly because the authors themselves have not been sincerely and deeply moved. They have found in their subjects nothing really significant, nothing that really stirs the imagination, almost nothing that a reader would not himself have felt when reflecting on the same themes. We wish poems to reveal new beauties, new truths, fresh aspects, what we should like to have perceived, what ever afterwards we shall think and feel when observing the previously commonplace. These things we want, and a perfect expression of what we had vaguely felt and could not put into words. Sir William Watson, in his poem "Wordsworth's Grave," speaks critically.

> Idly tuneful, the loquacious throng
>   Flutter and twitter, prodigal of time.
> And little masters make a toy of Song
>   Till grave men weary of the sound of rhyme.

In "Sleep and Poetry" Keats decries these poetasters.

Ah, dismal soul'd!
The winds of heaven blew, the ocean rolled
Its gathering waves—ye felt it not. The blue
Bared its eternal bosom, and the dew
Of summer night collected still to make
The morning precious: Beauty was awake!
Why were ye not awake? But ye were dead
To things ye knew not of,—were closely wed
To musty laws lived out with wretched rule
And compass vile; so that ye taught a school
Of dolts to smooth, inlay, and clip, and fit,
Till, like the certain wands of Jacob's wit
Their verses tallied. Easy was the task:
A thousand handicraftsmen wore the mask
Of Poesy.

Oliver Wendell Holmes gives in "A Familiar Letter to
Several Correspondents" a facetious recipe for writing this
kind of verse.

Yes, write if you want to—there's nothing like trying;
   Who knows what a treasure your casket may hold?
I'll show you that rhyming's as easy as lying,
   If you'll listen to me while the art I unfold.

Here's a book full of words: one can choose as he fancies,
   As a painter his tint, as a workman his tool;
Just think! all the poems and plays and romances
   Were drawn out of this, like a fish from a pool!

You can wander at will through its syllabled mazes,
   And take all you want—not a copper they cost;
What is there to hinder your picking out phrases
   For an epic as clever as "Paradise Lost"?

Don't mind if the index of sense is at zero;
   Use words that run smoothly, whatever they mean;
Leander and Lillian and Lillibullero
   Are much the same thing in the rhyming machine.

There are words so delicious their sweetness will smother
   That boarding-school flavour of which we're afraid;

> There is "lush" is a good one and "swirl" is another;
>     Put both in one stanza, its fortune is made.
>
> With musical murmurs and rhythmical closes
>     You can cheat us of smiles when you've nothing to tell;
> You hand us a nosegay of milliner's roses,
>     And we cry with delight, "Oh, how sweet they do smell!"
>
> Perhaps you will answer all needful conditions
>     For winning the laurels to which you aspire,
> By docking the tails of the two prepositions
>     I' the style o' the bards you so greatly admire.
>
> As for subjects of verse, they are only too plenty
>     For ringing the changes on metrical chimes;
> A maiden, a moonbeam, a lover of twenty,
>     Have filled that great basket with bushels of rhymes.

We know from their own reports that poets have different methods of composition. Wordsworth usually wrote after long contemplation and with revisions that often betrayed little critical faculty; Keats composed only when the mood of creation was in him, when he was pregnant with ideas, thoughts coming to him in troops, and his emendations, always felicitous improvements, were made mostly at the time of original composition; Robert Frost wrote out his poems much as they appear in printed form. Housman tells that he composed two stanzas of "I hoed and trenched and weeded" easily while on a casual walk, another at tea, and the fourth only after long and laborious effort, with twelve trials and failures; and yet, one reading the poem cannot tell which stanza almost wrote itself and which came after tedious effort.

William Cullen Bryant, in verses which, though failing themselves to evidence "lips quivering with the passionate thrill," gives sound advice as to how a poet should compose and revise.

> The secret wouldst thou know
>     To touch the heart or fire the blood at will?
> Let thine own eyes o'erflow;
>     Let thy lips quiver with the passionate thrill;

Seize the great thought, ere yet its power be past,
And bind, in words, the fleet emotion fast.

Then, should thy verse appear
  Halting and harsh, and all unaptly wrought,
Touch the crude line with fear,
  Save in the moment of impassioned thought;
Then summon back the original glow, and mend
The strain with rapture that with fire was penned.

From a poet's worksheets that have been preserved and from changes made after an original publication one can study a poet's "craftsmanship, watch his imagination at work on his materials, see what he was trying to do and how far he succeeded, watch him make his blunders and learn from them as he finds out by degrees how to use his tools and so approaches nearer and nearer to the ideal that still eludes him." Amy Lowell said that "Keats's corrections are a most important study for anyone who is learning the art of poetry," and, it may be added, for anyone who is learning to appreciate the taste and the artistry of a poet. "The most important criticism of art, as T. S. Eliot has maintained, is the criticism made by the artist himself during the process of creation— inventing, selecting, rejecting, harmonizing, contrasting, unifying, articulating, ordering, emphasizing, arranging, finishing."[2]

Fortunately one who wishes to pursue this interesting exercise in the appreciation of poetry can find an abundance of material. For a beginning and as a convenience several illustrations will now be given. The first is three versions of one section from a holographic copy that Milton made of "Lycidas." The words in italics are those which in the original were struck out by the poet. If still in the poem, they were restored. This version should be carefully compared line for line and even word for word with the final form (C).

[2] D. A. Stauffer, *Poets at Work*. Harcourt, Brace and Company, New York.

## LYCIDAS

### A

Bring the rathe primrose that unwedded dies
*collu* coloring the pale cheeke of uninjoyed love
and that sad floure that strove
to write his owne woes on the vermeil graine
next adde Narcissus y$^t$ still weeps in vaine
the woodbine and y$^e$ pansie freak't w$^{th}$ jet
the glowing violet
the cowslip wan that hangs his pensive head
and every bud that sorrows liverie weares
                          with
let Daffadillies fill thier cups   $\wedge$   teares
bid Amaranthus all his beautie shed
to strew the laureat herse &c

### B

Bring the rathe primrose that forsaken dies
the tufted crowtoe and pale Gessamin
the white pinke, and y$^e$ pansie freakt w$^{th}$ jet
the glowing violet      the well-attir'd woodbine
the muske rose and *the garish columbine*
w$^{th}$ cowslips wan that hang the pensive head
                     x       weare
and every flower that sad escutcheon   $\wedge$    beares
    x          weares
    imbroiderie *beares*
2   & *let* daffodillies fill thier cups w$^{th}$ teares
1   bid Amaranthus all his beauties shed
    to strew &c

### C

Bring the rathe Primrose that forsaken dies,
The tufted Crow-toe, and pale Gessamine,
The white Pinke, and the Pansie freakt with jeat,
The glowing Violet.
The Musk-rose, and the well attir'd Woodbine,
With Cowslips wan that hang the pensive hed,

And every flower that sad embroidery wears:
Bid *Amaranthus* all her beauty shed,
And Daffadillies fill their cups with tears,
To strew the Laureat Herse where *Lycid* lies

Wordsworth apparently wrote with ease and was well satisfied with what he had first set down on paper, but he did make revisions, many of them because of criticisms after first publication. In the poem "We Are Seven" an atrocious first line

A simple child, dear brother Jim,

he replaced with merely

A simple child

discarding the relative who had no meaning and no significance. Ordinarily Wordsworth was particularly faithful to his experiences and extraordinarily tenacious of them.

Following are four versions of the second stanza of Wordsworth's "To a Cuckoo," published in 1807, 1815, 1827, and 1845 respectively.

While I am lying on the grass,
I hear thy restless shout:
From hill to hill it seems to pass,
About, and all about!

. . . . .

Thy loud note smites my ear!
It seems to fill the whole air's space,
At once far off and near!

. . . . .

Thy twofold shout I hear,
That seems to fill the whole air's space,
As loud far off as near.

. . . . .

While I am lying on the grass
Thy twofold shout I hear,
From hill to hill it seems to pass,
At once far off, and near.

In the final version "there are three quite distinct observations of the cuckoo's song: the double note, the way in which it keeps coming unexpectedly from one direction and then another, and the odd and sudden variations in the volume of the sound."

In the 1807 version "the second of the two ideas—the restless, wandering voice, now here, now there—is more fully emphasized: but the double note is not expressed at all, and the fluctuating strength of the cuckoo's 'shout' is only suggested." In the 1915 version the poet "has got two of the three ideas included. . . . In 1920 he weakens the second point. . . . In 1827 the 'twofold shout' appears for the first time. . . . Here . . . Wordsworth has made a complete change in the meaning, an unusual proceeding with him."[3]

In the *Lyrical Ballads,* published in 1798, can be found the original versions of a number of poems written by Wordsworth and by Coleridge, each of which can be compared with the later ones in the collected work of each poet. A study of the changes in "The Ancient Mariner" will prove highly rewarding. By revision Coleridge got rid of commonplace lines and made the poem one of the most artistically perfect ballads in the English language. Only a few of the changes will be recorded here.

Before the present third stanza appeared these lines:

> He holds him the wedding-guest—
> There was a ship, quoth he—
> "Nay, if thou'st got a laughsome tale,
> "Marinere! come with me,"

and the third stanza originally ran as follows with the absurd last line:

> He holds him with his skinny hand,
> Quoth he, there was a Ship—
> "Now get thee hence, thou grey-beard Loon!
> "Or my staff will make thee skip."

[3] James Sutherland, *The Medium of Poetry*, pp. 57-58. The Hogarth Press, London, 1934.

Twice in the original version Coleridge began stanzas with "Listen, Stranger!" and instead of "It ate the food it ne'er had eat" there was the nauseating line "The Mariners gave it biscuit-worms." In the revision practically all of the artificial diction (*ne, uprist, wist, yspread, yeven*) disappeared, only *I wist, 'gan,* and *countree* being retained, and the superb gloss was added.

Also omitted was a weak stanza in Part V:

> Listen, O listen, thou wedding-guest!
> "Marinere! thou hast thy will:
> "For that, which comes out of thy eye, doth make
> "My body and soul to be still."

In Part III the lines

> And are these two all, all the crew,
> That woman and her fleshless Phere?

are replaced by the powerful suggestion of four startled questions:

> And is that Woman all her crew?
> Is that a Death? and are there two?
> Is Death that woman's mate?

Fortunately lost is the next original stanza:

> *His* bones are black with many a crack,
> All black and bare, I ween;
> Jet-black and bare, save where with rust
> Of mouldy damps and charnel crust
> They're patched with purple and green.

And

> She is far liker Death than he;
> Her flesh makes the still air cold.

becomes

> The nightmare Life-in-Death was she,
> Who thicks man's blood with cold.

Finally, compare two other passages from Part III. The first version read:

> And we look'd round, and we look'd up,
> And fear at our hearts, as at a cup,
> The life-blood seemed to sip—
>
> The sky was dull, and dark the night,
> The helsman's face by his lamp gleam'd bright,
> From the sails the dew did drip—
> While clombe above the Eastern bar
> The horned Moon, with one bright Star
> Almost between the tips.
>
> One after one by the horned Moon
> (Listen, O Stranger! to me)
> Each turn'd his face with a ghastly pang
> And curs'd me with his ee.

The final version, marvelously rid of the imperfections, runs:

> We listened and looked sideways up!
> Fear at my heart, as at a cup,
> The life-blood seemed to sip!
> The stars were dim, and thick the night,
> The steersman's face by his lamp gleamed white;
> From the sails the dew did drip—
> Till clomb above the eastern bar
> The horned Moon, with one bright star
> Within the nether tip.
>
> One after one by the star-dogged Moon,
> Too quick for groan or sigh,
> Each turned his face with a ghastly pang
> And cursed me with his eye.

It is from the revisions made by Keats during the fever of composition that one can learn most about the work of a skilled technician with exquisite taste. Keats delighted in his powers of expression, and he had "capacity for intense, sustained, and *general* excitement, . . . a state of heightened sensibility, in which thoughts and feelings pressed upon him, and his imagination became unusually active." He apparently composed when the strings of every sense were taut, ideas and images crowding into his mind and importunate for expression. It might have been Keats of whom Oliver Wendell Holmes wrote: "When one is in the receptive attitude of mind, the thoughts which are sprung upon him, the images which flash through his consciousness, are a delight and an excitement."

But Keats had unusual skill to revise, especially while in the creative mood. The lines in "Hyperion"

> No stir of air was there,
> Not so much life as on a summer's day
> Robs one light seed from the feather'd grass

were originally

> No stir of air was there,
> Not so much life as a young vulture's wing
> Would spread upon a field of green-ear'd corn.

But obviously a carrion-eating bird, however beautiful its silent soaring, is out of place in a poem about the god Saturn, and, besides, he would not be soaring above a field of grain; so first Keats substituted "eagle's" for "vulture's" and then discarded the grainfield altogether, writing

> Not so much life as on a summer's day
> Robs not at all the dandelion's fleece.

But the poet must have been dissatisfied with the definiteness of *dandelion* and the obtrusiveness of the figurative *fleece*, both words diverting attention from the intended effect of absolute stillness. So he rewrote the line, emphasizing the quiet with five lightly stressed words: "Robs not one light seed from the feather'd grass."[4]

Amy Lowell in her *John Keats*, notably on pages 503–504, discusses some of the revisions that the poet made; but the

[4] Much of the above is summarized from C. Day Lewis, *The Poetic Image*, pp. 75–77. Oxford University Press.

most complete and enlightening consideration will be found
in M. R. Ridley's *Keats' Craftsmanship* (Oxford University
Press). In this excellent treatise Ridley comments on the
changes made in nine of the major poems. From this volume
the following passage, the first paragraphs summarized, is
quoted.

In "To Autumn" Keats made only two changes in the opening
stanza as first written. In the fourth line he changed "The vines with
fruit" to "With fruit the vines"; in the sixth line "And fill all fruits
with sweetness to the core" to "And fill all fruit with ripeness to the
core"; and in the eighth line "With a white kernel" to "With a sweet
kernel."

In the second stanza the poet found difficulties, drawing on his
imagination instead of his observation. He began

> Who hath not seen thee? for thy haunts are many.
> Sometimes whoever seeks for thee may find. . .

But either at once, seeing that *many* is going to be awkward for
rhyme, or when he reaches the end of the third line, Keats alters,
feeling also no doubt a kind of thin abruptness in the half-line question, and a certain feebleness of both sound and sense in *for thee:*

> Who hath not seen thee oft amid thy stores?
> Sometimes whoever seeks abroad may find
> Thee sitting careless on a granary floor
> Thy hair soft lifted by the winnowing wing.

The final *s* of *stores* is deleted, and *wing* at once changed to the
intended *wind*.

However, whatever small points there may have been in the first
four lines, they were soon and easily solved. Now the real troubles
begin.
                                            husky
> While bright the Sun slants through the͜barn;
> Or sound asleep in a half reaped field
> Dosed with red poppies; while thy reeping hook
> Spares form Some slunbrous

At this point the lines, which have clearly been going from bad
to worse, have petered out altogether, and no rhyme for *field* is
in sight anyway. The next stage is some minor tinkering. The line
about the sun, and the next line, are deleted altogether, and the
second re-written as

on on a half reap'd furrow sound asleep

Then *Some slumbrous* is deleted, and under it written

minutes while wam slumpers creep

So that now he has in front of him

husky

While bright the Sun slants through the~barn
on on a half reap'd furrow sound asleep
~~Or sound asleep in a half reaped field~~
Dosed with read poppies; while thy reeping hook
Spares form ~~Some slumbrous~~

minutes while wam slumpers creep

That has at least achieved a rhyme; but if the line about the sun is
to disappear altogether, the rhyme is in the wrong place; none of it is
very satisfactory; and the *eep* sound has got out of hand. So Keats
cancels the whole passage with some vigorous cross-hatching, and
begins all over again, using the re-written sixth line as the fifth,
and improving the old seventh for use as the new sixth.

Or on a half reap'd furrow sound asleep
Dos'd with the fume of poppies, while thy hook
Spares for ~~one~~ some slunbrous minutes the next swath;

So far, so good; and as any troubles about a rhyme for the un-
promising *swath* are still four lines off he goes on his way rejoicing:

And sometimes like a gleans thost dost keep
Steady thy laden head across the brook
Or by a Cyder-press with patent look
Thou. . . .

Well, and now what about the swath, waiting four lines above for
its rhyme? But the Cyder-press is going as well as can be, so for
the moment confound the swath, and finish

watchest the last oozing hours by hours

and now go back and get the rhyme, even if we have to sacrifice
in the process the idea of the tenacious *slumpers* which has hung
onto existence through two corrections.

Spares the next swath and all its twined flowers . . .

The last stanza contains the picture that was the germ of the
whole poem. . . . The stanza starts easily enough:

Where are the songs of Spring? Aye where are they?
Think not of them thou hast thy music too—

> While a gold cloud gilds the soft dying day
> And touches

At this point he sees that, the cloud being singular, *And touches* is going to be awkward, so he deletes *And* and writes *Touching the,* and then, I think before completing the line, goes back to the third, which will clearly not do as it is with the redundance of *gilds* and *gold.* First he deletes *a,* makes *cloud* into *clouds* and cancels the *s* of *gilds,* and begins to emend *gold,* possibly to *yellow,* but before getting far with it scratches it out and writes *barred* above. Finally he finds a word which will give him the alliteration that led to the redundance, and cancels *gild* and writes in *bloom.* Then he goes back to the unfinished fourth line, finds that it will now do in its original form and so reverts to that. . . .

He began the last line "And new flocks still," but immediately canceled them and wrote "And gathering swallows twitter in the skies."

He found all his disciplined powers, of observation, of imagination, of craftsmanship, combining in one moment of power to produce the most serenely flawless poem in our language, "To Autumn."

## TO AUTUMN

> Season of mists and mellow fruitfulness,
>   Close bosom-friend of the maturing sun;
> Conspiring with him how to load and bless
>   With fruit the vines that round the thatch-eaves run;
> To bend with apples the moss'd cottage-trees
>   And fill all fruit with ripeness to the core;
>     To swell the gourd, and plump the hazel shells
>   With a sweet kernel; to set budding more,
> And still more, later flowers for the bees,
> Until they think warm days will never cease,
>     For Summer has o'er-brimmed their clammy cells.
>
> Who hath not seen thee oft amid thy store?
>   Sometimes whoever seeks abroad may find
> Thee sitting careless on a granary floor,
>   Thy hair soft-lifted by the winnowing wind;
> Or on a half-reap'd furrow fast asleep,
>   Drows'd with the fume of poppies, while thy hook
>     Spares the next swath and all its twined flowers:
> And sometimes like a gleaner thou dost keep

Steady thy head across a laden brook;
Or by a cyder-press, with patient look,
  Thou watchest the last oozings hours by hours.

Where are the songs of Spring? Ay, where are they?
  Think not of them, thou hast thy music too,—
While barred clouds bloom the soft-dying day,
  And touch the stubble-plains with rosy hue;
Then in a wailful choir the small gnats mourn
  Among the river sallows, borne aloft
    Or sinking as the light wind lives or dies;
And full-grown lambs loud bleat from hilly bourn;
  Hedge-crickets sing; and now with treble soft
  The red-breast whistles from a garden-croft;
    And gathering swallows twitter in the skies.

Tennyson could never compose poetry except when the mood was on him, but then he devoted all of his energies and enthusiasm to the task. Some subjects for poems, like tales of Arthur and his knights, lingered in his mind for years before he set them down; others he celebrated almost in a flash of inspiration. His son records that coming home from a walk in his eighty-first year Tennyson wrote out "Crossing the Bar" as it stands, unchanged. Some of the Idylls he first wrote out in prose—beautiful prose, too—before putting them into metrical form. One illustration of Tennyson's revisions is the substitution of "and the winds are dead" for the last half of the second verse in this passage from "Oenone."

    The lizard, with his shadow on the stone,
    Rests like a shadow, and the cicada sleeps.

And in "A Dream of Fair Women" he first made Iphigenia say

    One drew a sharp knife through my tender throat:
    Slowly, and nothing more.

In the revision he perfected the lines:

    The bright death quiver'd at the victim's throat;
    Touch'd; and I knew no more.

In the two-volume biography are included a number of verses not previously published, most of which do not heighten Tennyson's reputation as a poet, but the suppression does manifest his acumen as a critic.

The complete works of numerous authors edited by scholars contain the original and revised versions of poems. Especially recommended are the Virginia and the Stedman-Woodbury editions of Edgar Allan Poe.

Readers who are interested to consider the revisions made by contemporary poets will find in Stauffer's *Poets at Work* (Harcourt, Brace and Co., 1948) illuminating consideration of the processes used by Robert Bridges, Genevieve Taggard, Louis MacNeice, Conrad Aiken, and Stephen Spender. In this volume Stauffer says, "At some time every poem must have its vision; all the rest is revision." Phyllis Bartlett in *Poetry in Process* (Oxford University Press) devotes an entire volume to reporting how poets have composed and to the revisions which for various reasons they have made. The scholarly book is interestingly written.

It will be enlightening, too, to read the several poems from the same pen on the same topic; for example, Wordsworth's "To a Daisy" and the three versions of Shelley's "A Bridal Song."

# PART TWO

## The Means That Artists Use

## Chapter Five

## THE SENSUOUS APPEAL

WHAT are the means that artists use to get emotionally satisfying responses? In all of the arts they use three means: the sensuous, the technical, and the connotative or suggestive and imaginatively stimulating. The most satisfying, complete, and lasting pleasure comes from response to all three stimuli, each contributing its effect to one harmonious whole. But unfortunately, many who listen to music, look at pictures, or read poetry are unaware of or neglect one or two of those elements: to them music may be merely sensuous sound; painting must represent something while at the same time it is beautiful; and poetry uses rhythm to convey an intellectual message. Such people miss the fullest enjoyment that art can give. In this and in succeeding chapters will be discussed the three kinds of stimuli that artists use to arouse in others satisfying emotional responses.

The sensuous appeal depends largely on something innate, in varying degrees, in every human being. Without consciously being taught, people respond with pleasure to a gorgeous sunset, to the mysterious beauty of a full moon, to graceful form, and to rhythm. This is not to say that the pleasure from sensuous appeal cannot be intensified and made

more discriminating by instruction or that both instruction
and experience cannot make one more sensitive to sensuous
beauty. Art certainly does add to the appreciation of beauty
by pointing it out and by interpreting it, for

> We're made so that we love
> First when we see them painted, things we have passed
> Perhaps a hundred times nor cared to see.

But some sensuous response to sheer beauty is native and more
or less latent in everyone. Here again we must expect and
respect variations in kind and degree of responses to the
same stimulus. It is one function of poetry to quicken the
senses and to express as we would like to have them expressed
the feelings that beauty arouses.

The sensuous appeal is present to some degree in almost all
poetry. Sometimes it suffuses everything else, as in Poe's
"Ulalume," "Annabel Lee," and "The Raven." Who cares
what they mean? It is enough that they please the ear with
sonorous verse.

> For the moon never beams without bringing me dreams
>    Of the beautiful ANNABEL LEE.
> And the stars never rise but I feel the bright eyes
>    Of the beautiful ANNABEL LEE.
> And so, all the night-tide, I lie down by the side
> Of my darling—my darling, my life and my bride,
>    In the sepulchre there by the sea—
>    In her tomb by the sounding sea.

Coleridge's "Kubla Khan" is almost pure abstract music, the
sense being tenuous and of no importance.

> In Xanadu did Kubla Khan
>    A stately pleasure-dome decree:
> Where Alph, the sacred river, ran
> Through caverns measureless to man
>    Down to a sunless sea.
> So twice five miles of fertile ground
> With walls and towers were girdled round:
> And here were gardens bright with sinuous rills,
> Where blossomed many an incense-bearing tree,

And here were forests ancient as the hills,
Enfolding sunny spots of greenery.

And the song of the Echoes in Act II of Shelley's *Prometheus Unbound*, remindful of Titania's song in *A Midsummer Night's Dream*, depends little for its beauty on meaning.

O, follow, follow!
Thro' the caverns hollow,
As the song floats thou pursue,
Where the wild bee never flew,
Thro' the noon-tide darkness deep,
By the odour-breathing sleep
Of faint night flowers, and the waves
At the fountain-lighted caves,
While our music, wild and sweet,
Mocks thy gently falling feet,
Child of Ocean!

In "How the Waters Come Down at Lodore," Southey tried, not altogether successfully, to give the sound of a rushing stream, using single, double, triple, and eventually multiple rhymes. It begins quietly:

It runs and it creeps
For awhile till it sleeps
In its own little lake;

but in the end it is a brawling torrent:

Retreating and beating and meeting and sheeting,
Delaying and straying and playing and spraying,
Advancing and prancing and glancing and dancing,
Recoiling, turmoiling, toiling, and boiling,
And gleaming and streaming and steaming and beaming,
And rushing and flushing and brushing and gushing . . .
And so never ending, but always descending,
Sounds and motions for ever and ever are blending
All at once and all o'er, with a mighty uproar;
And this is the way the water comes down at Lodore.

Tennyson gives more delicately and with less apparent effort the music of the brook:

> I chatter over stony ways,
> In little sharps and trebles,
> I bubble into eddying bays,
> I babble on the pebbles. . . .

And Sidney Lanier, in his "Song of the Chattahoochee" is as much a sensuous musician as he is a poet making images.

> Out of the hills of Habersham,
> Down the valleys of Hall,
> I hurry amain to reach the plain,
> Run the rapid and leap the fall,
> Split at the rock and together again
> Accept my bed, or narrow or wide,
> And flee from folly on every side
> With a lover's pain to attain the plain
> Far from the hills of Habersham,
> Far from the valleys of Hall.
>
> All down the hills of Habersham,
> All through the valleys of Hall,
> The rushes cried "Abide, abide,"
> The wilful waterweed held me thrall,
> The laving laurel turned my tide,
> The ferns and the fondling grass said *Stay*.
> The dewberry dipped for to work delay,
> And the little reeds sighed "Abide, abide,
> Here in the hills of Habersham,
> Here in the valleys of Hall,"
>
> High o'er the hills of Habersham,
> Veiling the valleys of Hall,
> The hickory told me manifold
> Fair tales of shade, the poplar tall
> Wrought me her shadowy self to hold,
> The chestnut, the oak, the walnut, the pine
> Overleaning, with flickering meaning and sign,
> Said, "Pass not, so cold, these manifold
> Deep shades of the hills of Habersham,
> These glades in the valleys of Hall."
>
> And oft in the hills of Habersham,
> And oft in the valleys of Hall,

The white quartz shone, and the smooth brook-stone
Did bar me of passage with friendly brawl,
And many a luminous jewel lone
—Crystal clear or a-cloud with mist
Ruby, garnet, and amethyst—
Made lures with light of streaming stone
   In the clefts of the hills of Habersham,
   In the beds of the valleys of Hall.

But oh, not the hills of Habersham,
   And oh, not the valleys of Hall
Avail: I am fain for to water the plain.
Downward, to toil and be mixed with the main
The dry fields burn, and the mills are to turn,
And a myriad flowers mortally yearn,
And the lordly main from beyond the plain
   Calls o'er the hills of Habersham,
   Calls through the valleys of Hall.

With these poems one naturally thinks of Smetana's "Moldau," which in music without words follows the river from its source as a brook, past the hunt, the peasant wedding, the night with its water spirits in the shimmering moonlight, then after foaming rapids to a majestic stream that disappears in the quiet distance.

The sensuous appeal is seldom dominant in poetry, however, for usually the verses carry ideas which, beautified by expression, awaken the feelings all the more readily. The music may be grave and impressive, as in Milton, crisp and pungent, as in Pope, or gay and tinkling, as in many of the lyrists. It may have cadence that is almost formal music, with change of tempo and intensity, and with almost all of the devices in words that a musical composition uses with tones.

Numerous illustrations will be found by anyone who reads widely in poetry, the sensuous appeal occurring most noticeably in single lines or short passages, not because "beauty is its own excuse for being," but because sensuous beauty furnishes an appropriate setting for another kind of appeal or because it embellishes and intensifies a character or a situation. A landscape is painted as a place suitable for the action to be narrated; a heroine is presented as beautiful so that we may love her; an atmosphere is created by suggestive words for the sentiment that is to be expressed. Note how Tennyson appeals to the senses differently and appropriately in "The Bugle Song," in "The Lady of Shalott," and in the close of "The Coming of Arthur."

> The King will follow Christ, and we the King
> In whom high God hath breathed a secret thing.

> Fall battleaxe, and flash brand! Let the King reign.

Of course the art that appeals most directly and most completely to sensuous appreciation is instrumental music. Many hearers get nothing more from it than auditory pleasure, caring little if at all for the technical form or for suggestions that it may have to the intellect and imagination.

> Music which makes giddy the dim brain
> Faint with intoxication of keen joy.

But composers have supplemented this pleasure with "program music," which attempts to convey ideas by means of sounds, and they have supported melody and harmony by words for singing. Opera is the fusion of music, instrumental and vocal, and acting, the combination being more stimulating to pleasure than the orchestral music alone.

In pictorial and plastic art, too, there is a large element of pure, or almost pure, sensuous beauty. Who cares that Turner's glowing canvas is entitled "Dido and Aeneas," or that Corot called his paintings of delicate mist over the trees of spring "Bathers of Bellizona" or "Marriage of Isaac and Rebecca," or that the pale beauty of Watteau's canvas is labeled "Embarkment for Cytherea"? ("What's Hecuba to me, or me to Hecuba!") It is the harmony of color, the balance of details, the perfection of unity that arouse admiration and call us back to look at the paintings again and again, actually or in memory, always with renewed and often with increased pleasure. It is to the senses and not to one's sense that such paintings appeal.

Mere form, in line and in mass, may give sensuous pleasure without reference to meaning. Recall, for example, the graceful curve that William Blake drew of the soul reluctantly leaving the body of the good old man, or the solid monumentality of Michelangelo's "Moses," so substantial that it could be rolled downhill without breaking. Brancusi's "Bird in Flight" is a simple curve in brass so perfect that it entirely satisfies one's sense of form; and Mondrian's "Composition" is merely a rectangle with crossing lines, each one so perfectly placed that it could not be moved a hairsbreadth without ruining the symmetry. And there are vases which without decoration of color or figures ravish the senses by their mere beauty of form.

Like music, painting, and the plastic arts, poetry uses appeal to the sensitive appreciation of pure beauty. It may be wholly and pleasingly satisfying in its sound; indeed, the beauty of sound, as in "Tears, Idle Tears," may divert attention from such meaning as exists. But for the most part, as has already been said and as will be perceived in the subsequent discussion, the sensuous beauty of poetry is to support and intensify the beauty of expressed thought and to help stimulate imaginative response to the connotative appeal in words.

## The Diction of Poetry

Like prose, poetry uses words. But prose uses words primarily for the communication of ideas, whereas poetry, still communicating ideas, uses words primarily to arouse emotions.

Certain words, like *golden*, are sensuously beautiful, music pleasing to the ear regardless of what meaning they convey. Poets have traditionally sought and used words that are beautiful in their sounds. As Anna Hempstead Branch wrote,

> God wove a web of loveliness,
> Of clouds and stars and birds,

> But made not anything at all
> So beautiful as words.

The poet, as William Watson said of Tennyson, is the

> Master who crown'st our immelodious days
> With flower of perfect speech.

Unlike the artist who works in marble or colors, "the man who moulds his thought in verse has to employ the materials vulgarized by everybody's use," as Oliver Wendell Holmes noted in *The Poet at the Breakfast-Table*, "and glorify them by his handling."

As in everything else, fashions in words change. In one age words like *thou* and *ye*, *o'er* and *'twixt*, *wert* and *hast*, *erstwhile* and *anon*, *forsooth*, *ken*, and *lea* were the popular language of poetry; *azure* was generally used for *blue*, *beauteous* for *beautiful*, and *zephyr* for *breeze*. Such words are still occasionally found in rhymed verse, seldom in modern poetry. But, as the Russians use an early form of their language only in prayers, so in appeals to the Deity we still say, "O God, thou knowest that thy child hath been led astray," more modern diction seeming out of place and to many even sacrilegious. And there are poems in which even the most ancient, and in other situations obviously artificial, diction may seem appropriate, or at least not offensive. As Sutherland has pointed out, certain words "which have passed out of the living speech continue a ghostly existence by virtue of their memorable association with literature; words gain as well as lose by having fallen into disuse." As an example, he cites the word *twain*. Certainly no one would cavil at *doth*, *hath*, and *fro* in Arthur Symons' "Memory."

> As a perfume doth remain
> In the folds where it hath lain,
> So the thought of you, remaining,
> Deeply folded in my brain,
> Will not leave me: all things leave me:
> You remain.

Other thoughts may come and go,
Other moments I may know
That shall waft me, in their going,
As a breath blown to and fro,
Fragrant memories: fragrant memories
Come and go.

Only thoughts of you remain
In my heart where they have lain,
Perfuming thoughts of you, remaining,
A hid sweetness, in my brain.
Others leave me: all things leave me:
You remain!

When the use in verse of words that have gone out of fashion is excessive or without obvious artistic intent, however, feelings of the modern reader will seldom be moved. Today "finny prey" are just plain fish, "feathered choir" is an affected way of saying birds, and "whiskered vermin" are rats. It was a revered American poet who perpetrated the now ridiculous "In ocean sport the scaly herds." Many phrases which were once considered clever or amusing, and which in consequence were to some degree moving, have been used so often that they have worn off all the original sharp edges of suggestiveness. "Rosy dawn," "awful shriek," and "glittering dagger," along with tropes like "blind as a bat" and "patience on a monument" are now stereotypes with no radiation of feeling. It is against such clichés that protests have been made since the second generation tried its hand at verse.

Alexander Pope in "An Essay on Criticism" makes fun of phrases that were clichés even in his day and also throws the barbs of his wit into those who would emphasize the importance of diction to the neglect of meaning.

But most by numbers judge a poet's song,
And smooth or rough, with them, is right or wrong:
In the bright Muse, though thousand charms conspire,
Her voice is all these tuneful fools admire;

> Who haunt Parnassus but to please their ear,
> Not mend their minds; as some to church repair,
> Not for the doctrine, but the music there.
> These equal syllables alone require,
> Though oft the ear the open vowels tire;
> While expletives their feeble aid do join;
> And ten low words oft creep in one dull line:
> While they ring round the same unvaried chimes,
> With sure return of still expected rhymes:
> Where'er you find "the cooling western breeze,"
> In the next line it "whispers through the trees":
> If crystal streams "with pleasing murmurs creep,"
> The reader's threatened (not in vain) with "sleep."

William Cullen Bryant remonstrated with his brother, who had never been abroad, for writing verses in British diction to an English skylark. He himself wrote of our native fringed gentian and bobolink. But in the first stanza of the verses celebrating the bird he uses diction that is not indigenous: *dame* and *mead* destroy the simple naturalness that is appropriate.

> Merrily swinging on brier and weed,
> Near to the nest of his little dame,
> Over the mountain-side or mead,
> Robert of Lincoln is telling his name.

Many of Emerson's ideas might as well have been expressed in prose. True, he occasionally achieves an aphorism, like

> Blest is he, who, playing deep, yet haply asks not why,
> Too busied with the crowded hour to fear to live or die;

but it is memorable for the thought and not for the diction. His "Fable" of the mountain and the squirrel manifests, however, that verse does do something to elevate the commonplace. The poem contains no new idea, the diction is not euphonious, and "Little Prig" seems almost childish; but from the time when we read it in the elementary school it sticks in the memory. Does verse add anything to an idea expressed in such passages as the following from Byron?

On prince or bride no diamond stone
Half so gracious ever shone,
As the light of enterprise
Beaming from a young man's eyes.

In his "Fable for Critics" Lowell thus characterizes his venerated contemporary.

There comes Emerson first, whose rich words, every one,
Are like gold nails in temples to hang trophies on,
Whose prose is grand verse, while his verse, the Lord knows,
Is some of it pr— No, 'tis not even prose.

So perfect a balance there is in his head,
That he talks of things sometimes as if they were dead;
Life, nature, love, God, and affairs of that sort,
He looks at as merely ideas.

Emerson sits in a mystery, calm and intense,
And looks coolly round him with sharp common-sense . . .
Makes mysteries matters of plain every day.

Diction should be appropriate to the subject treated and also to the character of the poet. High sonorousness in Milton's poetry seems natural, as does the brilliant crackle of intellectualism in Pope's "Dunciad." When poets turned to nature and to lowly man as their prevailing interests, simple diction became their medium of expression. Wordsworth argued that any language was a proper vehicle for poetry if it aroused emotions that are pleasing. In his poetry he repeatedly demonstrated that his dictum was sound, but unfortunately in his revolt against artificialities he was led into an assumption that common language about anything is moving poetry. The diction in the following stanza certainly does not have poetic effect.

Suck, little babe, oh suck again!
It costs my blood, it costs my brain;
Thy lips I feel them, baby! They
Draw from my heart the pain away.

It is difficult to understand how a poet with a sensitive ear could write such bathos and also such sonorous and moving poetry as in the following quotations from Wordsworth:

> His little, nameless, unremembered acts
> Of kindness and of love.

> The heavy and the weary weight
> Of all this unintelligible world.

> The still sad music of humanity.

> It is a beauteous evening, calm and free,
> The holy time is quiet as a nun
> Breathless with adoration.

> Perhaps the plaintive numbers flow
> For old, unhappy, far-off things,
> And battles long ago.

> The light that never was, on sea or land,
> The consecration, and the Poet's dream.

Diction does not need to use uncommon words to become high poetry.

As William Watson declared:

> Often ornateness
> Goes with greatness;
> Oftener felicity
> Comes of simplicity.

Wordsworth's "Michael," tells the story of a highland shepherd who because of his poverty sent his only son to the city to seek success. As a memorial, before the parting the aged man and the boy started to build a sheepfold, and when later the lad became dissolute the father would go to the unfinished task, bowed with age and grief, and there on some days "he scarce lifted up a single stone." These simple words stir us as no elevated diction could. And an impression of Michael's solitude could not be better conveyed than by

They
Who journey hither find themselves alone
With a few sheep, with rocks and stones and kites
That overhead are sailing in the sky.

It is in truth an utter solitude.

He had been alone
Amid the heart of many thousand mists.

Poets from age to age experiment with diction, and each one who achieves success finds the style that is peculiarly fitting to what he has to express. Keats and Shelley and Byron wrote differently because each was a unique genius. Tennyson was peculiarly sensitive to delicacies in the music of language; Browning, though also on occasion similarly sensitive, was more masculine, using words to suit the vigor of his thought. And Swinburne was so intoxicated with mellifluous diction that one often revels in his verbal music with little or no attention to his thought, which sometimes is of small significance. The last two stanzas of "The Garden of Proserpine" are characteristic of his best sensuous poetry.

From too much love of living,
From hope and fear set free,
We thank with brief thanksgiving
Whatever gods may be
That no life lives forever;
That dead men rise up never;
That even the weariest river
Winds somewhere safe to sea.

Then star nor sun shall waken,
Nor any change of light:
Nor sound of waters shaken,
Nor any sound or sight:
Nor wintry leaves nor vernal,
Nor days nor things diurnal;
Only the sleep eternal
In an eternal night.

Though having styles more or less peculiar to themselves, poets are likely in most instances to be conventional in their diction. Experienced readers can usually see characteristic differences, but the great majority of poets are differentiated one from another by their thought and emotional content rather than by the diction that they use. There are of course outstanding exceptions: two lines from Poe will indicate their author, and one line will confidently assert that it was written by Walt Whitman.

Whitman was the most outstanding revolutionist in the history of our literature up to the beginning of the present century. Praised extravagantly by many who were tired of the conventional, he has been soundly denounced by others as a poseur who had a good idea but carried it to a disgusting extreme in diction as well as in his selection of subjects. One critic lauds his manly vigor, his independence, and his celebration of what is ordinarily not accepted as beautiful or emotionally moving. Another critic denounces his "barbaric yawp" and his open mention of vulgarities that offend sensitive culture. Whether he was a great poet or not is a matter of taste. Certainly since his time poetry has been more catholic in diction as well as in subject, but a reading of literature since his day will show that he has exerted much less influence than he or those who lauded him expected. And certainly his poems that are most often enjoyed today are those like "O Captain, My Captain" and "When Lilacs Last in the Dooryard Bloom'd," that most nearly conform to conventional patterns.

Whitman wrote, "I sound my barbaric yawp over the roofs of the world," and elsewhere, "My words itch at your ears till you understand them," and, "No one will ever get at my verses who insists on viewing them as a literary performance." Although he did emphasize a style of diction, it is evident that he thought his contribution was mostly in subject matter. His style is often confusing, the poems having no obvious unity and piling up details. One poem begins:

There was a child went forth every day,
And the first object he looked upon, that object he became,
And that object became part of him for the day or a certain
    part of the day,
Or for many years or stretching cycles of years.

The earliest lilacs became a part of this child . . .

Then he enumerates in rather tedious succession more than
fifty things that also "became a part of this child."

In recent years new cults of poetry have sprung up. Some
representatives run to one extreme in diction, following Whitman in choice of both subjects to celebrate and words and
phrases that never before have been thought fit to express the
admirable feelings of mankind. The new diction is sometimes
a hammer that beats one over the head, seldom a caress. But,
proving that these radicals have poetic souls, they also achieve
amazing effects and occasionally express beautiful sentiments
with rare felicity. Vachel Lindsay may be cited as a high
priest of one cult. Its future in our literature is uncertain.

Lindsay was the troubadour of America, interpreting his
country, which he had learned by tramping in his early man-
hood, exchanging chants of his poems for food and lodging.
Illustrative of the violence of style which he sometimes used
are the first two of five stanzas of his "Kallyope." Though its
diction is far different from what we are accustomed to in
poetry, it brings back something of the thrill that everyone
had when he heard the "steam piano" in the circus parade.

> Proud men
> Eternally
> Go about,
> Slander me,
> Call me the "Calliope,"
> Sizz . . . .
> Fizz . . . .
>
> I am the gutter dream,
> Tune-maker, born of steam,

Tooting joy, tooting hope.
I am the Kallyope,
Car called the Kallyope.
Willy, willy, willy wah HOO!
See the flags: snow-white tent,
See the bear and elephant,
See the monkey jump the rope,
Listen to the Kallyope, Kallyope, Kallyope!
Soul of the rhinoceros
And the hippopotamus
(Listen to the lion roar!)
Jaguar, cockatoot,
Loons, owls,
Hoot, Hoot.
Listen to the lion roar,
Listen to the lion roar,
Listen to the lion R-O-A-R!
Hear the leopard cry for gore,
Willy, willy, willy wah HOO!
Hail the bloody Indian band,
Hail, all hail the popcorn stand,
Hail to Barnum's picture there,
People's idol everywhere,
Whoop, whoop, whoop, WHOOP!
Music of the mob am I,
Circus day's tremendous cry:—
I am the Kallyope, Kallyope, Kallyope!
Hoot toot, hoot toot, hoot toot, hoot toot,
Willy, willy, willy wah HOO!
Sizz, fizz . . . .

That Lindsay was a master artificer in words is evidenced
by others of his poems, some (like "The Santa-Fe Trail,"
"General William Booth Enters Into Heaven," "The Congo,"
and "Daniel") after the general style of "Kallyope." Others
(like "The Broncho That Would Not Be Broken," "Abraham
Lincoln Walks at Midnight," and "The Leaden-Eyed") are
more conventional in subject and in diction. "The Chinese
Nightingale" has unusual imaginative tenderness and color.
Another cult is that of the Imagists. Instead of celebrating
the crude and the vulgar, they attempt to express feelings

aroused by refined and delicate beauties. Emily Dickinson was the forerunner of this cult, and H.D. (Hilda Doolittle) a later representative. Amy Lowell's "Patterns" is a brilliant illustration of Imagist diction.

The Imagists practiced an economy of expression, seeking the exact word, which often is hard, occasionally scintillant. As Florence Wilkinson noted, their diction is sometimes very good, sometimes very bad. It is so condensed that it demands much of a reader, who as often turns away baffled as perceives the delicate sheen of the poetry. This credit must be given the Imagists: they seldom or never use trite phrases or dull similes. To do so would to them be the first deadly sin.

Two poems by H.D. well illustrate the diction and style of the Imagists.

### NIGHT

The night has cut
each from each
and curled the petals
back from the stalk
and under it in crisp rows;

under at an unfaltering pace,
under till the rinds break,
back till each bent leaf
is parted from its stalk;

under at a grave pace,
under till the leaves
are bent back
till they drop upon earth,
back till they are all broken.

O night,
you take the petals
of the roses in your hand,
but leave the stark core
of the rose
to perish on the branch.

### STORM

You crash over the trees,
you crack the live branch—
the branch is white,
the green crushed,
each leaf is rent like split wood.

You burden the trees
with black drops,
you swirl and crash—
you have broken off a weighted leaf
in the wind,
it is hurled out,
whirls up and sinks,
a green stone.

"The imagists' admirable condensation, their attention to the matter in hand, their complete lack of literary dilution and confusion brought into immediate notice a clarity compared to which current 'magazine verse' seemed both soft and shabby."[1]

But whatever changes there may be in the fashions of poetic diction, one requirement remains steady: to be effective the diction used must arouse in readers emotions that are pleasing. It is obvious that words which make one person weep will stir another not at all—or even to laughter. There is always the danger that they will arouse the wrong kind of feelings in a reader because of peculiar associations. (The mad Lear and the drunken Roderigo were amusing on the Elizabethan stage.) The diction that sounded beautiful to us in adolescence may seem mawkish today; and even a change of mood may bring a different reaction to a verbal stimulus. So it is no wonder that poetic diction cannot be precisely defined or that readers disagree on effectiveness, or even on whether a passage of verse is poetry at all.

[1] Louise Bogan, *Achievement in American Poetry, 1900–1950.* Chicago, H. Regnery Co., 1951.

Who shall explain the mystery of the lyre? . . .
Demand of lilies wherefore they are white,
Extort her crimson secret from the rose,
But ask not of the Muse that she disclose
The meaning of the riddle of her might.[2]

Just as all of the other arts, poetry has its decorations, which, though not essential, are intended to increase its beauty. The decorations of poetry are euphony, cadence or rhythm, meter, stanzaic form, rhyme, alliteration, assonance, and onomatopoeia.

## DECORATIONS OF DICTION

*Euphony*, or sound pleasing to the ear, may be characteristic of a single word, but it is more likely to result from a felicitous combination of words in a phrase or a longer sequence. When not influenced by the association of pleasing ideas, it results from the predominance of open vowels or of liquid and soft consonants. Alliteration and assonance are effective means to euphony, as Tennyson demonstrates.

The moan of doves in immemorial elms,
And murmuring of innumerable bees.

As in music, the harmony of sound is intensified in words by contrast. "Why entered discords in but that harmony might issue forth?"

There are good illustrations of the effective swing from high diction to colloquialism in William Vaughn Moody's "The Menagerie." In this poem the speaker is a man befuddled with liquor, who, after the circus performance, lingers in the animal tent and gradually sees the great plan of evolution leading to the perfect man, which certainly, he realizes, he is not. The following selected stanzas, which should stimulate a reading of the entire poem, express the realization of the man's kindred with his evolutionary ancestors and his own inadequacy to exemplify the culmination of the aeon-long process. Though

2 William Watson, "Lachrimae Musarum."

none of the words are "poetic," a reader cannot fail to appreciate the appropriate differences between the diction of the first and last stanzas and that of the middle two.

## THE MENAGERIE

### WILLIAM VAUGHN MOODY

'Twas like a thunder-clap from out the clear,—
One minute they were circus beasts, some grand,
Some ugly, some amusing, and some queer:
Rival attractions to the hobo band,
The flying jenny, and the peanut stand.

Next minute they were old hearth-mates of mine!
Lost people, eyeing me with such a stare!
Patient, satiric, devilish, divine;
A gaze of hopeless envy, squalid care,
Hatred, and thwarted love, and dim despair.

Within my blood my ancient kindred spoke,—
Grotesque and monstrous voices, heard afar
Down ancient caves when behemoth awoke,
Or through fern forests roared the plesiosaur
Locked with the giant-bat in ghastly war.

Helpless I stood among those awful cages;
The beasts were walking loose, and I was bagged!
I, I, last product of the toiling ages,
Goal of heroic feet that never lagged,—
A little man in trousers, slightly jagged.

Of course euphony is not characteristic of all poetry. It would be inappropriate when not harmonious with the thought. "Clang battle-axe and clash brand!" is as harsh in sound as the indicated action is rough. Euphony is merely a decoration of diction, and sometimes even a beautiful decoration may be out of place and disturbing. Many an artistic effect is spoiled by the addition of curlicues. A tailored gown needs no flounces.

*Cadence*, the rhythmical flow of verse, is characteristic of all poetry. Rhythm is the language of the emotions. As Professor Winchester once wrote, "Laughter and sobbing, anger or gladness, impassioned entreaty, threat or endearment,—all have a more or less well-marked rhythm. The language of intense emotion, if thrown together out of meter, is sure to seem inflated, bombastic, ejaculatory, or in some other way unnatural, while if the same language and sentiments are put into metrical form, we feel nothing forced or unnatural in them."

Cadence may be mellifluous, as in the verse of the great majority of poets, or characterized by masculine vigor, as on occasion it is even in the verse of masters of music. It may be monotonously regular or subtly varied. It may be ordered into measured lines or subject to no apparent regulation. But it must satisfy the ear. There is always in the poet's brain a pattern, and this pattern will be perceived by a sensitive reader, however many departures are made from it. Unusual patterns often disturb the conventional reader, but if they produce cadence they justify themselves.

There is cadence in impassioned prose, some of which is poetry lacking formal meter. In this respect it is close to some adventurous modern verse and to what Amy Lowell called "polyphonic prose." The Bible, which has been the model for many a writer, contains much of cadence: "Lift up your heads, O ye gates; and be ye lifted up, ye everlasting doors; and the King of glory shall come in." The fact that such passages were poetry in the original, partly explains why they retain the moving quality in translation.

> Come, my beloved, let us go forth into the field;
>   Let us lodge in the villages.
>   Let us get up early to the vineyards;
> Let us see whether the vine hath budded,
>   And the tender grape appear,
>   And the pomegranates be in flower.
>
> There will I give thee my love.
>   The mandrakes give forth fragrance,

> And at our doors are all manner of precious fruits,
> New and old,
> Which I have laid up for thee, O my beloved.

*Rhythm* is characteristic of all the arts. Everybody recognizes it in music, and composers formally indicate what any listener can recognize, that a composition is in ¾ or ¼ time. A waltz may have its measures made up of three quarter notes or of combinations that are equivalent, the beat coming usually at the beginning of each measure; but however varied, the pattern persists in one's ear and in one's feet. Variations are pleasing breaks in what might otherwise be monotony. Goethe declared that architecture is frozen music, for it has its symmetry, its rhythm of form. And in painting there is rhythm in composition and in color. St. John balances the Infant Christ and a saint or an angel on both sides complete the composition; the red and blue of the Virgin's robe are repeated here and there or call out complementary colors that satisfy the demands of rhythm.

In some poems, of course, rhythm is more important than in others, which depend for their effects primarily on moving ideas or on connotation. Striking illustrations of the effectiveness of marked rhythm may be found in such well-known poems as "The Highwayman" by Alfred Noyes, "Cargoes" and "Spanish Waters" by John Masefield, "How They Brought the Good News from Ghent to Aix" by Browning, and "Atalanta in Calydon" by Algernon Charles Swinburne, who sometimes lost reason in rhapsody. The chorus from the last-named poem is quoted.

> Come with bows bent and with emptying of quivers
>     Maiden most perfect, lady of light,
> With a noise of winds and many rivers,
>     With a clamor of waters and with night;
> Bind on thy sandals, O thou most fleet,
> Over the splendor and speed of thy feet;
> For the faint east quickens, the wan west shivers,
>     Round the feet of the day and the feet of the night.

Organized rhythm is *meter*. There is no need to present here the names of the various "feet"—the iambus, the trochee, the anapaest, and so on. Nor, although these names are convenient to use, is it necessary for the enjoyment of poetry that they be known at all. It is the effect that must be appreciated, certainly not the means without the achievement. Ordered cadence is undoubtedly pleasing to the ear of everyone, as is evidenced by the popularity of the highest poetry and of the meanest doggerel. It has an effect of its own, regardless of the thought that is being conveyed, and it often gives an effectiveness that could not be achieved by prose. As Wordsworth wrote, "The tendency of meter is to divest language in a certain degree of its reality, and thus to throw a certain half-consciousness or unsubstantial existence over the whole composition."

A strict conformance to any pattern—in poetry as well as in music, painting, and architecture—would soon tire. That is why a modern reader so quickly becomes satiated with the poetry of the seventeenth century. The regular meter of Pope snaps his brief epigrams into our minds, but it is boring when continued page after page, as in his translation of Homer, and even so brilliant a narrative as the scintillating "Rape of the Lock" loses much of its effectiveness by its monotony of meter. This Pope no doubt recognized, for on occasion he introduced highly effective, though obviously conscious, variations.

Poets relieve monotony in verse and gain effectiveness by appropriate variations in meter. Note how the galloping of the horses is represented in Browning's "How They Brought the Good News from Ghent to Aix," and how, although this metrical pattern is preserved throughout, it is brilliantly varied when one horse "down on his haunches shuddered and sank" and another "rolled neck and croup over, lay dead as a stone," the regular rhythm being resumed as Roland gallops on to Aix. Variations may be found in almost any poem. They are effective when they reflect a change in thought or feeling; they fail, often miserably, when they evidence the author's lack of mastery of the vehicle of expression.

Note how the regular pattern is kept in the two following quotations from Tennyson, and yet effectiveness is achieved by the appropriate slowing up of the lines by words that demand full emphasis on each—by the substitution of spondees for iambs, if you wish to be technical.

> The tearful glimmer of the languid dawn
> On those long, rank, dark wood-walks drenched in dew.
>
> Between it and the garden lies
> A league of grass, wash'd by the slow broad stream.

To appreciate how the metrical pattern is preserved and at the same time is infinitely varied, read the following quotation from George Meredith's "Love in the Valley," first with an absurd emphasis on the words that the formal meter would normally require to be accented, and then in the way that your intelligence and musical ear demand.

> Under yonder beech-tree single on the greensward,
>   Couched with her arms behind her golden head,
> Knees and tresses folded to slip and ripple idly,
>   Lies my young love sleeping in the shade.
> Had I the heart to slide an arm beneath her,
>   Press her parting lips as her waist I gather slow,
> Waking in amazement she could not but embrace me:
>   Then would she hold me and never let me go.

Pleasing and effective variations of the metrical pattern are achieved not merely by the substitution of another "foot" for the one normally required, but also by use of pauses—caesuras—in the flow of the verse, and by run-ons of one verse to the next and even from one stanza to the next succeeding. The caesuras in a line from Browning's "Hervé Riel" emphasize the unexpectedness of a series of separate acts and the surprise that each one caused:

> For up stood/, for out stepped,/ for in struck amid all these.

A few lines from Tennyson's "Enoch Arden" illustrate how the use of pauses and the absence of them achieve quite different effects in the same metrical structure.

> He [Enoch] therefore turning softly like a thief,
> Lest the harsh shingle should grate underfoot,
> And feeling all along the garden-wall,
> Lest he should swoon and tumble and be found,
> Crept to the gate, and open'd it, and closed.

Note how the punctuation in the last verse, effective as caesuras, suggests the lingering pause after each act, and how the lack of punctuation in the preceding line implies the rapidity of tumbling and being found after the swooning.

The *run-on* of one verse or stanza to the next may contribute much to unity of thought and feeling or to rapidity of movement or to suspense if it is used for these effects. But if it is apparently a result of a lack of skill on the part of the author to use consistently the vehicle that he has chosen, the reader gains nothing and perhaps loses something by the not obviously justified departure from the pattern. Effective suspension of the thought to gain unity is repeatedly illustrated in Tennyson's "In Memoriam." In Part XII, which tells of the imaginary visit to the ship bearing his dead friend home, the flight of the dove is presented in one continuous narrative through the five four-verse stanzas; and Part LV, recognizing that science itself is not sufficient for comfort, runs on to the end without a significant break.

> The wish, that of the living whole
>   No life may fail beyond the grave,
>   Derives it not from what we have
> The likest God within the soul?
>
> Are God and nature then at strife,
>   That nature lends such evil dreams?
>   So careful of the type she seems,
> So careless of the single life,

That I, considering everywhere
Her secret meaning in her deeds,
And finding that of fifty seeds
She often brings but one to bear,

I falter where I firmly trod,
And failing with my weight of cares
Upon the great world's altar-stairs
That slope thro' darkness up to God,

I stretch lame hands of faith, and grope,
And gather dust and chaff, and call
To what I feel is Lord of all,
And faintly trust the larger hope.

The run-on so frequently found in Browning's poems is
the natural result of the complexity of his sustained thinking,
often introducing parenthetical ideas. Reread, for example,
the beginning of "Abt Vogler."

Would that the structure brave, the manifold music I build,
Bidding my organ obey, calling its keys to their work,
Claiming each slave of the sound, at a touch, as when Solomon
willed
Armies of angels that soar, legions of demons that lurk,
Man, brute, reptile, fly,—alien of end and of aim,
Adverse, each from the other heaven-high, hell-deep
removed,—
Should rush into sight at once as he named the ineffable Name,
And pile him a palace straight, to pleasure the princess he
loved!

Would it might tarry like his, the beautiful building of mine,
This which my keys in a crowd pressed and importuned to
raise!

This characteristic has stimulated numerous clever parodies
of Browning's style, but it cannot be doubted that it is highly
effective with a reader who has the intelligence to follow
through from beginning to end, with appreciation of the
subtleties and niceties of the workings of the poet's mind.

Not infrequently what is presented as verse, the lines manifesting a cadence and each beginning with a capital letter, could quite as well be printed as prose, so far as the conveyance of thought and the stimulation of feeling are concerned. One may read the long "Apology" of Bishop Blougram, in which the mighty man demolishes the idealistic petty journalist Gigadibs, and hardly realize that it is written in verse. The close, and at times fallacious, reasoning demands all of a reader's attention, and the numerous quotable passages obscure the art with which they are presented. Why did Browning use verse for such an intellectual tour de force? And why do we read it with impelled interest? Because, I think, verse is able, as prose seldom is, to challenge and hold attention by its very condensation of thought, which necessitates close and steady cooperation by a reader to get and to develop ideas that arouse emotions. The reader becomes a partner with the poet, and as such he has a feeling for the joint product.

Change only a word here and there and some of the noblest passages in such poems as Wordsworth's "Prelude" and "Excursion" could be printed as prose and a reader would never notice the difference. But they are poetry nevertheless, for they move us as we desire to be moved, and the beautiful diction gains, rather than loses, by the subtle effects of verse.

> We see but darkly
> Even when we look behind us . . .
>      If the mariner
> When at reluctant distance he hath passed
> Some tempting island, could but know the ills
> That must have fallen upon him had he brought
> His bark to land upon the wished-for shore,
> Good cause would oft be his to thank the surf
> Whose white belt scared him thence, or wind that blew
> Inexorably adverse.

Even if we cannot fully explain the effect of the verse form, we must recognize its superiority if we put such a passage as this into the best prose passage possible.

Simple diction is appropriate, of course, for telling a homely tale, which may become poetry because the story or the characters are appealing. Edgar Lee Masters' "Cato Braden" is a moving account in everyday diction of the gradual degeneration of a promising young man too weak to overcome the soporific effect of a small town. The following excerpt, printed as prose but with the verse ends indicated, has no poetic diction, but nevertheless it is entirely suitable to the story, which is poetry in its effect.

You see, old Jerry Ott/had left a son an interest in the Eagle/and Cato Braden died right at his table/while playing solitaire. This son came in/ and found him dead, a card clutched in his hand./ This card was, strange enough, the deuce of clubs!/ This son was glad that Cato died,/ for now he runs the Eagle by himself.

Because of, or in spite of, the diction, is not this quotation found near the end of the poem moving?

> He was like a nose half active
> Who enters in a room where gas escapes,
> Sits in the room unconscious of the gas
> Till he grows sluggish. So I say it's true
> That Winston Prairie ruined Cato Braden
> And killed him in the end. . . .
> They say a lung will turn to stone or steel
> When men work in the filings and the dust.
> At last the dust of Winston Prairie turned
> His soul to dust.

In Stephen Phillips' beautiful "Marsyas" there are passages, too, that might be printed as prose—that is, without measured lines, each beginning with a capital letter—because the construction is straightforward.

Pallas Athene in an hour of ease/ from guarding states and succoring the wise,/ pressed wistfully her lips against a flute/ made by a Phrygian youth from resonant wood/ cut near Saugarius.

But notice how the words *succoring, wistfully*, and *resonant* —good words anywhere—elevate the passage to poetry.

Even *Athene* and *Saugarius*, wherever that may be, tend to take the passage out of prose.

However varied, then, diction may be, it is an important element of poetry. It may be a mere vehicle for the conveyance of thought, which itself may stimulate emotional response, or for the characterization of persons whom we are made to admire, love, or hate; or, on the other hand, it may be beautiful in its own sonorousness or, raising an otherwise commonplace statement by the connotative effect of its words, singly or in happy combination.

It is easy to read poetry without pausing, as one should do if interested in technique, to consider the choice that the author has made of words—sometimes uniquely felicitous, sometimes merely to complete the sense or to fill out the meter. But the exact word, or combination of best words, is what goes far toward making verse poetry, and it is well worth consideration by the serious student. If one makes a careful comparison of the final draft of poems with tentative early versions,* his critical attention will be forced on details of diction. Or if one attempts a sort of completion test, supplying in blanks made in poetic passages by some cooperative friend words that satisfy the sense and the requirements of verse, he cannot fail to appreciate the skill or genius of the artist.

It is difficult, as one who tries it will find, to select passages that lend themselves well to such an exercise. Often an important word or phrase cannot be omitted with a preservation of enough of the meaning and feeling to challenge invention. Sometimes, it will appear, words that can fairly be left out have little importance, for poets frequently compromise ideals to satisfy technical requirements. But the game is well worth playing.

Several mutilated passages from poems are given below. On these a reader can try his hand at filling the blanks and then consider to what extent the poet has been more (or less) suc-

* See pages 95 ff. of this book.

cessful in finding the perfect diction. The words that the poets used will be found in Appendix D (page 321).

### 1

What can I give thee back, O liberal
And   1   giver, who has brought the gold
And   2   of thine heart,   3  , untold,
And laid them on the outside of the wall
For such as I to take or leave withal,
In unexpected   4   ? Am I cold,
  5  , that for these most   6
High gifts, I   7   nothing back at all?
Not so; not cold,—but very   8   instead.

### 2

From too much love of living,
  From hope and fear set free,
We thank with   1   thanksgiving
  Whatever gods may be,
That no life lives   2  ;
That dead men rise up never;
That even the   3   river
  Winds somewhere   4   to sea.

### 3

Sinuous southward and sinuous northward the
    1   band
Of the sea-beach fastens the   2   of the marsh
    to the   3   of the land.
Inward and outward to northward and southward the
    beachlines linger and   4
As a silver-wrought garment that   5   to and
    follows the firm   6   limbs of a girl.

One of the most commonly used decorations of poetry is *rhyme*. It was never intentionally used by the classic poets of Greece and Rome, but it was introduced sometime about the fourth century to aid worshipers in following the Latin services in the Catholic church. From that time onward it became popular, and was generally used in early English poetry. Toward the end of the sixteenth century it was resented by scholars who wished the influence of classical quantitative verse to be resumed. But though there were attempts by Spenser, Cowley, and others to write poetry without rhyme, it had no serious opposition except from blank verse. Although Milton used rhyme in his shorter poems, in the Preface to "Paradise Lost" he expressed violent opposition to it.

However, opposition was short-lived, and rhyme has been commonly used in poetry, especially in lyrics, from Milton's time to the present. There is a naive pleasure in rhyme, which is evidenced by its popularity in the jingles which we learned in childhood and which still linger pleasantly in the memory, and many proverbs and maxims are stamped in our minds by their rhymes, sometimes gaining more respect than their sense warrants. "Haste makes waste," "Red in the morning, sailors take warning; Red at night, sailors delight," and

> Early to bed early to rise,
> Makes a man healthy,
> Wealthy, and wise.

John Stuart Mill remarked that the practice makes a man conceited in the morning and stupid in the afternoon.

The use of rhyme is justified by the art principle of repetition with variety. Cathedral architecture affords numerous illustrations in its towers and saints and gargoyles, each repeating a dominant decoration with interesting variations. Music is built on this principle; and painting, especially the primitive, in which it is most easily seen, presents a sort of rhyme in the holy groups, each individual corresponding to another which balances it.

Rhyme is sensuously pleasurable to the ear because of the echo of sound, especially if it is mellifluous, giving what Pat-

more called "the closing kiss of rhyme." Beauty is "oft em-
balmed in amber of eternal rhyme," and, as Lowell said, "To
me rhyme's a gain, so it be not too jinglish." It intensifies
the effect of rhythm, giving a half sensual, half psychologi-
cal pleasure. The second verse of a couplet must be slightly
stronger than the first in order to support the enforcement
imparted by rhyme, and when rhymes are far apart, as notably in Collins' "Ode to the Passions," the effect is largely
lost.

Rhyme has an important function in binding together
verses that make up a stanza, often closing it like return in
music to the original key of a composition. It also may give
a snap to a statement, almost like an exclamation point. Dryden uses it to make effective his dagger thrusts into a poet
who was not as bad as depicted.

> Shadwell alone of all my sons is he
> Who stands confirmed in all stupidity.
> The rest to some faint meaning make pretense,
> But Shadwell never deviates into sense.

On the contrary, in an arrangement such as Tennyson uses
in "In Memoriam" (a b b a) the terminal rhyme-emphasis is
reduced. "The stanza is thus admirably adapted to that sweet
continuity of flow, free from abrupt checks, demanded by
the spiritualized sorrow which it bears along. Alternate
rhyme would have wrought an entire change in the poem."[3]

We get pleasure in rhyme from expectancy gratified, for in
it there is a mixture of anticipation, recognition, and surprise.
When the rhyme is unexpectantly felicitous it gives unusual
satisfaction, though sometimes the aesthetic pleasure is overcome by admiration for the author's cleverness. An interesting game is to anticipate the rhyme that a poet will use and
then compare what you expected with what he gives. One
can learn much in the way of appreciation by such comparisons, for poetry demands in rhyme not merely words that

[3] Hiram Corson, *A Primer of English Verse*. Ginn and Co., Boston, 1892

sound alike, but words that are exactly right, words that connote the feeling that the poet is trying to convey.

In the use of rhymes the principle that art should conceal
art is weakened, for no poet rhymes automatically and unconsciously, nor can any art wholly conceal the fact that
skill has been used to find and use the word that sounds right
and means right. It is true that occasionally a reader becomes
so absorbed in the expressed idea or in the beauty of the diction that he ignores the rhyme. When that occurs, much of
its potency is of course lost, though it must be admitted that
even then there is a subtle contribution to the effect as a
whole. A few lyrics are so lovely in thought and in music
that the presence or absence of rhyme may be wholly unnoticed.

An unusual use of rhyme may be noticed in the last two
lines of Mary Billings' "Cabin in the Snow." The verse moves
so smoothly that a reader is not likely to notice whether it
is rhymed or not. But

> If I were there this evening, I should know
> How silence fills a cabin in the snow

brings rhyme to keen consciousness. The concluding couplet
is italicized by rhyme. It has almost the effect of an octave in
a sonnet, emphasizing the speaker against the solitude of the
cabin.

> It would be quiet in the woods today
> From hemlock boughs that reach across the door
> Perhaps a small wind shook the new snow down
> To lie upon the doorsill, undisturbed.
> Today no wavering curl of smoke went up
> From the cold chimney. So perhaps a jay,
> Circling the roof, watching the windows, tried
> His cracked, discordant voice—or a gray squirrel
> Curled his plumed tail around the weather vane,
> And dropped a butternut, that bounced and rolled.
> Had I been there today, I could have seen
> How a gray daylight creeps between the trees,
> To press a gray face against the windowpanes—

And how it goes away in afternoon,
Taking the wind along, and leaves things still.
If I were there this evening, I should know
How silence fills a cabin in the snow.

Most rhyme, as everyone knows, is at the ends of lines, sometimes in immediate proximity and sometimes separated according to the requirements of the adopted stanza form. But there are many instances of inner-rhyme, which if not too frequent adds to the music of the verse.

I sift the snow on the mountains below,
And their great pines groan aghast;
And all the night 'tis my pillow white,
While I sleep in the arms of the blast.

Usually this internal rhyme regularly recurs somewhere near the middle of a verse, so that the above excerpt from Shelley's "The Cloud" might have been printed, though with less effect, in six lines.

In one edition of Poe's "Lenore," corrected by the author's own hand, the internal rhymes are made to end the verses. Evidently Poe could not quite make up his mind which form is the better, though the long lines with internal rhymes are likely to seem to modern readers more musical and harmonious with the theme.

Ah, broken is the golden bowl! the spirit flown forever!
Let the bell toll!—a saintly soul floats on the Stygian river;
And, Guy De Vere, hast *thou* no tear?—weep now or
    never more!
See! on yon drear and rigid bier low lies thy love, Lenore!
Come! let the burial rite be read—the funeral song be sung!—
An anthem for the queenliest dead that ever died so young—
A dirge for her the doubly dead in that she died so young.

But internal rhyme has been used at various places. Throughout "Dîs Aliter Visum" Browning used it in the latter half of the second verse of each stanza, for no apparent artistic purpose and with no obvious effect.

For boys say, "Love me or I die!"
  He did not say, "The truth is, youth
I want, who am old and know too much;
  I'd catch youth; lend me sight and touch!
Drop heart's blood where life's wheels grate dry!"

(Note the terrifying last line with hardly an unaccented syllable.)

Sidney Lanier, who "filled every cranny of his verse with lovely sound," in his intense pursuit of abstract music varied the position of internal rhyme in his poem "Sunrise" with lush sensuousness.

Oh, what if a sound should be made!
Oh, what if a bound should be laid
To this bow-and-string tension of beauty and silence aspring,—
To the bend of beauty the bow, or the hold of silence the string!
I fear me, I fear me yon dome of diaphanous gleam
Will break as a bubble o'erblown in a dream,—
Yon dome of too-tenuous tissues of space and of night,
Over-weighted with stars, over-freighted with light,
Over-sated with beauty and silence, will seem
But a bubble that broke in a dream,
If a bound of degree to this grace be laid,
Or a sound or a motion made.

Internal rhyme sometimes seems overdone, too artificial, as in Tennyson's

Whose free delight, from any height of rapid flight.

But there is good fun in such cleverness as George Macy displays in his "Daphne and Apollo":

Cried he, "My heart's aglow! Miss, I'll escort you to my
  *do*micyle
To live and love!"

Occasionally a poet will play with rhyme as if to show what he can do with it. Browning has written a number of tours de force of this kind. In "Through the Metidja to Abd-Ed-Kadr" he uses twenty-five words rhyming with the initial *ride*, which he gives fourteen repetitions. As Professor Corson once wrote, "When a rhyme is repeated a number of times, the emphasis gathers up to a certain point. Beyond that it pesters the ear and loses its effect." In "The Flight of the Duchess" Browning shifts from single- to double- and even triple-rhymed words, the rhyming sometimes in adjacent and sometimes in alternate verses. But the story is told so well that a reader scarcely notices the irregularity or the shift from rhymes of one syllable to those of two or three. It was in "The Pied Piper of Hamelin" that he ran riot with rhymes, some of them (*obese–robe-ease, council–gown sell, silence–mile hence, rich in–kitchen*) so intentionally far-fetched that they give an intended humor to the hilarious tale. Browning also plays with rhyme in "The Glove" and in "Pacchiarotto and How He Worked in a Distemper."

The breaking of a word so that one syllable is used at the end of a verse and the rest run on to begin the next * now and then occurs for comic effect, as in the rollicking song

> I think of those companions true
> Who studied with me at the U-
> -niversity of Göttingen.

And instances in Lowell's "Biglow Papers" and "A Fable for Critics" are well known.

> Guvener B. is a sensible man;
>   He stays to his home, and looks arter his folks,
> He draws his furrer ez straight ez he can,
>   An' into nobody's tater-patch pokes;
>     But John P.
>     Robinson he
> Sez he won't vote for Guvener B.

---

* In three of the *Carmina* (I.2,19; I.25,11; and II.16,8) Horace uses this break of a word for metrical effect.
    Vagus et sinistra
    Labitur ripa Iove non pedante u-
      xorius annis
(Spreading far and wide o'er the left bank without sanction of Jove, the uxorious river god.)

Thomas Hood had fun writing verses in which the last three words rhyme with each other.

> 'Tis eve and from the dark park, hark!
> The signal of the setting sun, one gun.

And George Herbert, a poet and clergyman in the early seventeenth century, showed his skill by dropping one letter of the rhyming words in successive lines.

> I bless thee, Lord, because I grow
> Among the trees, which, in a row,
> To thee both fruit and order ow.

> What open force or hidden charm
> Can blast my fruit, or bring me harm,
> While the inclosure is thy arm.

Some contemporary versifiers have gained amazing facility in their play with words, notably in using odd rhymes and in placing the rhymed words in unexpected places. Guy Wetmore Carryl tells the old Blue-Beard tale amusingly by the use of these devices. When reading the verses, notice how he shifts the position of the internal rhyme and cleverly contrives to match absurdities like *zealous, he–jealousy, did it, he–timidity* and *learn a–Smyrna.*

### HOW THE HELPMATE OF BLUE-BEARD
### MADE FREE WITH A DOOR

GUY WETMORE CARRYL

A maiden from the Bosphorus, with eyes as bright as phosphorus,
Once wed the wealthy bailiff of the Caliph of Kelat.
Though diligent and zealous, he became a slave to jealousy;
Considering her beauty 'twas his duty to be that.
When business would necessitate a journey he would hesitate,
But, fearing to disgust her, he would trust her with his keys,
Remarking to her prayerfully, "I beg you'll use them carefully,
Don't look what I deposit in that closet, if you please."
It might be mentioned casually, that blue as lapis-lazuli
He dyed his hair, his lashes, his mustaches, and his beard,

And, just because he did it, he aroused his wife's timidity;
Her terror she dissembled, but she trembled when he neared.
This feeling insalubrious soon made her most lugubrious,
And bitterly she missed her sister Marie Anne:
She asked if she might write her to come down and spend a night
    or two
Her husband answered rightly and politely: "Yes, you can."
Blue-Beard, the Monday following, his jealous feelings
    swallowing,
Packed all his clothes together in a leather-bound valise,
Then, feigning reprehensibly, he started out ostensibly
By traveling to learn a bit of Smyrna and of Greece.
His wife made but a cursory inspection of the nursery,
The kitchen and the airy little dairy were a bore,
As well as big or scanty rooms, and billiard, bath, and
    ante-rooms,
But not that interdicted and restricted little door.
For, all her curiosity awakened by the closet he
So carefully had hidden and forbidden her to see,
This damsel disobedient did something inexpedient
And in the key-hole tiny turned the shiny little key.
Then started back impulsively, and shrieked aloud convulsively;
Three heads of maids he'd wedded—and beheaded—met her eye.
And turning round much terrified, her darkest fears were
    verified,
For Blue-Beard stood behind her, come to find her on the sly.
Perceiving she was fated to be soon decapitated, too,
She telegraphed her brothers and some others what she feared.
And Sister Anne looked out for them in readiness to shout for
    them
Whenever in the distance with assistance they appeared.
But only from her battlement she saw some dust that cattle
    meant.
The ordinary story isn't glory, but a jest.
But here's the truth unqualified: her husband wasn't mollified;
Her head is in his bloody little study with the rest!

The Moral: Wives, we must allow, who to their husbands will
    not bow,
A stern and dreadful lesson learn when, as you've read, they're
    cut in turn.

Of course such extravagances are enjoyable because we all realize that the poet is master of his vehicle, and that he is having fun playing with it, a fun that we share in reading. It is when he strains at rhymes because he cannot find words which exactly satisfy his need and which seem naturally introduced that the intended decoration is obviously defective. John Masefield illustrates this defect in the verses included in his late volume *The Hill*. The verses of even great poets occasionally strain for rhyme with poor effect. Tennyson, though master of exactness and delicacy in the choice of words, rhymes *swallow–yellow, early–barley–cheerly, balcony–gallery, said–shade, alone–moon, wherefrom–foam*; and Byron, who, Bliss Perry declared, was unmatchable for sheer improvising cleverness of rhyme, in carelessness, haste, or sheer exuberance of spirit paired *stories–none is, damning us–magnanimous, Medea–be a, merry–vocabulary, from–tomb,* and *intellectual–hen pecked you all.* Etiam Homerus dormiet.

But Professor Mooney has pointed out that since the beginning of this century, poets, rebelling at the restrictions of rhyme, have experimented with "near rhymes" in an effort to produce pleasing effects. William Butler Yeats, Elinor Wylie, John Crowe Ransom, Wilfred Owen, Gerard Manley Hopkins, T. S. Eliot, Archibald MacLeish, Allen Tate, and W. H. Auden are examples of pioneers, though they were anticipated by Ralph Waldo Emerson and Emily Dickinson a hundred years ago.

Irked by the paucity of perfect rhymes in English, the experimentalists have asked, "In what ways can the sounds of a syllable be repeated with pleasing variation?" They have tried to answer the question by "near rhymes," like *another–bother, cowl–soul, sphere–air, arm–exclaim, gate–met,* and with other novelties like *brain–brine, hall–hill,* and even *sin–continues.* Mooney quotes as an example of what he calls "analyzed rhyme" Frank Kendon's verses:

> I spend my days *vainly*,
> Not in *delight;*
> Though the world is *elate*
> And takes her joys *finely.*

A reader may puzzle this out for himself. It does have a kind of logic, whether or not the scheme contributes to euphony.*

It is of course unfair to consider out of context the experiments in substitute for pure rhyme. Reading the entire poems in which they appear, one is likely to conclude that some of the daring ventures are aesthetically egregious failures. But there can be no question but that they do augment traditional rhyming, give a poet more freedom, and sometimes increase the range of musical effects. With these, as with other novelties, one should be tolerant, for adventuring, whether successful or not, is necessary for the advancement of poetry as well as of the other arts. An ear accustomed to the music of Bach and Beethoven has learned to enjoy Debussy, and perhaps a reader accustomed to Keats, Shelley, and Tennyson may come to detect finer harmonies in the verse of the modernists.

Extravagance in rhyme is peculiarly effective in humorous verse. Samuel Butler used it in the seventeenth century "Hudibras," which we can still read with pleasure for its pungency even though the persons satirized have long since been forgotten. Its opening lines are

> When civil dudgeon first grew high,
> And men fell out they knew not why;
> When hard words, jealousies, and fears,
> Set folks together by the ears,
> And made them fight, like mad or drunk,
> For dame Religion, as for punk;
> Whose honesty they all durst swear for,
> Tho' not a man of them knew wherefore;
> When gospel-trumpeter, surrounded
> With long-ear'd rout, to battle sounded,

---

* Most of the illustrations above are taken from Stephen L. Mooney's "New Devices in Sound Repetition," *Word Study*, April, 1949, and from subsequent comment by several authors.

And pulpit, drum ecclesiastick,
Was beat with fist instead of stick;
Then did Sir Knight abandon dwelling,
And out he rode a colonelling.

W. S. Gilbert is cleverness itself in the rhymed lyrics that he wrote for light operas, Sir Arthur Sullivan composing the music; in blank verse they would lose much of their effectiveness. It is in the extravagances of the contemporary Ogden Nash that we find hilarious and impossible rhymes that move the most serious sobersides to at least a grin at the dizzy blend of sense and nonsense. Nash has made peculiarly his own an unmetrical line, more suggestive of a cadence than actually giving one, and this seems exactly the medium for the outrageous rhymes with which he tickles the ear and shocks conventional sense.

## I DO, I WILL, I HAVE

### OGDEN NASH

Just as I know there are two Hagens, Walter and Copen,
I know that marriage is a legal and religious alliance entered into
  by a man who can't sleep with the window shut and a woman
  who can't sleep with the window open,
Also he can't sleep until he has read the last hundred pages to
  find out whether his suspicions of the murdered eccentric
  recluse's avaricious secretary were right,
And she can't sleep until he puts out the light,
Which when he finally does she is still awake and turns on hers,
And if he thinks she's going to turn it off before she finds out
  whether Janis marries the shy young clergyman or the sophisticated polo player, he errs.
Moreover, just as I am unsure of the difference between flora
  and fauna and flotsam and jetsam
I am quite sure that marriage is the alliance of two people one
  of whom never remembers birthdays and the other never
  forgetsam,
And the one refuses to believe there is a leak in the water pipe
  or the gas pipe and the other is convinced she is about to
  asphyxiate or drown,

And the other says Quick get up and get my hairbrushes off the
window sill, it's raining in, and the one replies Oh they're all
right, it's only raining straight down.
That's why marriage is so much more interesting than divorce,
Because it's the only known example of the happy meeting of
the immovable object and the irresistible force.
So I hope husbands and wives will continue to debate and
combat over everything debatable and combatable,
Because I believe a little incompatibility is the spice of life,
particularly if he has income and she is pattable.

Double rhymes are not confined to humorous poetry or to
extravaganzas. Tennyson uses them in his "Ode on the Death
of the Duke of Wellington," Hood in his "The Bridge of
Sighs," and Mrs. Browning, none too skillfully, in

> In a purple sublimity,
> And grind down men's bones
> To a pale unanimity.

The necessity of rhyme, particularly in poems of strict
form requirements, undoubtedly at times leads a poet into a
new line of thinking. Dryden confessed that rhyme often
"tickled him to a thought." Searching for a rhyme to meet
his need in developing an idea or an image, the poet finds another obtruding itself and insisting on being used. If its in-
sistence is strong enough and the original idea not too powerful, he finds himself wandering down a different, and perhaps
a more attractive, path.

When an old man and beloved in America as a popular
poet, Oliver Wendell Holmes in his *Over the Teacups* com-
mented humorously on the restrictions of rhyme. It is a high
tribute to skill that Holmes himself, along with many others,
overcame the obstacles and not only made rhyme contributory
to beauty but also made it seem natural expression.

When you write in prose you say what you *mean*. When you write
in verse you say what you *must*. Rhythm alone is a tether, and
not a very long one. But rhymes are iron fetters; it is dragging a
chain and ball to march under their incumbrance; it is a clog dance

you are figuring in, when you execute your metrical *pas seul*. Consider under what a disadvantage your thinking powers are laboring when you are handicapped by the inexorable demands of our scanty English rhyming vocabulary! You want to say something about the heavenly bodies, and you have a beautiful line ending with the word *stars*. Were you writing in prose, your invention, your fancy, your rhetoric, your musical ear for the harmonies of language, would all have full play. But there is your rhyme fastening you by the leg, and you must either reject the line which pleases you, or you must whip up your hobbling fancy and all your limping thoughts into the traces which are hitched to one of three or four or half a dozen serviceable words. You cannot make any use of *cars*, I will suppose; you have no occasion to talk about *scars;* "the red planet *Mars*" has been used already; Dibdin has said enough about the gallant *tars;* what is there left for you but *bars*? So you give up your trains of thought, capitulate to necessity, and manage to lug in some kind of allusion, in place or out of place, which will allow you to make use of *bars*. Can there be imagined a more certain process for breaking up all continuity of thought, for taking out all the vigor, all the virility, which belongs to natural prose as the vehicle of strong, graceful, spontaneous thought, than this miserable subjugation of intellect to the clink of well or ill matched syllables?

"If a poet is concerned with pouring out the richness of his mind rather than with communicating a definite experience," wrote James Sutherland, "he can afford to catch at any suggestion that comes to him in the course of the composition. . . . He will reject accidental suggestions afforded him by rhyme . . . because they make an inadequate contribution to his imaginative tapestry," for they may be too commonplace, or too bizarre, or simply unsuitable in the context.

Lowell warned

> Borne with the rush of the meter along,
> The poet may chance to go right or go wrong,
> Content with the whirl and delirium of song.

Closely akin to rhyme is *assonance*, which uses in words the same vowel sounds with different consonants, "muffled sounds of words which do all but rhyme." *Late* and *mate* are perfect rhymes; but *late–raise, nose–cloves, plenty–many* are assonantal. In several European languages assonance historically preceded rhyme in poetry, and in Spanish it is still important. Occasionally assonance is used, especially by modern experimenters, as a substitute for rhyme, but more often it is an added decoration to poetic diction. Of course it is less obvious than rhyme and certainly less effective. A keen ear may detect it, but many readers are likely to pass it by unnoticed, though subtly it may contribute something soothing and satisfying. On the other hand, if assonance is noticed and considered as a substitute for rhyme, it may to some be offensive as seeming evidence that the poet was unable to achieve the perfect correspondence of sound to which the ear is accustomed.

In serious poetry assonance is more likely to be used for its own sake than as a substitute for rhyme. An effective way to enhance the music of verse is illustrated in a line from Tennyson's early "Leonine Elegiacs":

> Low-flowing breezes are roaming the broad valley dimmed in the gloaming.

And in "The Princess" we find the elaborate assonantal verse

> Laborious orient ivory, sphere in sphere.

Assonance has long been successfully used as an ornament to poetic diction cast in conventional meters. It may be introduced unconsciously because the poet's ear demands the music that it subtly contributes, or it may be deliberately sought and carefully introduced by a skilled artificer in words. The absence of rhyme in Collins' "Ode to Evening" only makes him more susceptible to the association of similar sounds, subtle illustrations of which may be found in the poem, not at verse ends but placed internally. Though everybody knows *Mother Goose*, it is doubtful if many have noticed that assonance is substituted for rhyme in

> Little Tommy Tucker
> Sings for his supper.

> What shall he have
> But white bread and butter?

But so far in the progress of poetry, assonance has never justified itself to the popular ear as a substitute for rhyme, though some poets have attempted it. In George Eliot's "Spanish Gypsy" all of the interpolated songs but one are rhymed; that one uses assonance throughout.

> Maiden crowned with glossy blackness,
>     Lithe as panther forest-roaming,
> Long-armed maid, when she dances,
>     On a stream of ether floating.

Occasionally, especially in our time, writers have refused to be trammeled by rhyme, either because they consider natural expression more important or because they are unable easily to find rhymes that are satisfactory.

W. H. Auden, who, as he repeatedly evidences, possesses skill enough in rhyming, has experimented in using a kind of assonance as a substitute. Each reader must decide for himself whether the technique, as illustrated in the following two stanzas from a longer poem, "The Questioner Who Sits So Sly," contributes to the arousing of pleasant aesthetic feelings or not. If the experiment pleases, it will be copied; if not, it will be ignored and soon forgotten.

> Will you turn a deaf ear
> To what they said on the shore,
> Interrogate their poises
> In their rich houses;
>
> Of stork-legged heaven-reachers
> Of the compulsory touchers
> The sensitive amusers
> And masked amazers?

*Alliteration,* a decoration of diction as old as poetry itself, is the repetition of the same initial sound of syllables in words that are in close proximity. It was characteristic of Anglo-

Saxon poetry, in which rhymeless lines were divided in half by a caesural pause, each half having normally two strong accents and all or some of the accented syllables being alliterated. It was used commonly also in the unwritten minstrel poetry of the Middle Ages and was revived by Chaucer. Since his time it is frequent in English verse.

Usually, but by no means always, the alliteration is of consonants beginning stressed syllables; but, as will be seen in the illustrations given, it may be of vowels and, subtly, may occur anywhere within words. The oft-quoted line from the eighteenth century poet Charles Churchill alliterates with vowels: "Apt alliteration's artful aid," and in Thompson's "And murmurous with music not their own" the *n*'s in *not* and *own* are quite as contributory to the music as the more obvious initial *m*'s.

That alliteration pleases the ear and aids memory is evidenced by its use in proverbs and other popular sayings: "Look ere you leap," "Tide tarries for no man," "A cat may look at a king," "Forget and forgive," and scores of others.

Alliteration binds together phrases or verses, as it frequently did in Anglo-Saxon poetry and as may be commonly seen in much later and in contemporary verse. William Collins, in his well-known "Ode to Evening" not only uses alliteration at the beginning of words but also uses what may be called "internal alliteration," to effect unity in his stanzas and to enhance the delicate music of the verse. Only four stanzas are quoted.

### ODE TO EVENING

WILLIAM COLLINS

If aught of oaten stop, or pastoral song,
May hope, chaste Eve, to soothe thy modest ear,
  Like thine own solemn springs,
  Thy springs and dying gales;

O nymph reserved—while now the bright-haired sun
Sits in yon western tent, whose cloudy skirts,

With brede ethereal wove,
O'erhang his wavy bed;

Now air is hushed, save where the weak-eyed bat
With short, shrill shriek flits by on leathern wing,
Or where the beetle winds
His small but sullen horn.

As oft he rises, 'midst the twilight path
Against the pilgrim borne in heedless hum—
Now teach me, maid composed,
To breathe some softened strain,

When reading these stanzas, did you notice the absence
of rhyme? It is compensated for by the abundant use of
alliteration, nowhere obtrusive, and by the precision of diction
that suits the mood of evening. A reader will do well to
ponder Collins' felicity in his choice of words for his best
passages: with short, shrill shriek; small but sullen horn.

Alliteration is most effective with initial consonants like *s*, *l*,
*m*, and *w*. In the following sonnet by Shakespeare the *s* sound
occurs initially nine times, and elsewhere is twenty-two times
repeated. And, as any reader will note, other alliterative
sounds as well contribute to the musical diction.

When to the sessions of sweet silent thought
I summon up remembrance of things past,
I sigh the lack of many a thing I sought,
And with old woes new wail my dear time's waste:
Then can I drown an eye, unused to flow,
For precious friends hid in death's dateless night,
And weep afresh love's long since cancel'd woe,
And moan the expense of many a vanish'd sight:
Then can I grieve at grievances foregone,
And heavily from woe to woe tell o'er
The sad account of fore-bemoaned moan,
Which I new pay as if not paid before.
    But if the while I think on thee, dear friend,
    All losses are restored and sorrows end.

Ordinarily sibilants are dangerous threats to euphony. Tennyson declared that in all his poetry he never put two in close proximity. Note the cacophony of Thoreau's line:

> 'Tis peace's end, and war's beginning strife.

As the following illustrations will show, any sound may be skillfully repeated to beautify or intensify the music of verse. These selected passages are presented with no comment, as they speak for themselves, some subtly and some extravagantly. In context, of course, the value of the alliteration would in many cases be intensified.

> You have but fed on the roses and lain in the lilies of life.
>
> . . . . .
>
> Nobody learned the lady's name
> Nor the marvelous land from which she came.
>
> . . . . .
>
> The desert and illimitable air—
> Lone wandering, but not lost.
>
> . . . . .
>
> Where Claribel low-lieth
>   The breezes pause and die,
>     Letting the rose-leaves fall:
> But the solemn oak-tree sigheth,
>     Thick-leaved, ambrosial,
>     With an ancient melody
>     Of an inward agony,
> Where Claribel low-lieth.
>
> . . . . .
>
> Or the least little delicate aquiline curve
>   in a sensitive nose.
>
> . . . . .
>
> Thus were a match made, sure and fast,
>   'Mid the blue weed-flowers round the mound
> Where issuing, we shall stand and stay
>   For one more look at baths and bay,
> Sands, sea-gulls, and the old church last.
>
> . . . . .
>
> Far off from these a slow and silent stream,
> Lethe, the river of oblivion, rolls
> Her watery labyrinths, whereof who drinks

Forthwith his former state and being forgets,
Forgets both joy and grief, pleasure and pain.

. . . . .

Lancelot, who rushing outward lionlike
Leapt on him, and hurled him headlong, and he fell
Stunned, and his creatures took and bore him off
And all was still.

If occasional, apparently spontaneous, and with the obviously right word in the right place, alliteration is highly contributory to the music of verse, giving a grace that would otherwise be missed. If, however, it seems artificial, strained for, and obtrusive, it detracts from the aesthetic effect.

*Onomatopoeia* is imitation of the sense by the sound of a word, as *thud, tug, crack, pop, gurgle,* and *splash.* Many words in our language, such as *whippoorwill,* are derived from imitation. In common speech such words give picturesqueness and force (note how much more effective than *carry* are *lug* and *tote*), and in poetry they give vividness and beauty.

Onomatopoeia is achieved by both vowels and consonants and, of course, by both in combination. Professor Tolman said that *aw* (awe), *oo* (gloom), *o* (gone) express solemnity, horror, and deep grief as well as slow motion and great size, and that *i* (little), *e* (met), *a* (mat) express joy, gayety, triviality, rapid movement, delicacy, and physical littleness. Of the consonants he asserted that *p, t, k* express unexpectedness, vigor, explosive passion, and startling effects of all kinds; that *z* and *zh* are rich, pleasant colors; that *l* and smooth *r* are used for softness, liquidity, lingering, and love; and that the whispered consonants (*s, sh, h,* and *wh*) express fear, secrecy, deception, caution, and mystery.

Illustrations will be found in the quotations that follow.

The ponderous syllables, like sullen waves
In the half-glutted hollows of reef-rocks,
Came booming thus.

Compare the language that Milton uses in "Paradise Lost" to describe the opening of the gates of heaven and of hell.

> Heaven opened wide
> Her ever-during gates, harmonious sound,
> On golden hinges turning.

> On a sudden open fly
> With impetuous recoil and jarring sound,
> Th' infernal doors, and on their hinges grate
> Harsh thunder.

And, again, Milton by one line perfectly describes huge beasts "wallowing unwieldly, enormous in their gait."

Browning emphasizes the rebuff of the lover in "A Serenade at the Villa" by the harsh last line of the poem.

> Oh, how dark your villa was,
> Windows fast and obdurate!
> How the garden grudged me grass
> Where I stood—the iron gate
> Ground its teeth to let me pass.

The effect of light vowels is heard in the following quotations. Of Queen Mab as she rode, Shakespeare says:

> Her whip of cricket's bone; the lash of film.

And Tennyson gave us

> Crisping ripples on the beach
> And tender curving lines of creamy spray;

and the lines that tell how the little glass vessels of which he dreamed were destroyed.

> The brittle fleet. . .
> Touch'd, clink'd and clash'd and vanish'd.

Swinburne gave us

> The lisp of leaves and ripple of rain.

The short *a* also may express a harsh sound:

> The clattering flints batter'd with clanging hoofs

and

> So wrangled, brangled, jangled they a month,

whereas the long vowels are more mellifluous, as in the last line of Browning's "Garden Fancies."

> This flower she stopped at, finger on lip,
>     Stooped over, in doubt, as settling its claim;
> Till she gave me, with pride to make no slip,
>     Its soft meandering Spanish name:
> What a name! Was it love or praise?
>     Speech half-asleep or love half-awake?
> I must learn Spanish, one of these days,
>     Only for that slow sweet name's sake.

One word used by Benét makes anyone hear the sound that skates make on clear ice: the *skurr* of the steel.

A poem that illustrates onomatopoeia at its best and also is rich in striking imagery is Browning's "Meeting at Night."

> The gray sea and the long black land;
> And the yellow half-moon large and low;
> And the startled little waves that leap
> In fiery ringlets from their sleep,
> As I gain the cove with pushing prow,
> And quench its speed in the slushy sand.
>
> Then a mile of warm sea-scented beach;
> Three fields to cross till a farm appears;
> A tap at the pane, the quick sharp scratch
> And blue spurt of a lighted match,
> And a voice less loud, through its joys and fears,
> Than the two hearts beating each to each!

Although not onomatopoetic, "Parting at Morning" is quoted here because it is a complementary poem. It strongly stimulates the imagination. (What is the antecedent of *him*?)

> Round the cape of a sudden came the sea,
> And the sun looked over the mountain rim;
> And straight was a path of gold for him,
> And the need of a world of men for me.

Onomatopoeia may be subtle, seemingly natural, and almost inevitably the right expression of ideas and feelings, or it may be obvious as in Pope's well-known lines in his "Essay on Criticism."

> True ease in writing comes from Art, not Chance,
> As those move easiest who have learned to dance.
> 'Tis not enough no harshness gives offense;
> The sound must seem an echo to the sense.
> Soft is the strain when zephyr gently blows,
> And the smooth stream in smoother numbers flows;
> But when loud surges lash the sounding shore,
> The harsh rough verse should like the torrent roar.
> When Ajax strives some rock's vast weight to throw,
> The line, too, labors, and the words move slow:
> Not so when swift Camilla scours the plain,
> Flies o'er the unbending corn, and skims along the main.

Extended onomatopoetic passages are infrequent in poetry, but effect is commonly gained by the use of words which, although not imitative of the sense, are consonant with it, words like *dream, solemn, dusk, wrangle, soft, bright,* and *weary.* In Gray's "Elegy" there are numerous illustrations.

At times a whole poem is written with emphasis on imitative words. Dryden's "A Song for Saint Cecilia's Day" is such a poem. Here are four stanzas:

> The trumpet's loud clangor
>   Excites us to arms
> With shrill notes of anger
>   And mortal alarms.
>
> The double, double, double beat
>   Of the thundering drum
>   Cries, "Hark! the foes come;
> Charge, charge 'tis too late to retreat!"
>
> The soft complaining flute
> In dying notes discovers
>   The woes of hapless lovers,
> Whose dirge is whispered by the warbling lute.

Sharp violins proclaim
Their jealous pangs and desperation,
Fury, frantic indignation,
Depth of pains and height of passion,
For the fair disdainful dame.

Other notable illustrations of continuous onomatopoeia are Poe's "The Bells," Tennyson's "Brook," Lanier's "Song of the Chattahoochee," and Southey's "The Cataract of Lodore." Instrumental music, too, uses onomatopoeia. Compare with the poems just mentioned Smetana's "The Moldau." Other compositions that are illustrative are Beethoven's "Pastoral Symphony" and Chopin's "Raindrop Prelude," the introduction to the second act of Verdi's *Simon Boccanegra*, the opening of Puccini's *Gianni Schicchi*, Rachmaninoff's "Isle of the Dead," and numerous passages from Wagner's Ring Cycle, notably the coming of spring in *Siegfried*, and the singing of a bird in *Die Walküre*. Excellent examples of how music interprets and enforces the meaning of words are Schubert's "Gretchen am Spinnrade," Verdi's "O Patria Mia," the catalog in *Don Giovanni*, and Puccini's "Ah! fors 'è lui."

To appreciate the onomatopoetic effects that poets achieve, try your hand at substituting for each italicized word in the following quotations another word that expresses the sense by the sound. The words that the poets originally wrote are given in Appendix D.

1

The full-juiced apple, waxing over-mellow,
*Falls* in a silent autumn night.

2

To watch the *breaking* ripples on the beach.

3

The vessel *fills* her sails.

4

After the *flying* of the bats.

5
The ragged rims of thunder *hanging* low.

6
My long scythe *made a sound* and left the hay to make.

7
My soul
Smoothed itself out, a long-cramped scroll
Freshening and *waving* in the wind.

8
And Gareth loosed the stone
From off his neck, then in the mere beside
*Threw* it; *smoothly* bubbled up the mere.

Onomatopoeia is the chief means of securing *tone-color*, which is as important in poetry as it is in music. Tone-color is the quality by which one sound differs from another, not in pitch, length, or force, but in the way one shade or tint of a color differs from another. It is best observed in extended passages, where the sentiment demands an appropriate pitch and melody. It has been said that rhythm is the anatomy of verse, tone-color the flesh tint which clothes it with life and animation. The sound of the words sets the spirit of a poem. The first lines of Herrick's "Corinna's Going A-Maying,"

> Get up, get up for shame! The blooming morn
> Upon her wings presents the god unshorn,

and Sir Walter Scott's "Waken, lords and ladies gay" prepare us by the sound of the diction for something quite different from the beginning of Tennyson's "The Lotus-Eaters," two stanzas of which are quoted.

> "Courage!" he said, and pointed toward the land,
> "This mounting wave will roll us shoreward soon."
> In the afternoon they came unto a land
> In which it seemed always afternoon.
> All round the coast the languid air did swoon,
> Breathing like one that hath a weary dream,
> Full-faced above the valley stood the moon;

And like a downward smoke, the slender stream
Along the cliff to fall and pause did seem.

They sat them down upon the yellow sand,
Between the sun and moon upon the shore;
And sweet it was to dream of Fatherland,
Of child, and wife, and slave; but evermore
Most weary seem'd the sea, weary the oar,
Weary the wandering fields of barren foam.
Then someone said, "We will return no more";
And all at once they sang, "Our island home
Is far beyond the wave; we will no longer roam."

For additional illustrations of tone-color reread "The Eve
of St. Agnes," and the odes by Keats, Milton's "L'Allegro"
and "Il Penseroso," Poe's "Ulalume," Cowper's "John Gilpin's
Ride," and Oliver Wendell Holmes's occasional verses. The
first few lines of most poems set a tone that is developed
throughout.

When all is said about the diction of poetry there remains
an indefinable something that moves one like the music of
flute or trumpet. Certainly there must be naturalness in diction, what seems like the inevitable words in perfect order,
a naturalness that is destroyed by any suggestion of strain,
inversion, and padding especially. But beyond that are a
cadence and color, often heightened by connotative meaning.

Canst thou not minister to a mind diseas'd
Pluck from the memory a rooted sorrow,
Raze out the written troubles of the brain,
And with some sweet oblivious antidote
Cleanse the stuff'd bosom of that perilous stuff
Which weighs upon the heart?
                    . . . . .
Thou wast not born for death, immortal Bird!
   No hungry generations tread thee down;
The voice I heard this passing night was heard
   In ancient days by emperor and clown:
Perhaps the self-same song that found a path
   Through the sad heart of Ruth, when sick for home,

She stood in tears amid the alien corn;
The same that oft-times hath
Charm'd magic casements, opening on the foam
Of perilous seas, in faery lands forlorn.

. . . . .

Thou sawest, in thine old singing season, brother,
Secrets and sorrows unbeheld of us:
Fierce loves, and lovely leafbuds poisonous,
Bare to thy subtler eye, but for none other
Blowing by night in some unbreathed-in clime;
The hidden harvest of luxurious time,
Sin without shape, and pleasure without speech;
And where strange dreams in a tumultous sleep
Make the shut eyes of stricken spirits weep;
And with each face thou sawest the shadow on each,
Seeing as men sow men reap.

# Chapter Six

# THE CONNOTATIVE APPEAL

BESIDES its direct appeal to the senses, which results in what we have called sensuous appreciation, poetry, like other arts, has two other means of giving pleasure. One, which is intellectual and must be learned, is technique, which will be discussed at some length later. The other is connotation.

Words denote exact ideas, and they may also connote, or stimulate a person to contribute from his prior experience and from his imagination additions that amplify and enrich the original bare meaning. "July Fourth" *denotes* merely the fourth day of the seventh month; it generally *connotes* American independence, the battle of Bull Run, and several other historical events; and to individuals it may connote picnics, political oratory, personal anniversaries, or peculiar experiences that happened to them on that day. Obviously connotation is necessarily in large measure personal; but inasmuch as many experiences are common to the generality of mankind, the same or very similar extensions will be made by nearly everybody to many verbal stimuli. The greatest poet, declared Sainte-Beuve, is he who suggests the most, he not all of whose meaning is at first obvious, and who leaves you much to desire, to explain, to study, much to complete in your turn.

To illustrate the effect of emotionally toned connotative words, Robert H. Thouless rewrote Keats's lines

> Full on this casement shone the wintry moon
> And threw warm gules on Madeline's fair breast

as

> Full on this window shone the wintry moon
> Making red marks on Jane's uncolored chest.

Elene B. Weeks, a high school girl, saw, as others have seen time out of mind, beauties in nature, but to her they all connoted one thing which was at the time her own personal obsession.

> How do I know I love you?
> Because, today I have seen
> Dawn like a great symphony across a lake,
> A branch, shivered with sunlight,
> Hot, still noon, on a road
> Burning in the sun,
> The last swansong of golden light
> Flooding a hill turned toward the west,
> A pine, its arms holding little sighs, quietly dark and tall,
> With one still star in the sky yet light from the day—
> And the moon, slipping up, still, from a passion of light—
> All these, and more, I have seen,
> And every one made me think of you.
> That's how I know I love you.

Connotation is a common effect of all art. It calls upon those who would enjoy it to contribute, so that the result comes as much, perhaps, from the respondent as from the appealing technique. Poetry can mean much connotatively only to one who has a rich background of experience upon which he draws to supplement, enrich, and beautify what the artist has said or suggested. As the philosopher John Dewey wrote, "The function of art has always been to break through the crust of conventionalized and routine consciousness. Common things—a flower, a gleam of moonlight, the song of a bird, not things rare and remote—are means by which the deeper levels are touched so that they spring up as desire and thought." And it is perception, appreciation, and emotion that a reader must supply before any poem becomes art.

A poet may be able to see "books in the running brooks, sermons in stones, and good in everything," but unless he can stimulate a reader to imagine sermons and books from stones and running brooks, his verses remain mere denotative words on a printed page without becoming effective art. He must enable you

> To see a world in a grain of sand
> And a heaven in a wild flower,
> Hold Infinity in the palm of your hand
> And Eternity in an hour,

or he is merely a writer and not an artist. Robert Browning in "Balaustion's Adventure" asks, "What's poetry except a power that makes?" and then goes on:

> And speaking to one sense, inspires the rest,
> Pressing them all into its service; so
> That who sees painting, seems to hear as well
> The speech that's proper for the painted mouth; . . . .
> And who receives true verse at eye or ear,
> Takes in (with verse) time, place, and person too,
> So, links each sense on to its sister-sense. . . .
> Who hears the poem, therefore, sees the play.

## Connotative Sounds

There are sounds that are connotative of experiences and moods, pleasurable and unpleasurable according to the experiences and the mood of the one who hears them. The poet and the musician by skillful selection and combination of sounds suggest such recall as arouses feeling that is satisfying and thus create art. Even nonsensical combinations of verbal sounds, as in Lewis Carroll's "Jabberwocky," may be pleasurable.

> 'Twas brillig, and the slithy toves
> Did gyre and gimble in the wabe;

All mimsy were the borogoves,
And the mome raths outgrabe.

We may not agree on exactly what these verses mean, but no one could for a moment think that they express dignified thought or high passion. That they are pleasurable a world of readers have agreed. Much poetry, like Tennyson's "Tears, Idle Tears," that contains definite ideas, perfectly expressed, has by its musical beauty a sort of hypnotic effect on readers who are satisfied with a sensuous and indefinite connotation. Needless to say that their appreciation is incomplete.

It is by skillful choice and presentation of sounds that composers give us "program music." In contrast to "pure music," which depends for its effect solely on sensuous pleasure and on understanding of the techniques of composition, program music attempts by sounds to stimulate a hearer to imagine what a composer had in mind and to feel about it as he did. It is common for musicologists to sneer at program music, but it is the type that has given pleasure to the greatest number from primitive times to the present. It cannot justly be deprecated if masters like Brahms, Beethoven, Schubert, Schumann, and Wagner have felt it worth writing. "It is absurd and illogical that the concert-goer should, as some assert, be asked to listen to a piece of descriptive music in ignorance of its literary or pictorial or dramatic basis." It should be "a running comment or illustration of a sequence or a scheme already in the hearer's mind." If an incident or a scene was necessary for the poet's imagination, it is desirable for the hearer's; and without it he is likely to get no further than the outside of the composition.

Composers of music, like most painters, have felt the desirability of giving titles to their works to assure effective connotation. It is true they entitle some compositions of pure music Opus —— and Etude in E Flat Minor, but for other types we find titles that are definitely helpful in appreciation: Saint-Saëns' "Carnival of the Animals," with its tortoise, fish, and rattling dry bones; Dukas' "The Sorcerer's Apprentice," to which an outline of the story is appended by the composer.

Painters have always appreciated the advantage of giving titles to their pictures in order to assure understanding of what they intended. Usually the titles of primitive paintings, titles like "Madonna with Two Saints" or "St. George Slaying the Dragon," add nothing to what the symbolism tells or to what the priest says when using the picture as a text. But in Poussin's "Les Bergeres d'Arcadie," the inscription "Et in Arcadia Ego" ("I too was in Arcadia") gives a meaning that otherwise might be missed when one looks at healthy young shepherds observing the tomb of their dead companion. The titles of Rembrandt's "Death Appearing to a Newly Wedded Couple" and of Watts's "Sic Transit Gloria Mundi" are as connotative as the etching and the painting.

Unfortunately titles as meaningless as "Study" have sometimes been affixed to paintings, contributing nothing connotatively and in some cases actually diverting attention from what the artist was trying to express. "Ulysses Defying Polyphemus" and "The Sun of Venice Going to Sea" add nothing to one's appreciation of the glorious colors in Turner's compositions, whereas "The Fighting Temeraire" suggests tragic poetry as the gallant old battleship is towed away to be broken up. Sargent's "Man with a Pink Domino," Gainsborough's "Blue Boy," and most of Whistler's titles call attention to technique rather than give connotation. Modernistic art often uses titles that are intentionally mystifying and irritatingly mischievous. "Nude Falling Downstairs" and "Debris of an Automobile Giving Birth to a Blind Horse Biting a Telephone" direct one's attention to neither technique nor aesthetic significance.

Few laymen would agree with Mendelssohn when he wrote "Music that I love expresses to me thoughts not too *indefinite*, but too *definite*, to put into words," which he maintained do not mean the same thing to one person as to another; "only music can say the same thing to all, can awaken the same feelings, feelings which cannot be expressed in words." It is true that language cannot give the sense of peace, for example, that music can, but it can tell much more—exactly who is peaceful, why, and in what situation. Words can enrich music as music can enrich verbal meaning. Hence we have song and opera.

Beethoven's Seventh Symphony, to which he gave no title, has been variously interpreted. Wagner saw in it the apotheosis of the dance, Schumann a village marriage ceremony, Alberti the joy of Germany released from French yoke, and others have interpreted it as representing a knightly festival, the romantic Moors in Spain, a cathedral procession, and a battle of giants returning to the feasts of victory. Though these interpretations differ and no doubt are not precise expressions of what the composer felt, it will be noted that in a general way they do agree. Certainly the symphony is not expressing grief, humiliation, or a hope of immortality.

Besides giving titles to their compositions, titles such as have been supplied by popular agreement even to Mendelssohn's own "Songs without Words," composers have often written more or less detailed interpretations to guide hearers to proper appreciation. Here is Smetana's statement of what he tried to make "Vltava" (the Moldau River) say:

Two springs pour forth their streams in the shade of the Bohemian forest, the one warm and gushing, the other cold and tranquil. Their waves, joyfully flowing over their rocky beds, unite and sparkle in the morning sun. The forest brook, rushing on, becomes the River Moldau, which, with its waters speeding through Bohemia's valleys, grows into a mighty stream. It flows through dense woods from which come the joyous sounds of the chase, and the notes of the hunter's horn are heard ever nearer and nearer.

It flows through emerald meadows and lowlands, where a wedding feast is being celebrated with song and dancing. At night, in its shining waves, wood and water nymphs hold their revels, and in these waves are reflected many a fortress and castle—witnesses of bygone splendor of chivalry, and the vanished martial fame of days that are no more. At the Rapids of St. John the stream speeds on, winding its way through cataracts and hewing the path for its foaming waters through the rocky chasm into the broad river bed, in which it flows on in majestic calm toward Prague, welcomed by time-honored Vysehrad, to disappear in the far distance from the poet's gaze.

Commentators, some of them highly perspicacious, often write as program notes their own interpretations of music that is to be played. Such notes, as might be expected, vary widely in value, for of course the commentators themselves vary widely in background, in sensibilities, and in imaginative power. The best of program notes enhance the enjoyment of the music as performed, but others are hindrances, conflicting, as they must inevitably do, with the individualistic connotative responses of auditors. One of the most beautiful and on the whole most satisfying is the interpretation by Edmund Gosse, himself a poet, of Debussy's "L'Apres Midi d'Un Faune." If this is not what the composer was trying to say, it is at least an interpretation that gives to the majority of listeners to the music more beauty than they would get without it.

A faun—a simple, sensuous, passionate being—wakens in the forest at daybreak and tries to recall his experience of the previous afternoon. Was he the fortunate recipient of an actual visit from nymphs, white and golden goddesses, divinely tender and indulgent? Or is the memory he seems to retain nothing but the shadow of a vision, no more substantial than the arid rain of notes from his own flute? He cannot tell. Yet surely there was, surely there is, an animal whiteness among the brown reeds of the lake that shines out yonder. Were they, are they, swans? No! But naiads plunging? Perhaps! Vaguer and vaguer grows the impression of this delicious experience. He would resign his woodland godship to retain it. A garden of lilies, golden-headed, white-stalked behind the trellis of red roses? Ah, the effort is too great for his poor brain. Perhaps if he selects one lily from the garth of lilies, one benign and beneficent yielder of her cup to thirsty lips, the memory, the ever-receding memory, may be forced back. So when he has glutted upon a bunch of grapes, he is wont to toss the empty skins into the air and blow them out in a visionary greediness. But no, the delicious hour grows vaguer; experience or dream, he will never know which it was. The sun is warm, the grasses yielding; and he curls himself up again, after worshipping again the efficacious star of wine, that he may pursue the dubious ecstasy into the more hopeful boskages of sleep.

Charles O'Connell gives in *The Victor Book of the Symphony* what in addition this same music means to him. Differing somewhat because of the personalities of the interpreters, the two agree in general tone.

The late Lawrence Gilman was peculiarly able to express the connotative effects of music. From his column in the New York *Herald Tribune* in 1929 the following is quoted:

Why is it that when, in the second act of Wagner's *Tristan*, Isolde listens for the sound of King Mark's decrescent hunting-horns, and the orchestra responds to her listening with a hushed and delicate murmuring, the music floods our imaginations with a sudden and vivid sense of the glamour and magic of a summer night—a summer night in an Old World Garden? The musical means that Wagner uses here are of the utmost simplicity and transparency: violins, violas, and cellos play, pianissimo, a *tremolo sul ponticello* (an effect produced by drawing the bow across the strings close to the bridge); and then, through this vague and glamorous haze of tone, a solo clarinet traces an ascending melody of subdued chromatic tenderness. Yet, for all its simplicity, the passage is marvelous in its communicative potency; we stand beside Isolde in the garden, we hear with her the stirring of the wind in the tall trees. The music becomes the moment's poet, the scene's consummate painter, evoking for us its own exquisite image of that immortal trysting-place.

Nay, more: by virtue of the divine liberality of music, whose indefiniteness is a pattern of the absolute, we face the capping miracle of an unparagoned art, inexplicable and unique; for this music evokes for us, not only Isolde's garden, but every garden over which night and ecstasy have breathed enchantment; so that the imagination, magically enfranchised, wanders among all the gardens of which it has ever dreamt, knowing an immeasurable loveliness.

Unfortunately many concert program notes concern themselves with technical matters only: the instruments required in the orchestra, especially unusual instruments like the celesta and English horn, the architecture of the composition, biographic and historical facts, and the like. This type of commentary contributes little or nothing to connotative appreciation. It has been amusingly parodied by an anonymous writer in the *Atlantic Monthly*, September, 1930.

## From a Symphony Programme

The Roller Coaster Suite, Op. 23      Peter Pumpkin-Eater
(Born at West Hackensack June 1, 1898, living at West Hackensack)

Pumpkin-Eater did not depend on commentators to explain the meaning of his Roller Coaster Suite. He printed his own programme on the score:—

Night—The Ascent—The Wild Surmise—Lost in the Clouds—Moments of Danger—The Lost Hat—The Descent—Vision—Young Love—The Eternal Question—Night.

The work is in two movements, with a brief pause after the chief episode, "The Lost Hat."

The suite, dedicated "in profound gratitude" to Ruben Salzheimer (The inventor of the Roller Coaster), calls for these instruments: five flutes, two oboes, English horn and brake-lining, double bassoon, four tenor tubas, wind machine, cymbals, kettledrums, chewing gum, three soprano saxophones, for use at a considerable distance behind the scenes, and as many strings as can be conveniently seated on the stage.

This suite is frankly programme music. In the soft, slow measures of the introduction, Night is indicated. A Sicilian shepherd and his consort are discovered in a roller coaster chariot. Muted strings, horns, and wood winds have *(lento)* a slowly ascending figure. Against a chord (B-flat minor) the "mounting motive" is sounded by the brass. Philip Hale, the critic, believes that this theme is derived from the folk song, "All the Little Angels Ascend Up On High." There is development. What may be considered the main movement of the symphony follows, the "main" because, beginning with the Ascent, it has to do with the adventures of the couple on high. The movement begins (*"andante furioso* 4-4 time") with a theme played by the flutes, wind machine, and the full string choir. This is practically the chief theme of the work and is made much of. The English horn, now loud, now soft, indicates the traffic below. The chariot mounts higher and higher with the music. Saxophones, at a considerable distance, introduce the Moments of Danger, which, according to one of the wise men of Paris, represent the cries of the terrified female coasters.

A tonic part is now given to the tenor tubas, mounting to a crescendo. The Sicilian's hat has blown off! Here a noteworthy figure for brass, with a roll on cymbals with wooden drumsticks, bespeaks the wrath and lament of the young shepherd. "Arpeggios, glissandos, rapidly descending scales, bells, and brake-lining picture the dashing descent of the Roller Coaster."

Then begins that dulcet love passage so dear to concert-goers. From the composer's notes we are to understand that the Sicilian is now being comforted by his consort for the loss of his hat. Released from the peril and buffeting of Fate, the couple languish in each other's arms as their chariot comes gently to a stop. An appealing melody is given to the oboes over muted chewing gum.* This love melody is sustained for sixteen measures before it gives way to a brief interlude in which other roller coasters are heard in the distance. This threatens to grow ominous, then recedes as the music of endearment returns. For an ecstatic moment passion runs riot in a fugato movement in 6-8 time; then the love song fades, the chewing gum is heard no more. At the close, use is made of the Night material with which the suite begins.

There is a short coda.

* Many will challenge this use of an instrument not usually classified in the musical world. But though repeated efforts have been made to reproduce this gentle smacking by instruments, thus far no close likeness has been achieved. Where machines fail, nature must be employed.—EDITOR

Sounds are a potent characteristic of words, the raw material of poetry. The sounds of *moon* and *asleep* are more different in connotation than are the meanings of *celestial orb* and *dormant*. Sounds of words also have a connotative effect on people according to their associations with them. In Wordsworth's "Reverie of Poor Susan" a country girl hears a caged thrush singing at the corner of Wood Street in the crowded city, and

> She sees
> A mountain ascending, a vision of trees;
> Bright volumes of vapour through Lothbury glide,
> And a river flows on through the vale of Cheapside.

To her the sound brings up pictures of green pastures and of her humble home, for which her lonely heart yearns. To another person the song of the thrush might have suggested a feeling of pity for the caged bird, a refreshing memory of a beautiful experience on a summer morning, or a recollection of pleasure at seeing in a picture gallery Millet's "Song of the Lark." Sounds of all kinds are associated in human memories with experiences peculiar to them and brought into consciousness in the degree to which memory is intense and suffused by emotion.

The sound of some words is in itself especially pleasurable or unharmonious. Someone has said that *cellar-door* gives the most beautiful sound in our language, and there is a story that the word *Mesopotamia* in a sermon brought penitents to the altar, and another, that a vituperating fishwife was silenced when she was called a "parallelepipedon." *Harsh* and *grate* are as cacophonous as *smooth* and *roll* are musical.

"There is a fascination," wrote Oliver Wendell Holmes in *The Poet at the Breakfast-Table,* "in the mere sound of articulated breath; of consonants that resist with the firmness of a maid of honor, or half or wholly yield to the wooing lips; of vowels that flow and murmur, each after its kind; the peremptory *b* and *p*, the brittle *k*, the vibrating *r*, the insinuating *s*, the feathery *f*, the velvety *v*, the bell-voiced *m*, the tranquil broad *a*, the penetrating *e*, the cooing *u*, the emotional *o*, and the beautiful combinations of alternate rock and stream, as it were, that they give to the rippling flow of speech."

Tennyson and Fitzgerald quarreled in a friendly way over the authorship of what they agreed is the weakest possible line in English verse: "A Mr. Wilkinson, a clergyman," the feebleness of which is due altogether to the short vowels. "Laborious orient ivory" and "awful rose of dawn" are strong because the prominent vowels come from opposite ends of the scale. An experimental group of versifiers, calling themselves "Dadists," depended on the sound values of words, rather than on meaning, for producing aesthetic pleasure. However, that alone is not enough.

Several poets have made lists of words which appealed to them because of their sound or because of their connotation.

John T. McCutcheon, the versatile cartoonist of the *Chicago Tribune,* gave a specific list in his

## BALLAD OF BEAUTIFUL WORDS

Amethyst, airy, drifting, dell,
Oriole, lark, alone,
Columbine, kestrel, temple, bell,
Madrigal, calm, condone.

Emerald, swallow, tawny, dawn,
Silvery, starling, lane,
Radiance, rosary, garland, fawn,
Pastoral, valley, vane.

Crinoline, crimson, crystal, croon,
Troubadour, flagon, flown,
Caravan, amber, laurel, moon,
Tamarine, tendon, tone.

Chivalry, convoy, clamor, cling,
Hurricane, highland, dream,
Journeyman, mariner, sailor, wing,
Mandarin, tarn, redeem.

Imperial, ermine, helmet, lance,
Gondola, glory, glade,
Calendar, sultan, darling, dance,
Melody, minstrel, maid.

Dominion, destiny, danger, dare,
Revelry, drone, dragoon,
Tourmaline, treasure, fortune, fair,
Olden, gold, doubloon.

Smoldering, somber, tumbrel, tomb,
Indigo, ember, shorn,
Sonorous, sorrow, clover, doom,
Pendulum, dirge, forlorn.

Charity, gloaming, garnering, grain,
Curfew, candle, loam,
Benison, mother, lassie, swain,
Children, evening, home.

A poll of American and British writers resulted in the following list of words that to them are the most beautiful and also the most satisfyingly connotative: *dawn, lullaby, murmuring, tranquil, luminous, golden, melody, azure, moon, heart, and shadow.* It indicated that the writers think ugly and unpleasing in suggestion: *gangrene, scram, guzzle, mange, swell, gripe, spinach, jazz, and cacophony.*

Connotative names are popularly given to flowers (*buttercup, heartsease, goldenrod, jack-in-the-pulpit, forget-me-not, fireweed, black-eyed Susan, Johnny-jump-up*); to birds (*vesper sparrow, ruby-throat hummingbird, saw-whet owl*); to things (*skyscraper, dreadnaught*). If one knows the etymology of many common words he will perceive connotative poetry in their origin: *attention* means stretching out toward; *enthusiasm*, filled with the spirit of a god; *rival*, living on the opposite bank of a stream; *entomology* is the science of insects, small bugs that are nearly cut in two. Knowledge of the origin of many English words, such as *supercilious* and *hypocrite*, will give connotation unsuspected by the ignorant.

Poets often make use of geographical names for their musical and connotative qualities, with little or no concern for location on the face of the earth. Some geographical names that are musical are *Habersham, Vallombrosa, Salamis, Trebizond, Fontarabbia, Xanadu, Mogadore, Ulalume,* and *Aspramont*; and others, like *Arabia* and "*the ghoul-haunted woodland of Weir*," are by their sound suggestive of adventure and romance.

Poets also skillfully select for appropriate sound or for connotative effect names for their characters: *Bottom, Falstaff, Miniver Cheevy, Prufrock.* The names used by Edgar Lee Masters in his *Spoon River Anthology* are evidence of real genius.

## CONNOTATIVE THINGS

Inanimate things are often rich in connotation. Moonlight, spring, bird songs, and flowers, for example, are pleasantly connotative to practically everybody, and in consequence they are found frequently recurrent in poetry. The poet needs merely to mention them and he is assured that every reader will from memory give a supplementation that enriches meaning and heightens enjoyment. The reader becomes a partner with the poet. Choice of what is generally associated with pleasure or the ability to make pleasurable what had previously been known only as commonplace is the genius of the artist.

Raymond Alden truly says, "We are more likely to attach imaginative conceptions to things which are obviously beautiful than to those which are merely useful, and to things which are distant in place and time than to those recent and familiar; for this reason all the fine arts deal more largely with the former classes than with the latter. But after all, a poet may at anytime show the imaginative possibilities of objects in the other classes."

But though sounds and things may bring pleasure, for this purpose words are the tools of the poet. Every word has one or more exact or denotative meanings (*set* has nearly two hundred listed in the dictionaries), and many have in addition connotative meanings, suggestive significances that are determined by personal experiences. *Set* is ordinarily denotative only, but it may carry with it peculiar memories and emotions to a person who has recently failed to make his bid in a contract bridge game. *Angle, bone, rock, chair,* and *business* to most people most of the time carry a definite meaning with no halo of feeling. *Dawn, moonlight, kiss, death, baby,* and *courage,* on the other hand, are likely to be connotative, associated as they are with experiences, actual or vicarious, that have concomitant feeling.

Connotation must, of course, as already said, be highly personal. But fortunately for the poet all people have had many experiences in common, and it is by recall of these that the artist is most likely to get a generally satisfying response.

Practically everybody has had a home, the memory of which brings up details and feelings peculiar to the individual. Consequently the song "Home, Sweet Home" has been universally moving. To one person it recalls a farmhouse, the family sitting around the fire, Mother knitting, Father smoking his pipe, the old dog lying on the hearth, and the smell of supper permeating the atmosphere. It's winter, as in Whittier's description of his boyhood home in "Snow-Bound," or it's springtime, as in Bryant's home.

> There stand, in the clean-swept fireplace,
>     Fresh boughs from the wood in bloom,
> And the birch-tree's fragrant branches
>     Perfume the humble room.

To others, *home* brings back an elegant apartment or a hovel; but in every case memories are suffused with feeling. Consequently, in a boarding school the song "Home, Sweet Home" will melt to tears young girls who would be moved not at all by repetition of the denotative word *house*. "House, house, sweet, sweet house" would be ridiculously ineffective. The poet, then, uses words that are connotative of emotionally pleasurable experiences.

## IN THE OLD HOUSE

ARTHUR WILLIAM O'SHAUGHNESSY

> In the old house where we dwelt
>     No care had come, no grief we knew,
> No memory of the past we felt,
> No doubt assailed us when we knelt;
>     It is not so in the new.
>
> In the old house where we grew
>     From childhood up, the days were dreams,
>     The summers had unwonted gleams,
> The sun a warmer radiance threw
>     Upon the stair. Alas! it seems
> All different in the new.

Our mother still could sing the strain
In earlier days we listened to;
The white threads in her hair were few,
She seldom sighed or suffered pain,
Oh, for the old house back again!
It is not so in the new.

Not all connotative words are poetically useful. Parrington says, "Richer in poetry than any verses of Byron were the Latin words *habeas corpus* to one like this scholar. How packed they were with English history, how rich in suggestion to all who love English freedom!" It is true that to "this scholar" these words recall a wealth of history and perhaps a glow of pride, but most people are lacking in his background of knowledge and few have any emotional association with that Latin phrase. The poet chooses words that laugh or sing or weep for the majority.

Certain modern writers have attempted to present poetically the commonplace and what is ordinarily considered ugly and even disgusting. In this attempt they follow Wordsworth and Whitman, but they use a different diction—a diction that seems to them more appropriate to their subjects. It cannot be denied that their verses are picturesque and often strikingly memorable. The question that a reader should ask is, "Do they arouse in me pleasurable emotions?" If so, they are poetry to him. The first stanzas of T. S. Eliot's "Preludes" are an excellent illustration. The entire poem is quoted, for the penultimate stanza cannot fairly be neglected. Why do you think it was written? Does it give a significance to all that precedes?

## PRELUDES

THOMAS STEARNS ELIOT

(i)

The winter evening settles down
With smell of steaks in passageways.

Six o'clock.
The burnt-out ends of smoky days.
And now a gusty shower wraps
The grimy scraps
Of withered leaves about your feet
And newspapers from vacant lots;
The showers beat
On broken blinds and chimney-pots,
And at the corner of the street
A lonely cab-horse steams and stamps.
And then the lighting of the lamps.

(ii)

The morning comes to consciousness
Of faint stale smells of beer
From the sawdust-trampled street
With all its muddy feet that press
To early coffee-stands.
With the other masquerades
That time resumes,
One thinks of all the hands
That are raising dingy shades
In a thousand dingy rooms.

(iii)

You tossed a blanket from the bed,
You lay upon your back and waited;
You dozed, and watched the night revealing
The thousand sordid images
Of which your soul was constituted;
They flickered against the ceiling.
And when all the world came back
And the light crept up between the shutters,
And you heard the sparrows in the gutters,
You had such a vision of the street
As the street hardly understands;
Sitting along the bed's edge, where
You curled the papers from your hair,
Or clasped the yellow soles of feet
In the palms of both soiled hands.

(iv)

His soul stretched tight across the skies
That fade behind a city block,
Or trampled by insistent feet
At four or five or six o'clock;
And short square figures stuffing pipes,
And evening newspapers, and eyes
Assured of certain certainties,
The conscience of a blackened street
Impatient to assume the world.
I am moved by fancies that are curled
Around these images, and cling:
The notion of some infinitely gentle
Infinitely suffering thing.

Wipe your hand across your mouth, and laugh;
The worlds revolve like ancient women
Gathering fuel in vacant lots.

## CONNOTATIVE PHRASES

There are also numerous phrases that are highly connotative
and poetically suggestive. *Too late* is a perfect illustration.
Whittier wrote with an assurance of effect, despite the New
England rhyme,

For of all sad words of tongue or pen,
The saddest are these: "It might have been!"

Wordsworth's "The Solitary Reaper" is a great poem
largely because of the connotative phrases "plaintive numbers," "old, unhappy, far-off things," and "battles long ago."
In fact, without them the poem would hardly be more than
mere verse.

Behold her, single in the field,
Yon solitary Highland lass!
Reaping and singing by herself;
Stop here, or gently pass!
Alone she cuts and binds the grain,
And sings a melancholy strain;

O listen! for the vale profound
Is overflowing with the sound.

No nightingale did ever chaunt
More welcome notes to weary bands
Of travelers in some shady haunt,
Among Arabian sands:
A voice so thrilling ne'er was heard
In springtime from the cuckoo-bird,
Breaking the silence of the seas
Among the farthest Hebrides.

Will no one tell me what she sings?—
Perhaps the plaintive numbers flow
For old, unhappy, far-off things,
And battles long ago:
Or is it some more humble lay,
Familiar matter of today?
Some natural sorrow, loss, or pain,
That has been, and may be again?

Whate'er the theme, the maiden sang
As if her song could have no ending;
I saw her singing at her work,
And o'er the sickle bending;—
I listened, motionless and still;
And, as I mounted up the hill,
The music in my heart I bore,
Long after it was heard no more.

## Connotative Situations

There are situations that are powerfully connotative. When Stevenson puts Jim Hawkins in the apple barrel every reader of *Treasure Island* trembles with the boy at the approach of Long John Silver. In Rossetti's "The Blessed Damozel," the lover imagining his loved one at the gold bar of Heaven yearning for reunion with him is a highly connotative situation, as are the skeptical Orpheus followed by his recovered bride, a father sitting by his dead child, and hundreds of others that have been used by the poets.

In William Vaughn Moody's "The Death of Eve" we have a situation that challenges every imaginative reader. When Eve felt death coming on, she had one desire, to stand under the Tree of Life again and express her long-pent up feelings about the banishment from Eden. She asked Adam to go with her, but he was too old and too fearful of a repetition of the wrath of God; she asked Seth, but he was a respected citizen who dared not lose his reputation in the community. But Cain, the outcast, went with his mother. For once the gate was unguarded, and Eve re-entered the Garden, again stood underneath the Tree of Life, and with her last breath told God what her heart had harbored for nine hundred years. What did she say?

Browning in "Karshish" uses a situation that is connotative to the highest degree. A young Arab physician on his *Wanderjahr* has seen Lazarus, who had been raised from the dead. Karshish, of course, as a trained scientist cannot believe the story of his resurrection, and yet there are facts that he cannot get away from. Puzzled, he writes to his master, telling first of mottled spiders that are locally reputed to be efficacious remedies and other such details as would interest a physician of the time, but repeatedly he reverts to Lazarus, who has come back from the grave, who after vainly trying to tell of what he had learned in his three days of death had given up the attempt, and who had settled down with a perspective that no others, especially a scientist and an unbeliever, could understand, but with a peace of mind that all envied. The situation powerfully stirs the imagination, and the poet is masterful in expressing the conflict of doubt and unwilling conviction on the part of the young physician. Of course Browning himself had first strongly felt the connotation of a man returned to life after three days of death, and by his art he sets us to wondering what such a man would say and do when his friends came eagerly questioning, how he would feel and act when he realized that no words could explain, and what new values he would see in life.

The skillful poet endeavors to present a connotative situation quickly so that the cooperative imagination of the reader
is challenged and made active. Keats begins one ode with

O wild West Wind, thou breath of Autumn's being

and another ode with

> Hail to thee, blithe spirit!
>   Bird thou never wert,
> That from heaven or near it,
>   Pourest thy full heart
> In profuse strains of unpremeditated art.

Scott begins his "Hunting Song" with the stirring

> Waken, lords and ladies gay.
> On the mountains dawns the day,

and "The Lady of the Lake" with

> The stag at eve had drunk his fill.

Browning's first stanza of "Childe Roland to the Dark Towei
Came" effectively brings a reader into the horrible situation
that confronts the adventurer.

> My first thought was, he lied in every word,
>   That hoary cripple, with malicious eye
>   Askance to watch the working of his lie
> On mine, and mouth scarce able to afford
> Suppression of the glee, that pursed and scored
>   Its edge, at one more victim gained thereby.

Coleridge begins his famous ballad abruptly: "It is an ancient mariner," not "an old sailor," and "He stoppeth one of
three," who wonders why he alone was addressed when he
and his companions were on their way to a joyous wedding
feast, the merry din of which he has already heard. We
wonder, too, and like the unwilling listener we shrink from
the skinny hand and glittering eye and listen like a three years'
child to the weird story of the man on the mystic ship. The

intriguing word *last* in "That's my last Duchess painted on the wall," the arrogant egotism of "I celebrate myself; and sing myself," the opening line "When in disgrace with fortune and men's eyes," as everybody has at times felt himself to be, the welcome advice "Gather ye rosebuds while ye may," and the question " 'What are the bugles blowin' for?' said Files-on-Parade"—all invite us to cooperate with the poet by imaginatively sharing his feelings and adding to them from our own experiences. And Edgar Lee Masters sets the mood for his *Spoon River Anthology* in the first lines of the poem "The Hill":

> Where are Elmer, Herman, Bert, Tom and Charley,
> The weak of will, the strong of arm, the clown, the boozer,
> the fighter?
> All, all are sleeping on the hill.

Often the poet uses for his poem a title that suggests the situation; and occasionally, as in this cinquain by Adelaide Crapsey, it is essential to meaning and effect.

### THE GUARDED WOUND

> If it
> Were lighter touch
> Than petal of flower resting
> On grass, oh, still too heavy it were,
> Too heavy!

It is interesting to turn through a volume of verse and consider the connotative value of the titles used and that of the opening lines. Which titles are conventional and commonplace and which, on the other hand, immediately start one's connotative response off on the right road? Often a title that has little connotation when first seen has much after the poem is known, and its recall sets up memories and stimulates the imagination anew. "Address to the Unco Guid" and "Tam o' Shanter," "La Belle Dame Sans Merci," "Ozymandias," and "The Blessed Damozel" are such titles.

## CONNOTATIVE SETTINGS

Artists know that their appeal to sympathetic appreciation depends to a large extent on the setting that their work has, the conditions under which it is seen or heard or perceived. Paintings that were deeply moving when placed in a mediaeval church may in a modern museum be mere exhibits of technical and historical interest, though efforts are often made to invest them with an appropriate atmosphere, as when the Sistine Madonna was given a room of quiet in the Dresden Museum, and, as the Cloisters in New York was built to furnish an appropriate setting for mediaeval church art. A statue may have been charming in a garden, surrounded by green foliage, but cold under artificial light indoors. Imagine what feelings the Winged Victory of Samothrace would stir if it were seen mounted on the prow of a ship instead of at the end of a long corridor in the Louvre. To get its intended effect Mahler's Eighth Symphony, with its immense orchestra and chorus, must be heard in a great auditorium, whereas Mendelssohn's "Canzonetta" there would lose the effectiveness that it has when played in the intimacy of a small chamber by a string quartette.

The artist in words must build up his setting, for he cannot require that his poem or story be read in the quiet of a study, under a tree in the woods, or with a sympathetic companion. As DeQuincey said, a situation must invite ghosts—or they will not come. The poetry of a situation is not likely to be perceived unless it has a suitable setting.

In the theater a dramatist knows that the audience has come in many moods, far too varied to give immediately sympathetic attention and desired response to what will be presented. So when the curtain goes up there is scenery which suggests tragedy or comedy or romance, and the actors come on in costumes that are appropriate to the characters that they represent. In almost every play the first scenes are largely for the purpose of tuning the audience, as it were, to the pitch that will respond sympathetically to the story and the lines as they are to be given. If the balcony scene in "Romeo and Juliet," printed as an excerpt from the play, were read for the first time on a crowded subway, the chances are that some of the lines would seem sentimental, and certainly the effect would be far different from that resulting from seeing the play built up from the opening curtain and developing in the entire audience an appreciative mood. The antics of Bottom and his companions may seem silly when considered in isolation, but in the third act of *A Midsummer Night's Dream* they are very amusing.

In the analysis of "The Bugle Song" (in Appendix A) one can see how Tennyson builds up with detail a setting in which he can present the situation that is the central point of the poem. Usually the setting is given briefly, sometimes it is to be surmised, if necessary, from the poem as a whole; and sometimes, as in Walter de la Mare's well-known "The Listeners," and in the following poem by Harold Monro, only a setting is given, but it so strongly connotes a situation that it impels a reader to supply from his imagination one that he feels is suitable.

### SOLITUDE

When you have tidied all things for the night,
And while your thoughts are fading to their sleep,
You'll pause a moment in the late firelight,
Too sorrowful to weep.

The large and gentle furniture has stood
In sympathetic silence all the day
With that old kindness of domestic wood;
Nevertheless the haunted room will say:
"Someone must be away."

The little dog rolls over half awake,
Stretches its paws, yawns, looking up at you,
Wags his tail very slightly for your sake,
That you may feel he is unhappy too.

A distant engine whistles, or the floor
Creaks, or the wandering night-wind bangs a door.

Silence is scattered like a broken glass.
The minutes prick their ears and run about,
Then one by one subside again and pass
Sedately in, monotonously out.

You bend your head and wipe away a tear.
Solitude walks one heavy step more near.

In Browning's "Fra Lippo Lippi" there are twelve lines
which are a poem in themselves. Not only is the picture
clear, it also penetrates into the meaning of moods and of
motives. Its connotations are so powerful that the least imaginative reader must be impelled to develop for himself stories
about the breathless murderer at the altar-foot, the vengeful
son of the victim, and the poor girl with the intense eyes.

To the breathless fellow at the altar-foot,
Fresh from his murder, safe and sitting there
With the little children round him in a row
Of admiration, half for his beard, and half
For that white anger of his victim's son
Shaking a fist at him with one fierce arm,
Signing himself with the other because of Christ. . . .
Till some poor girl, her apron o'er her head,
(Which the intense eyes looked through) came at eve
On tiptoe, said a word, dropped in a loaf,
Her pair of ear-rings and a bunch of flowers
(The brute took growling) prayed, and so was gone.

Setting for a poem is usually given by images, for the creation of which the artist calls on the senses of sight, sound,
touch, taste, and even smell. Sometimes an image is built up
carefully by the presentation of details logically arranged and
skillfully presented; sometimes, like a picture painted by
Monet, they are flashed upon one all at once. Compare the
developing setting in Keats's "Ode on a Grecian Urn" and the
impressionistic effect in Tennyson's

> Willows whiten, aspens quiver,
> Little breezes dusk and shiver
> Through the wave that runs forever
> By the island in the river
> Flowing down to Camelot.

"In Keats's 'La Belle Dame Sans Merci,'" Professor Fairchild observed, "the images are vague and intangible, and carry merely an emotional suggestiveness; in Wordsworth's 'Resolution and Independence' they are definite and vivid, and imply, in their grouping, an important idea; in Pope's 'Essay on Criticism' they are subdued and colorless, and are weighted with ideas; in 'Paradise Lost' they are graphic and imposing, and signify a world theme." And yet, however different, they are all in their own way effective.

A distinction must be made between images that are suggested as a setting for a character or an incident and images that are presented for their own sake. But the words and phrases used in each type are connotative, calling on the reader to draw on his experience and imagination for full realization. Amy Lowell in the Preface to her *Towns in Color* said, "I have endeavored to give the color, a light and shade of certain places and hours, stressing the purely pictorial effect, and with little or no reference to any other aspect of the places described."

An illustration of images presented because they are in themselves interesting and because they create a feeling or mood is John Gould Fletcher's "The Windmills," which is quoted below. Each detail is in itself vivid, bringing reality strikingly to the reader; and though there seems to be no logical order in the presentation, a feeling for the barren, arid, hot Arizona country is effected. The reader is challenged, if he is interested, to put the details into some arrangement, as one would arrange spots of color on a canvas, to get a coherent picture.

> The windmills, like great sunflowers of steel,
> Lift themselves proudly over the straggling houses;

And at their feet the deep blue-green alfalfa
Cuts the desert like the stroke of a sword.

Yellow melon flowers
Crawl beneath the withered peach-trees;
A date-palm throws its heavy fronds of steel
Against the scoured metallic sky.

The houses, double-roofed for coolness,
Cower amid the manzanita shrub.
A man with jingling spurs
Walks heavily out of a vine-bowered doorway,
Mounts his pony, and rides away.

The windmills stare at the sun.
The yellow earth cracks and blisters.
Everything is still.

In the afternoon
The wind takes dry waves of heat and tosses them,
Mingled with dust, up and down the streets,
Against the belfry with its green bells:

And, after sunset, when the sky
Becomes a green and orange fan,
The windmills, like great sunflowers on dried stalks,
Stare hard at the sun they cannot follow.

Turning, turning, forever turning
In the chill night-wind that sweeps over the valley,
With the shriek and the clank of the pumps groaning beneath
    them,
And the choking gurgle of tepid water.

Poetic images to be effective must be fresh, vivid, and intense, pointing out some previously unrecognized beauty or
truth or relationship, coming to consciousness with something
of a revelation, "inwardly working a stirre to the mind," as
old Puttenham said. Moreover, they should evoke some feeling, as Walt Whitman's do in the simple line:

I see the battle-fields of the earth—grass grows upon them,
blossoms and corn.

Another illustration of imagery for its own sake is Tennyson's vivid fragment "The Eagle."

> He clasps the crag with crooked hands;
> Close to the sun in lonely lands,
> Ring'd with the lonely world, he stands.
>
> The wrinkled sea beneath him crawls;
> He watches from his mountain walls,
> And like a thunderbolt he falls.

Images are often realized by tropes, of which more later.
Here only two illustrations of the picturing effect of figurative
language will be given. The first is by Stephen Vincent
Benét; the second, as all will recognize, by Shakespeare.

### 1

> The buildings reeked with vapor, black and harsh
> Against the deepening shadows of the sky;
> And each lamp was a hazy yellow moon,
> Filling the space about with yellow motes.

### 2

> What envious streaks
> Do lace the severing clouds in yonder east:
> Night's candles are burnt out, and jocund day
> Stands tiptoe on the misty mountain tops.

## CONNOTATIVE IMAGES

### *Visual Images*

The skill of the poet in selecting and arranging words so
as to suggest, almost to force, a reader to see and hear and feel
and taste what the artist has experienced is amazing. Even
though one has not had exactly the same experiences as the
poet, he can hardly fail to get a vivid and beautiful picture
and also to feel the mood when he reads Keats's "Ode on a
Grecian Urn."

In his dreamy "Ode to Autumn," which is quoted on page 104, Keats also gives images which are marvelously vivid and which create in a reader a mood as few other poems have ever done. With it one may like to compare William Watson's gorgeousness of language matching the gorgeousness of color, the spirit of regret at the dying year replacing the quiet joy in mellow fruitfulness and in the music of full-grown lambs and robin redbreasts. The first stanza of his poem follows.

### AUTUMN

Thou burden of all songs the earth hath sung,
  Thou retrospect in Time's averted eyes,
  Thou metaphor of everything that dies,
That dies ill-starred, or dies beloved and young
  And therefore blest and wise—
O be less beautiful or be less brief,
  Thou tragic splendour, strange and full of fear!
  In vain her pageant shall the Summer rear.
At thy mute signal, leaf by golden leaf,
  Crumbles the gorgeous year.

It is interesting to read in this connection Edna St. Vincent Millay's "God's World" and "Death of Autumn" and also the two following poems.

### A VAGABOND SONG

BLISS CARMAN

There is something in the autumn that is native to my blood—
Touch of manner, hint of mood;
And my heart is like a rhyme,
With the yellow and the purple and the crimson keeping time.

The scarlet of the maples can shake me like a cry
Of bugles going by.
And my lonely spirit thrills
To see the frosty asters like a smoke among the hills.

There is something in October sets the gypsy blood astir;
We must rise and follow her,

When from every hill of flame
She calls and calls each vagabond by name.

## AUTUMN

EMILY DICKINSON

The morns are weaker than they were,
The nuts are getting brown;
The berry's cheek is plumper,
The rose is out of town.

The maple wears a gayer scarf,
The fields a scarlet gown.
Lest I should be old-fashioned,
I'll put a trinket on.

Poets describe what they have seen, but they also have
powers to imagine what they have not seen. In these verses
Emily Dickinson manifests this power.

I never saw a moor,
I never saw the sea;
Yet know I how the heather looks,
And what a wave must be.

I never spoke with God,
Nor visited in heaven;
Yet certain am I of the spot
As if the chart were given.

Stephen Phillips wrote this setting for his "Marpessa," in
which the earth maiden, whose life had been

The history of a flower in the air
Liable but to breezes and to time,
As rich as perpetuates a rose,

given her choice, took the mortal Idas instead of the god
Apollo for her lover.*

* If you do not know the poem, look it up and compare the promises
made by Apollo and then by Idas, and consider the reasons that Marsyas
gave for her choice of the mortal.

So
When the long day that glideth without a cloud,
The summer day, was at her deep blue hour
Of lilies musical with busy bliss,
When very light trembled as with excess,
And heat was frail, and every bush and flower
Was drooping in the glory overcome.

One more illustration of the thousands that could be quoted is the miracle that is wrought by poets in making visual images out of words carefully chosen and skillfully combined. This is from Robert P. Tristram Coffin's "Crystal Moment."

A buck leaped out and took the tide
With jewels floating past each side.
With his high head like a tree,
He swam within a yard of me.

I have never seen a buck swimming past my boat, but I know that this is just how he would look.

Occasionally a poet writes description apparently more for its own sake than for a necessary setting of his characters and story. The opening section of Tennyson's "Enoch Arden" is illustrative. Its vividness of imagery is amazing, but the story of Annie and Philip and Enoch could be well told without the introduction, however beautiful and harmonious.

Long lines of cliff breaking have left a chasm;
And in the chasm are foam and yellow sands;
Beyond, red roofs about a narrow wharf
In cluster; then a moulder'd church; and higher
A long street climbs to one tall-tower'd mill;
And high in heaven above is a gray down
With Danish barrows; and a hazelwood,
By autumn nutters haunted, flourishes
Green in a cuplike hollow of the down.

Readers often skip rapidly over passages of description. Read properly, they give tremendous connotative effect. But in poetry skipping won't do. The poet has sensed something that has moved him by its beauty or by its novelty and he is trying to share with others his discovery. He uses his best skill to present the picture and his own sensations; to profit, a reader must take time, considering each detail with constructive imagination and building up a picture which he too can see and which is likely to move him to new perceptions of beauty in the world.

## Auditory Images

Poets also use auditory images, making a reader hear sounds that are beautiful, impressive, and usually contributory to the general effect of the passage in which they occur. Skillfully presented, often by onomatopoeia, which has already been discussed, they are both effective and memorable: "Dying rolls of deathless thunder," the thin and clear notes of a bugle across a rippling lake, "the mumble of the hummin'-birds and buzzin' of the bees," "the moan of doves in immemorial elms, and murmuring of innumerable bees," and "the iron gate ground its teeth to let me pass."

Sounds are strongly connotative if they have in the past been associated with experiences that are tinged with feeling. Anyone who has slept as a child in the attic and heard the rain dropping on the roof above him will have nostalgic memories revived by Nixon Waterman's "Dream-Song." And even if a reader has never had such an experience, the poem will make it so real that he can hardly fail to be moved by it.

> Oh, the drip, drip, drip of the rain, the rain,
>   The drip, drip, drip of the rain;
> The sweet, sad song the whole night long
>   Is sung in my drowsy brain.
> In a dream I rest in the old home nest,
>   And my mother comes again
> As came she oft with step as soft
>   As the drip, drip, drip of the rain,
>     The rain
>   The drip, drip, drip of the rain.
>
> Oh, the drip, drip, drip of the rain,
>   The drip, drip, drip of the rain;

As it weaves the woof of the song on the roof
  With the warp of the sound at the pane.
And my dream-ship sails with the happy gales
  That ripple the broad, blue main,
While the waves soft-tossed, in my dreams are lost
  Mid the drip, drip, drip of the rain,
        The rain,
  The drip, drip, drip of the rain.

Oh, the drip, drip, drip of the rain, the rain,
  The drip, drip, drip of the rain;
Like the drowsy croon of bees in June
  Is the song and the soft refrain.
And I drift away through a golden bay
  By the shores of my castled Spain,
While my soul grows young in the dream song sung
  Mid the drip, drip, drip of the rain
        The rain,
  The drip, drip, drip of the rain.

Some of the most effective auditory images are those that emphasize sound by contrast, like Hood's sonnet "There is a silence where no sound hath been," Elinor Wylie's "Velvet Shoes," Edgar Lee Masters' "Silence," and the lines "For now the noonday quiet holds the hill," "Low-winging moth-owl, home to your sleep." And to every reader will occur Idella Purnell's "A Shot in the Night," Walter de la Mare's "The Listeners," and Alfred Noyes's "The Highwayman," in the last of which are the vivid verses

  Ay, they heard his foot upon the stirrup,
  And the sound of iron on stone,
  And how the silence surged softly backward
  When the plunging hoofs were gone.

And in "Endymion" Keats gives us

            . . . a whispering blade
  Of grass, a wailful gnat, a bee bustling
  Down in the blue-bells, or a wren light-rustling
  Among sere leaves and twigs, might all be heard.

Auditory and visual images are often, perhaps usually, combined, as in Browning's "Meeting at Night." After reading Browning's verses who will ever again beach a boat without recalling the perfect line "And quench its speed in the slushy sand"? And as a final illustration of auditory images connoting other sensations as well we may recall the stanza from Gray's "Elegy Written in a Country Churchyard."

> The breezy call of incense-breathing morn,
>   The swallow twitt'ring from the straw-built shed,
> The cock's shrill clarion or the echoing horn,
>   No more shall rouse them from their lowly bed.

## Images of Touch

Less often artists use suggestions of touch. Sorolla's colorful painting "The Bathers" recalls the satisfaction of limpid water laving the body, the thrill of mastery over invited danger, the joy of vigor, and the pleasure of physical exercise in sunshine and beauty. Certain marble statues invite a caress of the hand over their smoothness. And poets also effectively present tactile images, some of them beautiful and some repulsive. "Jellies soother than the creamy curd" and "Pillowed in silk and scented down" are pleasing in idea and in diction. In contrast, we have the horrible images in "The Ancient Mariner"

> Yea, slimy things did crawl with legs
> Upon the slimy sea

and

> We could not speak, no more than if
> We had been choked with soot.

Stanzas in "Childe Roland," especially the one that describes the crossing of the spiteful little river in which there are suspected corpses, are as terrifying as anything in literature; and in "Caliban on Setebos" Browning gives tactile images that make us actually feel as the savage did:

Will sprawl, now that the heat of the day is best,
Flat on his belly in the pit's much mire,
With elbows wide, fists clenched to prop his chin.
And, while he kicks both feet in the cool slush,
And feels about his spine small eft-things course,
Run in and out each arm, and make him laugh.

### Images of Smell and Taste

And poets use olfactory images too. Psychologists tell us that the sense of smell in these modern days is degenerating, but they also tell that the memory of odors is remarkably persistent. When these memories are associated with experiences that were touched with feeling, an olfactory image brought up by the exact word may be strongly connotative.

On a more poetic plane Tennyson gives us

And the woodbine spices are wafted abroad
And the musk of roses blown,
For a breeze of morning moves,
And the planet of Love is on high,
Beginning to paint on the light that she loves
On a bed of daffodil sky.

And there are the even more connotative verses by Wordsworth:

The smell of violets, hidden in the green,
Poured back into my empty soul and frame
The times when I remember to have been
Joyous and free from flame

We have passages in poems combining images of sight, sound, and smell, as when Shakespeare gives an opulent description of the approach of the sensuous Queen Cleopatra.

The barge she sat in, like a burnished throne,
Burned on the water: the poop was beaten gold;
Purple the sails, and so perfumed that
The winds were love-sick with them; the oars were silver,
Which to the tune of flutes kept stroke, and made
The water which they beat to follow faster
As amorous as their strokes.

In poetry there are occasionally even connotative taste images that make our mouths water as they do at the actual sight of tempting foods. Recall the midnight feast set out by the lover in Keats's "Eve of St. Agnes" and note the appeals not only to the senses of sight and touch and smell, but also to that of taste.

> And still she slept an azure-lidded sleep,
> In blanched linen, smooth and lavendered,
> While he from forth the closet brought a heap
> Of candied apple, quince, and plum, and gourd;
> With jellies soother than the creamy curd,
> And lucent syrups, tinct with cinnamon;
> Manna and dates, in argosy transferred
> From Fez; and spiced dainties, every one
> From silken Samarcand to cedared Lebanon.

It is interesting to compare with this quotation from Keats the passage from "Paradise Lost" (Book V, 337–47) in which Milton describes food in sonorous diction but with practically no sense appeal whatever.

> And from each tender stalk
> Whatever Earth all-bearing mother yields
> In India East or West, or middle shore
> In Portus or the Punic coast, or where
> Alcinous reign'd, fruit of all kinds, in coat
> Rough or smooth rind, or bearded husk, or shell
> She gathers, tribute large, and on the board
> Heaps with unsparing hand; for drink the grape
> She crushes, inoffensive must, and meaths
> From many a berry, and from sweet kernels prest
> She tempers dulcet creams.

Much less pleasant are the taste images that Milton presents in appropriately harsh diction.

> Greedily they pluck'd
> The Fruitage fair to sight, like that which grew
> Near that bituminous Lake where Sodom flam'd;
> This more delusive, not the touch, but taste
> Deceav'd; they, fondly thinking to allay

Their appetite with gust, instead of Fruit
Chewed bitter Ashes, which th' offended taste
With spattering noise rejected; oft they assayed,
Hunger and thirst constraining, drug'd as oft,
With hatefulest disrelish writh'd their jaws
With soot and cinders fill'd.

## Kinesthetic Images

And finally to be noted of images used by poets are those
that are kinesthetic, causing a feeling of muscular strain or
of motions in one who reads them. In John Jarvis Holden's
"The High Jump" not only "Foeman and friend were flying
when he flew," but the reader of the verses tenses his own
muscles and helps the jumper get over the bar.

He slowly paced his distance off, and turned,
    Took poise, and darted forward at full speed;
Before the bar the heavy earth he spurned,
    Himself an arrow. They who saw his deed,
Tensed muscles, poised and ran and leapt, and burned
    With close-drawn breath, helping him to succeed:
Now he is over; they were over, too;
Foeman and friend were flying when he flew.

William Rose Benét so presents his "Skater of Ghost Lake"
that we feel ourselves gliding over the ice with him.

Leaning and leaning, with a stride and a stride,
Hands locked behind him, and scarf blowing wide,
Jeremy Randall skates, skates late,
Star for a candle, moon for a mate.

Black is the clear glass now that he glides,
Crisp is the whisper of long lean strides,
Swift is his swaying . . .

This is not inferior to Wordsworth's famous lines in "The
Prelude."

                I wheeled about,
Proud and exulting like an untried horse
That cares not for his home. All shod with steel,
We hissed along the polished ice.

The following excerpt from Louis Untermeyer's "The Swimmers" connotes much that everyone who has plunged into ocean breakers has felt but has been unable to express with any such clarity and vigor. His playful victory over "The cat-like sea" is our victory; his grin at being master of the breakers spreads upon our faces.

> Then the quick plunge into the cool, green dark,
> The windy waters rushing past me, through me;
> Filled with the sense of some heroic lark
> Existing in a vigor clean and roomy.
> Swiftly I rose to meet the cat-like sea
> That sprang upon me with a hundred claws,
> And grappled, pulled me down and played with me.
> Then, held suspended in the tightening pause
> When one wave grows into a toppling acre,
> I dived headlong into the foremost breakers,
> Pitting against a cold and turbulent strife
> The feverish intensity of life.
> Out of the foam I lurched and rode the wave,
> Swimming, hand over hand, against the wind;
> I felt the sea's vain pounding, and I grinned
> Knowing I was master, not its slave.

Poets have the power through kinesthetic images of making us enter into a feeling with even animals, to mimic sensibly as we read their muscular movements. Keats illustrates and effects this empathy in a passage from "I Stood Tiptoe Upon a Little Hill."

> Swarms of minnows show their little heads,
> Staying their wavy bodies 'gainst the streams,
> To taste the luxury of sunny beams
> Temper'd with coolness. How they ever wrestle
> With their own sweet delight, and ever nestle
> Their silver bellies on the pebbly sand!

## Images Create a Mood

As was earlier said, images in poetry are sometimes presented solely for their own connotative power to represent the beautiful or the novel, often to help build up a setting

for a tale that is to be told. They are also used to create a
mood. Wordsworth is highly successful in using images for
this purpose in his sonnet "Composed upon Westminster
Bridge." In fact, the images and the mood *are* the poem: they
prepare for nothing; they are justified by their own beauty.

Earth hath not anything to show more fair:
Dull would he be of soul who could pass by
A sight so touching in its majesty:
The city doth now, like a garment, wear
The beauty of the morning; silent, bare,
Ships, towers, domes, theaters, and temples lie
Open unto the fields, and to the sky;
All bright and glittering in the morning air.
Never did sun more beautifully steep
In his first splendor, valley, rock, or hill;
Ne'er saw I, never felt, a calm so deep!
The river glideth at its own sweet will:
Dear God! the very houses seem asleep;
And all that mighty heart is lying still!

In his sonnet "On the Beach at Calais," on the other hand,
Wordsworth first in the octave creates a mood by the use of
images, and then in the sestet explains that the "dear child"
appears unmoved by the tranquillity because she "lies in
Abraham's bosom all the year, God being with her when we
know it not."

In Tennyson's "Oenone" images are very definitely used
to create in the reader a mood of sympathy for the grief of
the nymph forsaken by Paris for the mortal Helen. After a
description of the vale of Ida, the mournful Oenone begins
her complaint in a stanza full of the most exact and suggestive
images.

O mother Ida, many-fountained Ida,
Dear mother Ida, hearken ere I die.
For now the noonday quiet holds the hill:
The grasshopper is silent in the grass:
The lizard, with his shadow on the stone,
Rests like a shadow, and the winds are dead.
The purple flower droops: the golden bee

Is lily-cradled: I alone awake.
My eyes are full of tears, my heart of love,
My heart is breaking, and my eyes are dim,
And I am all aweary of my life.

Mood is created at once at the beginning of John Masefield's "Spanish Waters" not by images but by the connotative power of the romantic diction.

Spanish waters, Spanish waters, you are ringing in my ears,
Like a slow sweet piece of music from the gray forgotten years;
Telling tales, and beating tunes, and bringing weary thoughts
    to me
Of the sandy beach at Muertes, where I would that I could be.

The most potent means that the poet has for creating mood,
however, is images. One may never have enjoyed an English
April, but Browning's poem conveys the mood that makes
everyone long to share the experience and even to thrill more
appreciatively at spring wherever he may be.

Oh, to be in England
Now that April's there.
And whoever wakes in England
Sees, some morning, unaware,
That the lowest boughs and the brush-wood sheaf
Round the elm-tree bole are in tiny leaf,
While the chaffinch sings on the orchard bough
In England—now!

And after April, when May follows,
And the whitethroat builds, and all the swallows!
Hark, where my blossomed pear-tree in the hedge
Leans to the field and scatters on the clover
Blossoms and dewdrops—at the bent-spray's edge—
That's the wise thrush; he sings each song twice over,
Lest you should think he never could recapture
The first fine careless rapture!
And though the fields look rough with hoary dew,
All will be gay when noontide wakes anew
The buttercups, the little children's dower,
—Far brighter than this gaudy melon-flower!

## *Images Characterize*

Poetry uses images not only to describe but also to characterize a person. Compare, for instance, the following two passages. In the first Tennyson conveys an understanding of the sort of girl the gardener's daughter was; and in the second he introduces us to the aloof Princess.

### 1

One arm aloft—
Gowned in pure white, that fitted to her shape—
Holding the bush, to fix it back, she stood.
A single stream of all her soft brown hair
Pour'd on one side: the shadow of the flowers
Stole all the golden gloss, and, wavering,
Lovingly lower, trembled to her waist.

### 2

There at the board the Princess Ida sat,
With two tame leopards couch'd beside her throne,
All beauty compassed in a female form,
The Princess; liker to the inhabitant
Of some clear planet closer to the Sun,
Than our man's earth; such eyes were in her head,
And so much grace and power, breathing down
From over her arch'd brows, with every turn
Lived thro' her to the tips of her long hands,
And to her feet.

## SELECTION AND RESTRAINT FOR CONNOTATION

To be effective, connotation requires much skill from the artist in selection and in restraint; enjoyment requires sympathetic supplementation. "Right from the heart, right to the heart" art springs. "One word with blood in 't," said Lowell, "'s twice ez good ez two." The painter chooses for presentation the one right moment, from which the spectator can and will imagine the significance of what precedes and of what is likely to follow. Many pictures of course are of static scenes, but look at Botticelli's "Spring" and "The Birth of

Venus," for instance, or at El Greco's "Casting out the Money Changers from the Temple" and "The Burial of Count Orgaz," and note with care the exact moment in action that the artist chose to fix on the canvas. And the artist must not show too much, for "the presentation of extremes clips the wings of fancy." Japanese prints in the classic period are admirable examples of restraint. In the Metropolitan Museum of Art is an etching of a man with a 'cello, the instrument indicated by a few lines which at first glance seem carelessly sketchy, but closer inspection will show that they are most carefully chosen; the only lines that would make a person looking at the picture complete from his memory or from his constructive imagination the instrument. The poise of the player indicates his intensity and also the music that will momently be drawn out by the bow hovering above the strings. Looking at a number of paintings, other than posed portraits of people or natural scenery, will emphasize that the great artist has chosen exactly the right moment to perpetuate and that he has exercised such restraint of details that he invites, and even forces, the spectator to become a partner in the creation.

> For much imaginary work was there;
> Conceit deceitful, so compact, so kind,
> That for Achilles' image stood his spear,
> Grip'd in an armed hand: himself behind
> Was left unseen, save to the eye of mind.
> A hand, a foot, a face, a leg, a head
> Stood for the whole to be imagined.

The Japanese in their tanka and hokku were masters of restraint. Fletcher in his Preface to *Japanese Prints* quotes

> An old pond
> And an old frog leaping
> Into the water

and comments on it as follows:

To the Japanese it [this poem] means all the beauty of such a life of retirement and contemplation as Basho practiced. If we permit our

minds to supply the details Basho deliberately omitted, we see the
moldering temple enclosure, the sage himself in meditation, the ancient
piece of water, and the sound of the frog's leap—passing vanity—
slipping into the silence of eternity. The poem has three meanings.
First, it is a statement of fact. Second, it is an emotion deduced
from that. Third, it is a sort of spiritual allegory. And all this Basho
has given us in his seventeen syllables.

A similar achievement in restraint is found in the twelfth
century Chinese poem "Village News."

> "You come from my village?
> Tell me quickly all the things
>    That have happened there since I left."

> "Your plum tree has blossomed,
> And a goat ate the little bamboo
>    Which you planted at the edge of the pool."

The musician and the poet have more freedom, for after
selecting a pregnant moment or incident or character, they
can use the more fluid medium of sounds and of words for
development. But, like painter and sculptor, they are re-
strained from presenting too much. Lowell said that we must

> Measure their writings by Hesiod's staff,
> Which teaches that all has less value than half.

The failure of many versifiers is that they try to tell everything, leaving nothing to be supplied by the reader. Their
verses may give a passing pleasure, but they are exhausted at
one reading. They give no opportunity for the reader to draw
on his own experience and imagination; they do not stimulate
response. Of course such verses may appeal to those whose
lives are shallow, whose experiences are superficial, and whose
imaginations are too sluggish to enjoy being stirred. But there
is no great art, no lasting and growing art, that does not invite
a partnership in creation and in imaginative extension.

Edward Arlington Robinson's "Richard Cory" is a perfect
example of the effectiveness of restraint. A lesser poet might

have expanded the story into exhausting pages, but Robinson gives only the barest outline, challenging the reader to clothe it with such details as he will.

> Whenever Richard Cory went down town,
>     We people on the pavement looked at him:
> He was a gentleman from sole to crown,
>     Clean favored, and imperially slim.
>
> And he was always quietly arrayed,
>     And he was always human when he talked;
> But still he fluttered pulses when he said,
>     "Good Morning," and he glittered when he walked.
>
> And he was rich—yes, richer than a king—
>     And admirably schooled in every grace:
> In fine, we thought that he was everything
>     To make us wish that we were in his place.
>
> So on we worked, and waited for the light,
>     And went without the meat, and cursed the bread;
> And Richard Cory, one calm summer night,
>     Went home and put a bullet through his head.

Even the poets that achieve masterpieces of restraint not infrequently are ineffective because they tell too much. Of all the great poets, Wordsworth is in this respect the major sinner. Most of his long poems become boring, largely because he forgets that the reader must be a partner in the most effective creation of satisfying emotions. In the short *Lucy* series of poems there is only one that in its restraint approaches perfection.

> She dwelt among the untrodden ways
>     Beside the springs of Dove,
> A maid whom there were none to praise
>     And very few to love.
>
> A violet by a mossy stone
>     Half hidden from the eye.
> Fair as a star when only one
>     Is shining in the sky.

She lived unknown, and few could know
　　When Lucy ceased to be;
But she is in her grave, and, oh,
　　The difference to me.

## CONNOTATION REQUIRES IMAGINATION

Active and sensitive imagination is what all true poets have. To them it opens new worlds and to them it reveals meanings and significances, which they try to convey connotatively to readers of their verses. Elizabeth Coatsworth tells that romance had come to her through a quickened imagination.

To think I once saw grocery shops
With but a casual eye,
And fingered figs and apricots
As one who came to buy.

To think I never dreamed of how
Bananas sway in rain,
And often looked at oranges
But never thought of Spain.

And in those wasted days I saw
No sails above the tea,
For grocery shops were grocery shops—
No hemispheres to me.

And John Drinkwater writes in "Symbols":

I saw history in a poet's song,
In a river reach and a gallows-hill,
In a bridal bed, and a secret wrong,
In a crown of thorns: in a daffodil.

I imagined measureless time in a day,
And starry space in a wagon-road,
And the treasure of all good harvests lay
In a single seed that the sower sowed.

My garden-wind had driven and havened again
All ships that ever had gone to sea.
And I saw the glory of all dead men
In the shadow that went by the side of me.

And imagination is what a reader of poetry must have too.
With it

> Oh, the little more, and how much it is!
> And the little less, and what worlds away!

Man's reach of imagination must exceed his intellectual grasp
—or what is the reading of poetry for?  Imagination draws
a poignant pathos from Browning's "Andrea del Sarto" when
it comes to the lines

> Inside the melancholy little house
> We built to be so gay with.

In much poetry it is not what is said, but, rather, what is
suggested, what a reader must supply by his active imagination.  As Coleridge wrote,

> We receive but what we give
> And in ourselves alone does nature live.
> Ours is her wedding garment, ours her shroud!
> And would we aught behold of higher worth
> Than that inanimate cold world allowed
> To the poor loveless, ever-anxious crowd,
> Ah! from the soul must issue forth
> A light, a glory, a fair luminous cloud
> Enveloping the earth.

Nature itself has no sentiment, but it is constantly connotative to the sensitive imagination, as George Meredith points
out.

> They have no song, the sedges dry,
> And still they sing.
> It is within my breast they sing,
> As I pass by.

> Within my breast they touch a spring.
> They wake a sigh.
> There is but sound of sedges dry;
> In me they sing.

Florence Wilkinson has a whole poem in two lines of verses that are otherwise commonplace. Who can ever see again a crowd at a railway station without being made to wonder by her simple statement?

> Some set out for a whole new world—
> And some for a change of weather.

And in her poem "Genius" she clearly points out the difference between those who possess imagination and those who do not.

> What seest thou on yonder desert plain,
>     Large, vague, and void?
> *I see a city full of flickering streets,*
> *I hear the hum of myriad engine beats.*
>         *What seest thou?*
>     I see a desert plain
>     Large, vague, and void.
>
> What seest thou in yonder human face,
>     Pale, frail, and small?
> *I read a page of poetry, of sin,*
> *I see a soul by tragedy worn thin.*
>         *What seest thou?*
>     I see a human face,
>     Pale, frail, and small.
>
> What seest thou at yonder dim cross-roads
>     Beside that shuttered inn?
> *Untravelled Possibility,*
> *The Inn of Splendid Mystery.*
>         *What seest thou?*
>     I see the dim cross-roads
>     Beside a shuttered inn.

Dorothy Wellesley illustrates in the first stanza of her poem "Horses" how the commonplace appears to the imaginative person.

## HORSES
### (*Newmarket or St. Leger*)

DOROTHY WELLESLEY

Who, in the garden-pony carrying skeps
Of grass or fallen leaves, his knees gone slack,
Round belly, hollow back,
Sees the Mongolian Tarpan of the Steppes?
Or, in the Shire with plaits and feathered feet,
The war-horse like the wind the Tartar knew?
Or, in the Suffolk Punch, spells out anew
The wild grey asses fleet
With stripe from head to tail, and moderate ears?
In cross sea-donkeys, sheltering as storm gathers,
The mountain zebras maned upon the withers,
With round enormous ears?

The unimaginative, who can never enjoy art of any kind,
is one who when he reads Tennyson's lines from "Maud"

He pestles a poisoned poison
Behind his crimson lights

questions the apparent tautology. He may be able to scan the
lines metrically and to recognize the effective alliteration, but
unless he gets a picture of the drug clerk behind lights that
were conventional a generation ago and responds with indignation to the adulteration of medicines already ineffi-
cacious, he entirely fails to get the intended effect.

### CONNOTATION REQUIRES EXPERIENCE

Connotation requires much of a reader. In the first place,
he must willingly and wholly put himself into the mood suggested by the artist. No poet can successfully evoke laughter
or tears or arouse sentiments that are tender or heroic in a
person who resists or who fails to cooperate wholeheartedly.
When a reader is not in a mood for sentiment and cannot
yield himself easily to such a mood, he would better lay aside
poetry until a more propitious time.

Those who cannot read poetry are like the old servitor in "Balaustion's Adventure."

> So there he stood, a much-bewildered man.
> Stupid? Nay, but sagacious in a sort:
> Learned, life-long, i' the first outside of things,
> Though bat for blindness to what lies beneath.

However willing one may be to cooperate with a poet, connotation will fail unless a reader has a necessary background of information or experience. Failure results when a poet uses references and allusions, rich in significance as they may be to him, that draw from a reader's memory no answering and enriching details. One must know Helen of Troy, the patient Job, the tragic Lear, and the complex life of Abraham Lincoln to appreciate references to them. Mrs. Browning's

> What was he doing, the great god Pan,
> Down in the reeds by the river,
> Spreading ruin and scattering ban?

means something, but not a great deal, to one who knows merely that Pan was a Greek demigod, half goat and half man in form, and reputedly the inventor of the syrinx. But real appreciation of the poem can come only if one has read widely in the literature of mythology, if he knows the "Hymn to Hermes" beginning

> To Hermes's son awake the trembling string,
> The horned goat-foot Pan, ye Muses sing,

and especially if he has enjoyed Kenneth Grahame's "Piper at the Gates of Dawn" in his delightful *Wind in the Willows*.

And what would Edgar Lee Masters' highly condensed "Anne Rutledge" mean to one who does not know the story of Lincoln's early love and of his later glories?

> Out of me unworthy and unknown
> The vibrations of deathless music:
> "With malice toward none, with charity for all."

Out of me the forgiveness of millions toward millions,
And the beneficent face of a nation
Shining with justice and truth.
I am Anne Rutledge who sleep beneath these weeds,
Beloved in life of Abraham Lincoln,
Wedded to him, though not through union,
But through separation.
Bloom forever, O Republic,
From the dust of my bosom!

Love, spring and autumn, bird songs and blossoming flowers, achievement and failure, admiration for courage, hope—these are examples of the common experience of all men, and these are the subjects that poet after poet selects, confident that they will awaken in readers memories that are necessary for conveying and enriching the expressed emotion. Whistler used a similar technique in his "Arrangement in Gray and Black" (his portrait of his mother, or, for that matter, of anybody's mother) and in his "Carlyle," but the former is vastly more moving because it connotes associations that do not exist to be evoked by the latter. Tchaikovsky "was the first musician to drag out and give voice to the frightened child there is somewhere in each of us." Consequently, when we hear the "Pathetique" we respond with understanding.

The religious paintings of Giotto, Cimabue, and Fra Angelico cannot move us today as they did the unlettered worshipers in the Middle Ages who got their spiritual inspiration from pictures instead of from books. The more humanly beautiful the Madonna became, as those by Fra Lippo Lippi and Mainardi, the less she moved to religious worship, for the connotation was different.

In numerous primary schoolrooms there are pictures of the Christ child. They may, and doubtless do, have values, but they cannot have on young children the effect that the artist was attempting to produce. Having more understanding of animal pets, of circuses, and of games, children can bring to pictures of them more from their pleasurable experiences. To them, pictures of such things are connotative; they do not have a background to understand and to respond to paintings of saints, even St. Christopher, any more than they can to the father's grief in Eugene Field's "Little Boy Blue."

Any reader can get certain pleasures from Field's poem, but only a father who has lost his beloved child can respond as the poet did in

> The little toy dog is covered with dust,
> But sturdy and stanch he stands;
> The little toy soldier is red with rust,
> And his musket moulds in his hands.

And it requires a father, especially one bereft of his wife, to read connotatively Coventry Patmore's "The Toys."

> My little son, who looked from thoughtful eyes
> And moved and spoke in quiet grown-up wise,
> Having my law the seventh time disobeyed,
> I struck him, and dismissed
> With hard words and unkissed,
> —His mother, who was patient, being dead.
> Then, fearing lest his grief should hinder sleep,
> I visited his bed,
> But found him slumbering deep,
> With darkened eyelids, and their lashes yet
> From his late sobbing wet.
> And I, with moan,
> Kissing away his tears, left others of my own;
> For, on a table drawn beside his head,
> He had put, within his reach,
> A box of counters and a red-veined stone,
> A piece of glass abraded by the beach,
> And six or seven shells,
> A bottle with bluebells,
> And two French copper coins, ranged there with careful art,
> To comfort his sad heart.
> So when that night I prayed
> To God, I wept, and said:
> "Ah, when we lie at last with tranced breath,
> Not vexing Thee in death,
> And Thou rememberest of what toys,
> We made our joys,

How weakly understood
Thy great commanded good.
Then, fatherly not less
Than I whom Thou hast molded from the clay,
Thou'lt leave Thy wrath and say,
'I will be sorry for their childishness.' "

Contrast "On a Dead Child" by Robert Bridges, a poet laureate of England. Do you feel that this poem is more "artful" than the ones on the same subject by Eugene Field, James Whitcomb Riley, and Coventry Patmore? What do you think of the sincerity in the four poems? Which affects you most?

## ON A DEAD CHILD

### ROBERT BRIDGES

Perfect little body, without fault or stain on thee,
    With promise of strength and manhood full and fair!
        Though cold and stark and bare,
The bloom and the charm of life doth awhile remain on thee.

Thy mother's treasure wert thou;—alas! no longer
    To visit her heart with wondrous joy; to be
        Thy father's pride;—ah, he
Must gather his faith together, and his strength make stronger.

To me, as I move thee now in the last duty,
    Dost thou with a turn or gesture anon respond;
        Startling my fancy fond
With a chance attitude of the head, or a freak of beauty.

Thy hand clasps, as 'twere wont, my finger, and holds it:
    But the grasp is the clasp of death, heartbreaking and stiff;
        Yet feels to my hand as if
'Twas still thy will, thy pleasure and trust that enfolds it.

So I lay thee there, thy sunken eyelids closing,—
    Go lie thou there in thy coffin, thy last little bed!—
        Propping thy wise, sad head,
Thy firm, pale hands across thy chest disposing.

So quiet! doth the change content thee?—Death, whither hath he
    taken thee?
  To a world, do I think, that rights the disaster of this?
    The vision of which I miss,
Who weep for the body, and wish but to warm thee and awaken
    thee?

Ah! little at best can all our hopes avail us
  To lift this sorrow, or cheer us, when in the dark,
    Unwilling, alone we embark,
And the things we have seen and have known and have heard
    of, fail us.

As repeatedly emphasized, connotation requires active recall and relation of experience and also a constructive imagination. The trouble with most people who say that they
do not appreciate the arts is that they are unwilling to put
forth the effort necessary to cooperate with the artist and
contribute what will educe and extend the feeling that is
suggested and stimulated. The young man who said that some
summer he would lie in a hammock and read Browning was
properly rebuked and advised, "When you tackle Browning,
read him in the winter time standing up."

## Connotation Requires Time

And, finally, connotation requires time in which understanding may come and imagination may work. The spirit
of a painter must be scarified when he observes visitors at
an exhibition of his pictures, over which he has labored long
and painstakingly to express what life has meant to him. In
a publication of the American Association of Museums E. S.
Robinson reports the time spent by over two hundred visitors
to one gallery. They stopped before from 23 to 45 pictures,
spending on each one an average of nine seconds. The maximum time given by these two hundred men and women to
any picture was forty-four seconds! What could they see
in that time? What understanding could be got in less than
a minute? What contribution could be evoked? What could

they feel? What could they carry away from such casual and unresponsive inspection? Appreciation of any art demands plenty of time.

In reading of any kind the average person spends too much time with his eyes on the pages and too little with his finger between them, reflecting on ideas that he has acquired, finding significances in them and applications that might enrich his life.

Being condensed expression, the distilled quintessence, as it were, of beauty and wisdom, poetry, more than any other form of expression, requires time for understanding of what the artist has felt and is trying to express, and time for drawing from experience, however rich or however narrow that may be, a personal supplementation and extension of the feeling. Occasionally a poem will gain an instantaneous response, like a sudden electric shock, but ordinarily it requires time for the active exercise of all one's powers to make the emotion one's own and to extend its implications, especially those that are personal. One may give a sensuous response to beauty, one may have learned to understand the techniques that the artist uses to express himself and his feelings; but unless the reader himself responds to the connotations expressed by poetry in words, settings, situations, and incidents, he fails in the one essential of appreciation. Of course the highest form of appreciation is that which combines the sensuous, the technical, and the connotative.

## TROPES FOR CONNOTATION

Poets have another shorthand means of connotation, the use of tropes, or figures of speech. A trope is a word or group of words used in an unusual way to enrich an idea by stating or suggesting a likeness with something already in the reader's mind. ("Silent as a snowfall," "his lightning flashes of wit," "the wind howled awhile and died.") The comparison contributes reality, vividness, emphasis, beauty, or humor to the original idea.

Rhetoricians have made long lists of tropes, lists that include simile, metaphor, synecdoche, metonymy, epizeuxis, hendiadys, anacrusis, metaphrasis, and a score of others with names hard to remember and with definitions of distinctions utterly unimportant to one who seeks merely to enjoy poetry. As a matter of fact, most of these technical terms concern matters that make little or no contribution to poetic values. Though they may be neglected by all but specialists, it is important for a reader to get the effect that the use of indirect means of expression is intended to convey. When one comes upon a trope he should be able to answer these questions:

1. What is the bare idea?
2. What is the bare image?
3. What is the exact likeness between the image and the idea?
4. What does the image add to the idea?

When we read that King Richard was a lion (or like a lion) in battle, we realize that the writer is trying to emphasize some qualities of the king, notably strength and courage. To do this, he calls up the image of a lion, the king of beasts, supreme in strength, lithe, unafraid, and menacing, expecting us to ignore all other characteristics—that the lion is a quadruped, tawny, with a tail and a shaggy mane, and so on. But if our image of the lion advancing upon his victim is vivid and terrifying, as it is likely to be, the strength and courage in King Richard are emphasized and even exaggerated. A reader is likely to imagine the terror of his enemies as he feels the terror of a victim threatened by the animal.

Seldom will one need to answer the above four questions formally, fundamental as they are, for the effect of a good trope is usually felt immediately without such procedure. If an intellectual process is necessary, a trope is likely to be a hindrance instead of a help to enjoyment, diverting attention from the substance of the poem to the decoration. The con-

tribution of a good trope is likely to come as a flash of illumination.

> And the sudden flurries of snow-birds,
> Like brown leaves whirling by.

But occasionally, as in one passage of Shelley's elegy
"Adonais," analysis will be called for, with resultant appreciation of the beautiful image and added enjoyment of the poem.

> The One remains, the many change and pass;
> Heaven's light forever shines, earth's shadows flee;
> Life, like a dome of many-colored glass,
> Stains the white radiance of Eternity,
> Until Death tramples it to fragments.

"Adonais" is unusually rich with tropes that require no such
formal analysis.

> And others . . .
> Came in slow pomp—the moving pomp might seem
> Like pageantry of mist on an autumnal stream.
>
> . . . . .
>
> And the green lizard, and the golden snake,
> Like unimprisoned flames, out of their trance awake.

The passages just quoted contain tropes so striking that they
call attention to themselves as they decorate the thought.
But many tropes are, as it were, concealed in single words or
phrases. In the following three lines there are at least ten,
which in combination present interpreted auditory, visual,
and feeling images.

> Afar the melancholy thunder moaned,
> Pale Ocean in unquiet slumber lay,
> And the wild winds flow round, sobbing in their dismay.

Common speech is full of figurative language, much of it
so long used that the sharp edge of its significance has been
worn away and it no longer gives the pleasure that novelty
once brought. Names of flowers, like "buttercup," proper

names and especially nicknames, like "Bones" and "Sawed Off," and colloquialisms like "cut throat," "flat tire," "all washed up," are originally figurative, as etymologically are "heliotrope," "sarcasm," and "supercilious." Because of its original picturing power, slang has been called "the illegitimate sister of poetry."

"I don't understand," said the Divinity Student in Holmes's *Autocrat of the Breakfast Table*, "how it is that some minds are continually coupling thoughts and objects that seem not in the least related to each other, until all at once they are put in a certain light, and you wonder that you did not always see that they were alike as a pair of twins." With his unusual keenness the poet perceives these likenesses to which ordinary mortals are blind. He has the taste to select those that contribute beauty or emphasis, and he has the skill so to phrase them that they add what is pleasing to the bare idea. Instead of saying "As a man grows older, he grows wiser," Waller said,

> The soul's dark cottage, batter'd and decay'd,
> Lets in new light through chinks that time has made.

Instead of "evening brings twilight," Collins wrote

> Thy dusky fingers draw
> The gradual dusky veil.

Coleridge made the Ancient Mariner express his fear in

> Fear at my heart, as at a cup,
> My life-blood seemed to sip.

By tropes the poet gains an effect that is far more pleasing and emotionally inspiring than plain statement. By surprise he stimulates a reader to see what he saw: "Leaves on the paths ran like rats."

Emily Dickinson thus interprets for us a snake. Nothing could be more nearly perfect than "It wrinkled and was gone," or than the last stanza, which tells exactly how you must have felt at a similar sudden adventure.

### THE SNAKE

A narrow fellow in the grass
Occasionally rides;
You may have met him,—did you not?
His notice sudden is

The grass divides as with a comb,
A spotted shaft is seen;
And then it closes at your feet
And opens further on.

He likes a boggy acre,
A floor too cool for corn.
Yet when a child, and barefoot,
I more than once, at morn,

Have passed, I thought, a whip-lash
When, stooping to secure it,
Unbraiding in the sun,—
It wrinkled, and was gone.

Several of nature's people
I know, and they know me;
I feel for them a transport
Of cordiality;

But never met this fellow,
Attended or alone,
Without a tighter breathing,
And zero at the bone.

The poet uses tropes to emphasize beauty, as Elizabeth
Coatsworth does in "A Lady Comes to an Inn."

The lovely woman was long and slim
As a young white birch or a maple limb. . . .
Her great silk skirts like a silver bell
Down to her little bronze slippers fell.

Tennyson conveys beauty and his feeling for it in the
mellifluous tropic passage from "The Lotus-Eaters."

> There is sweet music here that softer falls
> Than petals from soft roses on the grass,
> Or night-dews on still waters between walls
> Of shadowy granite, in a gleaming pass;
> Music that gentler on the spirit lies
> Than tir'd eyelids upon tir'd eyes.

It is in making images vivid that tropes are perhaps most often used. Even if we have never noticed sheep quiet on a hillside, we are made to see them clearly by the lines

> Flung on a tufted range the crinkled sheep
> Stand like a scattering of stones.

The poet did not need to tell the color of the sheep, for gray motionless stones are in everyone's experience, but notice what he adds by "tufted" and "crinkled."

A trope can enhance amazingly the vividness and proportions of an idea, as in Browning's

> Has gained an abyss where a dewdrop was asked.

Vividness by tropes is not always elegant; sometimes it is homely, as when Jim Bludso's boat burned.

> The fire bust out as she clared the bar,
> And burnt a hole in the night,

and as in Lowell's "The Courtin'"

> All ways to once her feelin's flew
> Like sparks in burnt-up paper.

Edgar Lee Masters in "Autochthon" thus characterizes Lincoln's arguments:

> A country lawyer with a solid logic,
> And gift of prudent phrase that has a way
> Of hardening under time to rock as hard
> As the enduring rock you seal it with.

The poet can use tropes to give a touch of humor, too, sometimes interpolated to lighten the verse, and sometimes an integral part of the general tone. Note the boisterous tropes in Cowper's "John Gilpin's Ride" and the gentle humor in Oliver Wendell Holmes's "The Last Leaf." In "Hudibras" we find

> The sun had long since in the lap
> Of Thetis taken out his nap,
> And like a lobster boyl'd, the morn
> From black to red began to turn.

In "The Pied Piper" Browning gives us

> Not brighter than his eye, nor moister
> Than a too-long-opened oyster.

And with questionable humor Holmes wrote in "The Ballad of the Oysterman"

> Her hair drooped round her pallid cheeks like seaweed on a clam.

Nathalia Crane gives a light and humorous touch by her homely figure:

> My heart is all a-flutter
> Like the washing on the line.

An appreciative reader cannot fail to get pleasure from tropes that add surprise, vividness, strength, or humor to an idea which unadorned might be less impressive. And, unconsciously, he is likely to feel a little proud of himself that he has the background and the imagination to appreciate what the poet is attempting to convey. He must be on his guard, however, against being carried away by figurative language, in verse or in prose, for, as Prior wrote in "Alma,"

> In argument
> Similes are like songs in love:
> They much describe; they nothing prove.

Most often tropes flash forth—briefly like a shooting star, or like sparks to set going a flame in the imagination of the reader. In verb or adjective or daring noun they seem spontaneous and right.

Thus I set my printless feet
O'er the cowslip's velvet head,
That bends not as I tread.

But they are built up, too, consciously cumulative, as in Shelley's "Ode to a Skylark," in which he compares the bird to "a poet hidden in the light of thought," to

A high-born maiden
In a palace-tower,
Soothing her love-laden
Soul in secret hour
With music sweet as love, which overflows her bower,

to "a glow-worm golden," and to "a rose embowered." It will increase a reader's appreciation if he will attempt to complete with details the last two comparisons and then read the tenth and eleventh stanzas. What does each trope add to the bare idea of the skylark singing? Which to your taste is best? Do all of the comparisons together give a unified contribution of beauty?

Compare parts of two poems (Amy Lowell's "A Lady" and Alice Corbin's "Una Anciana Mexicana"), both rich in tropes. Which combination of tropes gives you the most vivid and the most pleasing impressions?

1

You are beautiful and faded
Like an old opera tune
Played upon a harpsichord;
Or like the sun-flooded silks
Of an eighteenth-century boudoir.
In your eyes
Smoulder the fallen roses of out-lived minutes,
And the perfume of your soul
Is vague and suffusing,
With the pungence of sealed spice-jars. . .

2

I've seen her pass with eyes upon the road—
An old bent woman in a bronze-black shawl,

> With skin as dried and wrinkled as a mummy's,
> As brown as a cigar-box, and her voice
> Like the low vibrant strings of a guitar. . .

And Robert Browning in "Saul" builds up by an extended trope a picture of the great King as he is recalled by David's song from the profound melancholy that had possessed him.

> Have ye seen when Spring's arrowy summons goes right to the
>     aim,
> And some mountain, the last to withstand her, that held (he alone
> While the vale laughed in freedom and flowers) on a broad bust
>     of stone
> A year's snow bound about for a breastplate,—leaves grasp of
>     the sheet?
> Fold on fold all at once it crowds thunderously down to his feet,
> And there fronts you, stark, black, but alive yet, your moun-
>     tain of old,
> With its rents, the successive bequeathings of ages untold—
> Yet, each harm got in fighting your battles, each furrow and scar
> Of his head thrust 'twixt you and the tempest—all hail, there
>     you are!
> —Now again to be softened with verdure, again hold the nest
> Of the dove, tempt the goat and its young to the green on its
>     crest
> For their food in the ardors of summer.

An extended comparison, called a Homeric simile because so often used in the "Iliad" and in the "Odyssey," is seldom found in modern poetry, though it was commonly used by earlier writers. The presentation of the image usually begins with "As" and that of the idea with "so." Two illustrations of the Homeric simile are given below, the first from Book III of Dante's "Purgatorio" and the second from Book X of Milton's "Paradise Lost."

### I

> As sheep come forth from the pen, in ones, in twos, in threes, and the others stand all timid, casting eye and nose to earth, and what the first one doeth, the others do also, huddling up to her if she stand still, silly and quiet, and they know not why, so saw I then the head of that happy flock move to come on, modest in countenance, in movement dignified.

## II

As when a flock
Of ravenous fowl, though many a league remote,
Against the day of battle, to a field,
Where armies lie encampt, come flying, lur'd
With scent of living carcasses design'd
For death, the following day, in bloody fight:
So scented the grim Feature [Death], and upturn'd
His nostril wide into the murky air,
Sagacious of his quarry from so far.

Though the extended trope is now out of fashion, Shakespeare not infrequently used it, especially in speeches of dignity, as when old Nestor argues in *Troilus and Cressida.*

In the reproof of chance
Lies the true proof of men: the sea being smooth,
How many shallow bauble boats dare sail
Upon her patient breast, making their way
With those of nobler bulk?
But let the ruffian Boreas once enrage
The gentle Thetis, and, anon, behold
The strong rock-ribb'd bark through liquid mountains cut,
Bounding between the two moist elements,
Like Perseus' horse: where's then the saucy boat,
Whose weak untimber'd sides but even now
Co-rivall'd greatness? either to harbour fled
Or made a toast for Neptune.

James Russell Lowell in his impressive "Commemoration Ode," delivered at Harvard University in 1865, introduced tropes that were highly effective and in every case attuned to the spirit of the occasion, the honoring of soldiers who had died in battle, whose names were "dream-footed as the shadow of a cloud." It is remarkable that this great ode was written almost overnight.

We seem to do them wrong,
Bringing one robin's-leaf to deck their hearse
Who in warm life-blood wrought their nobler verse,
Our trivial song to honor those who come
With ears attuned to strenuous trump and drum,

And shaped in squadron-strophes their desire,
Live battle-odes whose lines were steel and fire;
    Yet sometimes feathered words are strong.

One of the most perfect sonnets written by an American
is Longfellow's "Nature," in which he gives an extended
trope in the octave, and in the sestet applies it to strengthen
and beautify the idea that he had in mind.

As a fond mother, when the day is o'er,
Leads by the hand her little child to bed,
Half willing, half reluctant to be led,
And leave his broken playthings on the floor,
Still gazing at them through the open door,
Not wholly reassured and comforted
By promises of others in their stead
Which, though more splendid, may not please him more;
So nature deals with us, and takes away
Our playthings one by one, and by the hand
Leads us to rest so gently, that we go
Scarce knowing if we wish to go or stay,
Being too full of sleep to understand
How far the unknown transcends the what we know.

Theodosia Garrison's "A Love Song" will close the illustrations of tropes effectively used. Notice how naturally she
introduces each comparison and how the contrast in the two
stanzas adds to the vividness.

My love it should be silent, being deep,
And being very peaceful should be still,
Still as the utmost depths of ocean keep,
Serenely silent as some mighty hill.

Yet is my love so great it needs must fill
With very joy the inmost heart of me,
The joy of dancing branches on the hill,
The joy of leaping waves upon the sea.

A trope does not always come off successfully, however.
Though picturesque in itself, it may add nothing to the bare
idea. When a poet says of gulls

> They stretched and shook their wings, and folded them
> Feather by feather to their sides

we get a felicitous picture, but he gains nothing of vividness or beauty by the strained added comparison "Like old housewives storing their linen into drawers." "Midnight shakes the memory" is a powerfully connotative line, but the addition of "as a madman shakes a dead geranium" diverts the attention and destroys the effect. Even Wordsworth adds little if anything to our conception of Lucy when he writes that she was "fair as a star when only one is shining in the sky." And Tennyson fails to increase the beauty of the child's laughter when he writes "It laughed like a dawn in May."

Contemporary writers are addicted to an exhibition of cleverness and affectation in tropes, especially when given in isolation from any context, that amuse but divert attention from any idea significant to the author. "They simply lived in one another's pockets" causes a smile, but it does nothing else. This sort of exhibitionism frequently distorts a well-known maxim: "She was torn between love and booty." It is found in collections of tropes published in magazines and heard every night on the radio.

However clever or however beautiful and even apt, a trope is likely to be ineffective if it is obviously studied and strained after.

> She winks a feeble eye,
> She smiles into corners.
> She smooths the hair of the grass.
> The moon has lost her memory,
> A washed-out smallpox cracks her face.

Tropes fail, too, when they compare the greater to the lesser. When Longfellow wrote that stars are forget-me-nots in the infinite meadows of heaven he added nothing to the beauty of the stars or to one's impression of their number. But Wordsworth, reversing the comparison, is eminently successful when he wrote that the daffodils are

> Continuous as the stars that shine
> And twinkle on the milky way.

By calling on the lesser to illumine the greater, poets are likely to become ridiculous. The words "eyelash" and "cheek" destroy the beauty of the dawn in

> Morn
> Had lifted the dark eyelash of the Night
> From off the rosy cheek of waking Day.

At the other extreme, tropes fail by being too strong, by comparing some slight or commonplace thing with that which is grand, remote, or vague.

> Her hair is like the gleaming gold of dawn

or

> The snow sails round him as he sings,
> White as the down on angels' wings

or Milton's

> What mean those colour'd streaks in heaven,
> Distended as the brow of God appeas'd?

When tropes are obscure to a reader, they obviously can contribute nothing to him except confusion and a probable prejudice against the poem as a whole. Gascoyne may have had clearly in his own mind images that were impressive to him, but he has not written poetry unless he succeeds in making them impressive to others.

> The face of the cliff is black with lovers;
> The sun above them is a bag of nails; the spring's
> First rivers hide among her hair.

Though poets perceive more likenesses than ordinary people, their taste is not always impeccable. Certainly questionable is the selection of the trope in

> While green grass beneath me lies,
> Pearled with dew like fishes' eyes.

And the relationship in the following two quotations is not close enough to make the tropes effective.

> The hooded beehive, small and low,
> Stands like a maiden in the snow.
>
> . . . . .
>
> Keen as the ivoried hoofs of antelopes,
> A gilt-edged wind blows over the divide.

Everyone has sat indoors at night and heard the wind outside. How did it sound? Of what did it make you think? How did it make you feel? Was the author of the following lines successful in your opinion in characterizing the wind? Try your hand at improvement.

> All night the wind ran round the house
> Hugging his sides with laughter

And Kipling's tropes are striking and, unfortunately, memorable.

> And love's torch stinking and stale
> Like the butt of a dead cigar.

The "mixed metaphor," especially as used by florid orators, has been ridiculed from time immemorial. Only a confused mind insensitive to words could tolerate "I smell a rat! I see it floating in the air! We must nip it in the bud," or would, in an attempt to be picturesque, write "She set sail with angry feet pounding the pavement like hailstones." But occasionally real poets come perilously near confusing the senses by tropes. When Swinburne writes "Prince of song more sweet than honey" his emphasis on the cloying sweetness of honey is a far cry from the sweetness of the poet's song. And a modernist who wrote of

> The apple tree's gnarled hands
> Caressing the weathered shingles

transfers to the leaves and tips of the branches the adjective that is appropriate only to the old trunk. And giving arms

to an amorphous fog ("The fog received him in its arms")
violates any concept that one may have of a mist.

Of course one may be too finicky about poetic language,
but, nevertheless, it should make sense while it is connoting
by tropes beauty or emphasis that would not otherwise be
had. One should not surrender his own judgment or his
own sense of good taste, for the poet is writing to give
pleasure to the reader; and the reader alone, by exercising such
intelligence as he has approves or condemns, is pleased or is
offended by the product offered him.

In one of his amusing "versus" Ogden Nash cleverly exhibits to what extent literalness may go in reading figurative
language. It is interesting after going over "Very Like a
Whale" to review Byron's poem to see if the implied criticism
is at all justified. What virtues in the original poem outweigh
any defects that it may have?

### VERY LIKE A WHALE

OGDEN NASH

One thing that literature would be greatly the better for
Would be a more restricted employment by authors of simile
  and metaphor
Authors of all races, be they Greeks, Romans, Teutons, or Celts,
Can't seem just to say that anything is the thing it is but have
  to go out of their way to say that it is like something else.
What does it mean when we are told
That the Assyrian came down like a wolf on the fold?
In the first place, George Gordon Byron had had enough experi-
  ence
To know that it probably wasn't just one Assyrian, it was a *lot*
  of Assyrians.
However, as too many arguments are apt to induce apoplexy
  and thus hinder longevity,
We'll let it pass as one Assyrian for the sake of brevity.
Now, then, this particular Assyrian, the one whose cohorts were
  gleaming in purple and gold,
Just what does the poet mean when he says he came down like
  a wolf on the fold?

In heaven and earth more than is dreamed of in our philosophy
   there are a great many things,
But I don't imagine that among them is a wolf with purple and
   gold cohorts or purple and gold anythings.
No, no, Lord Byron, before I'll believe that this Assyrian was
   actually like a wolf I must have some kind of proof;
Did he run on all fours and did he have a hairy tail and a big red
   mouth and big white teeth and did he say Woof woof woof?
Frankly I think it very unlikely, and all you were entitled to
   say, at the very most,
Was that the Assyrian cohorts came down like a lot of Assyrian
   cohorts about to destroy the Hebrew host.
But that wasn't fancy enough for Lord Byron, oh dear me, no,
   he had to invent a lot of figures of speech and then interpolate
   them,
With the result that whenever you mention Old Testament soldiers to people they say Oh yes, they're the ones that a lot of
   wolves dressed up in gold and purple ate them.
That's the kind of thing that's being done all the time by poets,
   from Homer to Tennyson;
They're always comparing ladies to lilies and veal to venison,
And they always say things like that the snow is a white blanket
   after a winter storm.
Oh it is, is it, all right then, you sleep under a six-inch blanket
   of snow and I'll sleep under a half-inch blanket of unpoetic
   blanket material and we'll see which one keeps warm,
And after that maybe you'll begin to comprehend dimly
What I mean by too much metaphor and simile.

Appreciation of tropes requires a background that includes
a vivid realization of the image to which the poet refers.
"Houses brown as stale whalemeat" means nothing to most
of us, for we have never seen whalemeat, fresh or stale. But
we have all observed the humming bird, and although we
may not actually have seen "downs" and although we recognize that "bowers" is used only for rhyme, experience tells
us that Nathalia Crane gives a marvelous description. "Dip-
ping," "pivoted on emptiness," and "scrutinize" are perfect.

> Across the downs a humming bird
>    Came dipping through the bowers,

He pivoted on emptiness
To scrutinize the flowers.

Appreciation also demands that a reader must have perspicacity to see the likeness, stated or implied, between the bare idea and the image, and the ability to recognize the contribution that the latter makes in enriching the former. When the value of a trope is not immediately perceived, the poet should be given the benefit of an assumption that he has recognized a likeness which has given him pleasure and which he is trying to convey to us. But if, after reasonable effort, we do not get it, let us pass on. There is beauty ahead.

For those who wish to increase their appreciation of poetry, the following exercises are suggested.

## A

In this list of tropes which do you applaud for their contribution to some idea and which merely for the cleverness of expression? If a pleasing contribution is made, what is it?

1. Yellow dandelions buttoning the green sod to earth.
2. A canyon filled to the brim with hush.
3. No more memory than a mirror.
4. I buttoned up the pockets of my sympathy.
5. A mind like a flash of lightning, quick but crooked.
6. From the slowly changing tapestry of life the old people ravel out at one end, while the babies are woven in at the other.
7. Worry had autographed her face.
8. A wild rose tree pavilions him in bloom.
9. I have (as when the sun doth light a storm)
   Buried this sigh in wrinkle of a smile.

## B

Following are passages quoted from different poets, unnamed lest you be influenced in your judgments by the authorship. What do you know and what do you need to do to gain as fully as possible what the poet intended? How do you respond to each one at a first reading? Are there any that require formal analysis for understanding? By intent there are included tropes which may seem in poor taste or which for some other reason are ineffective. Be honest in making your judgments.

1. Storm and darkness, ye are wondrous strong,
   Yet lovely in your strength, as is the light
   Of a dark eye in woman.

2. From you, Ianthe, little troubles pass
   Like silver ripples down a sunny river;
   Your pleasures spring like daisies in the grass,
   Cut down, and up again as blithe as ever.

3. I am: yet what I am none cares or knows;
   My friends forsake me like a memory lost.

4. He rose, faint smiling as like a star
   Through autumn mists.

5. She was as white and silent as an egg.

6. The wroth sea's waves are edged
   With foam, white as the bitten waves of hate.

7. Its soft meandering Spanish name . . .
   Speech half-asleep or song half-awake.

8. When the dead man is praised on his journey—
   "Bear, bear him along,
   With his faults shut up like dead flowerets."

9. Snow-banked windows faintly holding
   The feathery filigree of frost.

10. A hundred winters snowed upon his breast,
    From cheek and throat and chin.

11. My soul is an enchanted boat
    Which, like a sleeping swan, doth float
    Upon the silver wings of thy sweet singing.

12.             His sacred shaft
    Pierced the red circlet of one ravening eye
    Beneath the brute brows of the sanguine boar,
    Now bloodier from one slain; but he so galled
    Sprang straight, and rearing cried no lesser cry
    Than thunder and the roar of wintering streams
    That mix their own foam with the yellower sea.

13. Love's feeling is more soft and sensible
    Than are the cockled horns of tender snails.

14. But that old man, now lord of the broad estate and the Hall,
    Dropt off gorged from a scheme that had left us flaccid and
    drained.

15. That time of year thou mayst in me behold
    When yellow leaves, or none, or few, do hang
    Upon those boughs which shake against the cold,
    Bare ruin'd choirs, where late the sweet birds sang.

16.                    'Tis her breathing that
    Perfumes the chamber thus: the flame o' the taper
    Bows toward her, and would under-peep her lids,
    To see the enclosed lights, now canopied
    Under these windows, white and azure, lac'd
    With blue of heaven's own tinct.

17. Slowly, as when the walking-beam
    First feels the gathering head of steam,
    With warning cough and threatening wheeze
    The stiff old charger crooked his knees.

18. And multitudes of dense white fleecy clouds
    Were wandering in their flocks along the mountains
    Shepherded by the slow unwilling wind.

### C

What do you think of the trope that Milton used to describe the flight of the hosts of Hell?

> Thither
> They hastened with glad precipitance, uproll'd
> As drops of dust conglobing from the dry.

And of the tropes in this passage from Shakespeare's *Lucrece?*

> Without the bed her other hand was,
> On the green coverlet; whose perfect white
> Show'd like an April daisy on the grass,
> With pearly sweat resembling dew of night.

### D

Try your hand at completing the comparison in the following quotations and then consider what the poets wrote. The poets' words are given in Appendix D.

1. There is sweet music here that softer falls

    Than ———

2. Music that gentler on the spirit lies
    Than ———

3. And one an English home—gray twilight pour'd
   On dewy pastures, dewy trees,
   Softer than ⸻

4.        I think I never saw
   Such starved ignoble nature; nothing throve: . . .
   As for the grass, it grew as scant as

   ⸻

5. Coleridge describing the weird Woman in "The Ancient Mariner":

   > Her lips were red, her looks were free,
   > Her locks were yellow as gold:
   > Her skin was as white as ⸻

6. The scarlet of the maples can shake me like a cry
   Of ⸻

7. Are there no water-lilies, smooth as ⸻?

8. As a perfume doth remain
   In the folds where it hath lain,
   So the ⸻

### E

Of the following pairs of comparisons, which to you is more pleasingly connotative?

1. Swallows like dark petals blown from a tree *or* Falling leaves that dart like swallows in the wind.

2. Swarm of fireflies sparkle like the Pleiades *or* The Pleiades sparkle like a swarm of fireflies.

3. The sea moans like distant thunder *or* The distant thunder rumbles like the moan of the sea.

4. The docile sheep seek their lodging as star after star into eve far above us *or* Star after star seeks its lodging as the sheep return to their fold.

5. She leaned on my heart as a bird clings to a spray of blossoms *or* A bird clings to a spray of blossoms as my love leaned on my heart.

### F

What is
1. as playful as a pup?

2. as wet as a washcloth?
3. as dismal as a rainy November?
4. as joyous as a robin in spring?
5. as unexpected as a serpent?
6. as restless as a worm?
7. as quiet as dawn?
8. as gentle as April rain?
9. as dream-footed as the shadow of a cloud?
10. like charred paper blown by a breeze?
11. a nervous naked sword on little feet?
12. as silent as a cat?

## G

Add tropes to strengthen each idea:
1. A trust as strong as ———
2. The eyes of a widow, like ———
3. As frank as ———
4. A cricket song, like ———
5. Red berries in the snow, like ———
6. I started from sleep like ———
7. Cowbells at dusk, like ———
8. A mother's hand, like ———

## H

Mention of the eyes of a snake, a fawn, an ox, an infant, a mother would emphasize the expression in the eyes of what kinds of persons?

## REFERENCE AND ALLUSION IN POETRY

We have seen that appreciation of poetry depends largely on its connotative power and that connotation is not achieved unless a reader has not only the necessary background of information and experience, but also a lively constructive imagination to which he allows ample time for its exercise. In his sermon a preacher elaborates a text, presumably telling what it means and what it implies beyond ordinary interpretation, and for music programs, commentators expound the connotation to them of the selections to be performed. A reader must learn to be his own commentator on a poem, respecting his honest reactions as more important to him at the time than what anyone else, "authority" or not, reports that he understands it to mean and to suggest. He must become a partner with the poet in developing emotionalized responses so satisfactory that he will store them away in his treasury of memory and be stimulated to return again and again to the source of inspiration for renewed and added pleasures.

To the person who experiences art it appeals to him to do for himself what the priest or the commentator does for those who are limited in information and imagination or who are too lazy to use their own resources and powers. Art suggests, stimulates, and guides one to begin thinking and feeling as the artist did, but it puts no limit on where he shall end. Titian painted Pope Paul III as a crafty old man, not as a holy representative on earth of the Deity, but the painting may be revered by one who, misled by the title of the portrait, cannot abandon his own confirmed concept of archpriests.

Spoken words are supplemented by gesture and by intonation. A lifting of the eyebrows or a shrug of the shoulders can change the entire meaning of a spoken sentence. And intonation of a simple word like the affirmative "Yes" may suggest suspicion or even make it a sarcastic negation. In *Macbeth* the faltering King says, "But if we fail . . ." and his Lady replies "We fail." What does she mean? By intonation one actor makes her mean "If we fail, we fail, and that is all there is to it." Another implies by emphasis on the first word, "*We* fail!" that for them failure was impossible. And in *Hamlet* Shakespeare implies in one word more than any human voice can adequately express. To the Ghost's "If thou didst ever thy dear father love . . ." the Prince interrupts with "O heavens!" and when the Ghost continues "Revenge his foul and most unnatural murder," Hamlet exclaims "Murder!" That one word conveys, or should convey, satisfaction at the confirmation of his suspicion, horror, grief, and perhaps a determination on revenge. A wonderful thing is language! Meaning depends on many things besides dictionary definitions.

What is true of gesture and intonation is true also of symbols. Probably an ankh, a tau cross with a loop at the top, means nothing to most of us. But to the ancient Egyptians it was a symbol of enduring life, repeatedly used in their art and presumably conveying not only meaning, but also emotional reaction, as the cross of the Crucifixion and the communion chalice do to Christians.

But the poet has neither gesture, intonation, nor concrete symbol to interpret his printed page. He must rely on an exquisite choice of words harmoniously related to convey both meaning and feeling. They are like the male cells seeking a female egg, which when fertilized produces a living embryo that will develop of itself.

When the poet uses a simple word like "bird" he knows that it will convey a denotative meaning to everybody, but also that it will produce different images—of a nightingale, an eagle, a starling, or a buzzard—each connoting feelings that are pleasant or unpleasant. Even the name of a person carries different impressions of an individual, as Oliver Wendell Holmes explains in *The Autocrat of the Breakfast Table*. John is more than three Johns: he is as many Johns as there are people who know him. In literature on the other hand, the characters are essentially the same to all who read of them, for they are known as heroes or villains or romantic lovers by the carefully selected experiences that are presented in connotative words.

But art does have its own shorthand of expression. Wagner, after associating his motifs with the ring, Valhalla, and the Rhine, introduces them from time to time to recall all that each one has previously meant in the music drama. And poets use a shorthand of reference and allusion to characters, stories, and situations that are presumably well known. If they are not known, the allusions are no more intelligible than the hen-scratches of a stenographer to one who has not learned the system. When Byron writes "To snatch the Rayahs from their fate" he conveys neither meaning nor feeling to one who does not know that a rayah is a subject of the sultan who is not a Mohammedan. Such a reference not only adds nothing to a poem, it actually baffles and offends, for no one likes to be made conscious of his ignorance. And although Matthew Arnold's "To a Friend" contains the notable line "who saw life steadily and saw it whole," which makes it memorable, it is to most readers occult in its references: Asian fen, Tmolus Hill, Smyrna Bay, Nicapolis, Arrian, Vespasian's brutal son, and Singer of sweet Colonus.

The unpopularity of "Paradise Lost" and of Milton's superb "minor poems" today is doubtless due in large part to the many references that the modern reader has inadequate background for understanding. The voluminous editorial notes to these poems are evidence of the poet's vast learning, but they are an obstacle to a reader who has to turn to them at every third line. Young people often rebel at assignments to learn of the ancient myths and to read the "Iliad" and the "Odyssey," but without the knowledge that such study gives them, much of later poetry must remain a closed book.

## References to Literature

Poetry is studded with reference to myths, the Bible, history, and classic literature. When containing such references, it is written for the literate; it can mean little to a reader who is not prepared to understand and thus to appreciate it. "Looking up notes" will help, but that is a sorry substitute for an accumulated rich background of knowledge. Fortunately even information acquired for a special poem may later be used for pleasure when the same or a similar reference is made in another poem, and of course a later rereading will bring a pleasure that the tedious original study could hardly give.

To a reader with a broad knowledge of the ancient myths, the very titles of many poems are highly connotative—are, indeed, poems in themselves because of what they recall. Compare such titles as "Ulysses," "The Lotus-Eaters," "Oenone," "The Death of Oenone," "Tiresias," "Tithonus,"

"Demeter and Persephone" with "Fatima," "Audley Court," "Sir John Oldcastle," and "Kapiolani." The latter group may represent stirring stories, but they create no aura and stimulate no curiosity in most readers. What can many paintings by the primitives connote unless one knows the stories of saints and martyrs, like Ursula, Lucy, Sebastian, Christopher, and Jerome? Also, to appreciate many references and allusions in any of the arts, one must have a wide background of literature. Without a memory of Dante, one may find William Blake's "Wood of Self Murderers" only grotesque or amusing.

A reader can get pleasure from the mellifluous language in Tennyson's "Tithonus" and he can gradually learn from it the condition in which the unfortunate mortal found himself. But what an advantage one has who knows beforehand that Tithonus, beloved of the goddess Aurora, asked for and was given immortality, never realizing that continued life would not bring continued youth. Even the reference to the swan assumes knowledge of the popular belief that it lived for a hundred years, and a reader is supposed to know that Troy rose to the magical music of Apollo.

Shelley ("Orpheus," "Hymn of Apollo," "Song of Proserpine"), Keats ("Hyperion" and "Endymion"), and numerous other poets have drawn on the classic myths for subjects, and there are innumerable references to them in single phrases and lines.

A high school girl manifested in the following poem a rich imagination and by her reference awakens similar connotations for the reader who has known Catullus.

### ON FIRST READING "LESBIA'S SPARROW"

LEAH LEVINGER

Rain dripping on the naked trees. Beyond
I watch the draggled sparrows bickering
Perched on the barren wires. They try to sing;
A gray cat listens wistfully, as though he's fond

Of gutter minstrelsy. I turn the pages
  Of a worn book, and read of other days
  Until I am cut loose from modern ways
And from my shoulders slip the weary ages

Men passed through, uselessly. I enter in
  Most joyously a golden winding street
  Of heavy Latin laughter, songs, and meet
A godlike group of men, and midst the din

A togaed Roman, black eyes filled with fire—
For Lesbia's sake I love the sparrows on the wire!

Margaret Sherwood combines classic reference, which she assumes will bring to a reader a rich setting, with expression of her tender love for a dead pet.

### IN MEMORIAM—LEO: A YELLOW CAT

If in your twilight land of dream—
  Persephone, Persephone,
Drifting with all your shadow host—
Dim sunlight comes, with sudden gleam
And you lift veiled eyes to see
Slip past a little golden ghost,
That wakes a sense of springing flowers,
Of resting birds, and lambs new-born,
Of spring astir in quickening hours,
And young blades of Demeter's corn;
For joy of that sweet glimpse of sun,
O Goddess of unnumbered dead,
Give one soft touch—if only one—
To that uplifted, pleading head!
Whisper some kindly word, to bless
A wistful soul who understands
That life is but one long caress
Of gentle words and gentle hands.

The Bible is a rich source of reference in poetry. Tennyson's "The Palace of Art" is studded with references to it: Herod "struck thro' with pangs of hell," and

> The airy hand confusion wrought,
> Wrote "Mene, mene," and divided quite
> The kingdom of her thought,

as well as references to "the maid-mother by a crucifix," "St. Cecily," and "the dying Islamite." Henry Van Dyke in his *Poetry of Tennyson* gives a list of more than three hundred references by the poet to the Bible.

Readers ignorant of the New Testament will miss the point in the second quoted stanza of Gilbert K. Chesterton's "The Donkey."

> With monstrous head and sickening cry
> And ears like errant wings,
> The devil's walking parody
> On all four-footed things.
>
> I also had my hour;
> One far fierce hour and sweet;
> There was a shout about my ears,
> And palms before my feet.

Poets assume that every reader is familiar with the stories and the characters in the Bible, and that a reference or even an allusion will call up something more than knowledge, often a feeling of reverence, a halo of holiness. In Sidney Lanier's poem the soothing influence of the woods is made more impressive because they comforted Christ in his hour of agony.

> Into the woods my Master went,
> Clean forspent, forspent.
> Into the woods my Master came,
> Forspent with love and shame.
> But the olives they were not blind to Him;
> The little gray leaves were kind to Him;
> The thorn-tree had a mind to Him
> When into the woods He came.
>
> Out of the woods my Master went,
> And he was well content.
> Out of the woods my Master came,
> Content with death and shame.

> When Death and Shame would woo Him last,
> From under the trees they drew Him last:
> 'Twas on a tree they slew him—last
> When out of the woods He came.

The story of Ruth in the Bible has moved everyone who has truly read it. Its beautiful prose is as connotative as any poem. "Intreat me not to leave thee, or to return from following after thee; for whither thou goest, I will go; and where thou lodgest, I will lodge: thy people shall be my people, and thy God my God." Assuming that this story is in the heart of every reader, Keats adds to the connotative effect of his "Ode to the Nightingale" by the lines:

> Perhaps the self-same song that found a path
> Through the sad heart of Ruth, when, sick for home,
> She stood in tears amid the alien corn.

How much more moving is this passage because of its reference than it would be if the poet had told an original story of a girl who had left her people to follow her mother-in-law into a foreign land!

## References to History

It is not to classic myths and the Bible alone that poets make reference. They use history of all periods and of almost all nations, complimenting a reader, as it were, by the assumption that his previously accumulated knowledge will bring a richness of background. Enjoyment is assured much more by what one brings to the reading than by looking up the reference. Readiness brings a sort of self-gratulation; ignorance brings some resentment and a tendency to disparage or to neglect the poem. Respect is due the young woman who laid aside Benét's "John Brown's Body" until she had reviewed her history of the War Between the States.

Browning's "Pheidippides" is a more thrilling story because one has read the incident in Herodotus, and Tennyson's "Revenge" because it refers to a great battle of which we already know. In rewriting such stories, however, the poet adds something that the originals did not contain, giving a new point of view, an interpretation, an extension, or a connotation that would otherwise not be gained.

References in poems succeed or fail because of what a reader brings, or fails to bring, in response. The following passage from Shelley's "Adonais" is rich in connotation to one who has a stored up wealth of literature; to others it is likely to be merely a list of names vaguely familiar and by no means connotatively effective.

> Chatterton
> Rose pale, his solemn agony had not
> Yet faded from him; Sidney, as he fought
> And as he fell and as he lived and loved
> Sublimely mild, a spirit without spot,
> Arose; and Lucan, by his death approved;
> Oblivion as they rose shrank like a thing reproved.

Without a memory of the Wars of the Roses and of the symbols that identified its contestants, one loses much in reading James Somerville's dainty poem:

### THE WHITE ROSE

*Sent by a Yorkshire Gentleman to His Lancastrian Mistress*

> If this fair rose offend thy sight,
>     Placed in thy bosom bare,
> 'Twill blush to find itself less white,
>     And turn Lancastrian there.
>
> And if thy ruby lips it spy,—
>     As kiss it thou mayst deign,—
> With envy pale 'twill lose its dye,
>     And Yorkist turn again.

Artists in music, painting, and sculpture, as well as those in words, have enriched their works by references to what is well known, respected, admired, reverenced, and loved. Beethoven wrote his "Eroica" with reference to Napoleon; on the walls of every gallery are paintings of the Annunciation, the Crucifixion, and the Resurrection, as well as of the classic Graces, the fall of Icarus, and the rape of Europe; and sculpture gives numerous Pietàs, Daphnes, and winged-foot Mercurys. The sensuous beauty of music, painting, and sculpture brings enjoyment, which is increased by appreciation of the technical skill exhibited. But for the great majority of people the connotation, heightened by reference to familiar things, brings the greatest pleasure. Enjoyment depends on what one brings to the stimulus. Without a satisfying emotional response there can be no art.

## Dialect

A final kind of shorthand that some authors use for connotation is dialect. Everyone, from experience or from previously read literature, has built up toward certain races or nations attitudes of sympathy, affection, reverence, or respect, and associations of humor, gentleness, romance, or penuriousness. Mention of these people or use of their dialects calls up in readers the developed associations with them and thus creates an atmosphere hospitable to the story to be told, the sentiment to be expressed, or the character to be presented.

Of course the associations vary greatly with individuals. The Irish may to one person be a persecuted people to be pitied; to another, a race rich in sentiment and folklore; and to still another, something else entirely. Many Jews have resented the character of Shylock in *The Merchant of Venice* because they feel that he is an unfair representative of their race. But the common sentiment in England in the early seventeenth century was such that it could be counted on to supply what would have had to be said in the play if the money-lender had been a Hungarian, a Persian, or a Pole.

There is enough of common attitude toward races to warrant an author's depending on it to supplement what he says about them. Whether the attitude is justified or not, he knows that general sentiment, developed by experience or by previous reading, will supply much that he does not need to say directly. So we find connotative a setting in Italy, Ireland, or our Old South, extended dialect, or even use of dialect phrases or words. Of course Burns used the Scotch dialect because it was his natural tongue, not artistically because he expected it to draw on the attitudes of the English toward their northern neighbors, and Wordsworth similarly used, or professed to use, the language of the common man because he thought it the natural expression for poetry. But many, many authors have resorted to dialect as a means of creating atmosphere and as a short cut to effects. Whether they do this purposefully or not, the result is the same.

Probably literature has had more influence in building up attitudes toward peoples than experience has had. The poems of Burns, the old ballads, stories by Barrie and Ian Maclaren have created in millions of readers an attitude toward the Scotch that materially influences their response to anything written in the dialect. Try putting into plain English a few lines from Burns and you will see what is lost—not in the sense of the poem, but in one's response to it. We may not know precisely what some of the words mean, but all evoke the sentiment that we have associated with Scotland.

> Inspiring bold John Barleycorn!
> What dangers thou canst make us scorn!
> Wi' tippenny, we fear nae evil;
> Wi' usquebae, we'll face the Devil!
> The swabs sae reamed in Tammie's noddle,
> Fair play, he cared na deils a boddle.
>
> · · · · ·
>
> Wi' lightsome heart I pu'd a rose,
>     Frae aff its thorny tree;
> And my fause luver staw the rose,
>     But left the thorn wi' me.

### JEAN

> Of a' the airts the wind can blaw,
>     I dearly like the west,

For there the bonie lassie lives,
    The lassie I lo'e best:
There wild woods grow, and rivers row,
    And mony a hill between;
But day and night my fancy's flight
    Is ever wi' my Jean.

I see her in the dewy flowers,
    I see her sweet and fair:
I hear her in the tunefu' birds,
    I hear her charm the air:
There's not a bonie flower that springs
    By fountain, shaw, or green,
There's not a bonie bird that sings,
    But minds me o' my Jean.

In "Sea Love," by Charlotte Mew, the dialect may be indefinite as to nationality or specific locality, but nevertheless, being obviously the expression of a humble woman deeply moved by feeling, it is connotative. The poem would lose much if written in the conventional idiom.

Tide be runnin' the great world over:
    'Twas only last June month I mind that we
Was thinkin' the toss and the call in the breast of the lover
    So everlastin' as the sea.

Here's the same little fishes that sputter and swim,
    Wi' the moon's old glim on the gray, wet sand;
And him no more to me nor me to him
    Than the wind goin' over my hand.

Probably few American readers have had firsthand contact with the inhabitants of Ireland, but most have built up attitudes toward them from the songs of Thomas Moore, the satires of Swift, the biting wit of Shaw, the dramas and poems of Synge and Dunsany—attitudes that are complex and confusing, perhaps, but ready to add connotation to anything written about the modern Gaels. Certainly most of what we know of the British soldier in India has come from reading, but that has cloaked the "Tommy" in an atmosphere that is effective when Kipling's *Barrack-Room Ballads* use the idiom that we think is peculiarly his.

Dialect is effective when one associates it with a rich background, however it may have been developed. If it was familiar to one in childhood, its use brings a nostalgia that is highly emotional: the stories and songs of Uncle Remus affect most those who are Southern-born. But if dialect is difficult and has few if any associations, like that in some of Masefield's sailor poems and especially in Tennyson's "Northern Farmer," it may effectually inhibit enjoyment, whatever the content of the poem. Few performances are more offensive than the vocal rendering of dialect by those who do not feel its spirit. Pronunciation and mispronunciation are less important than the rhythm of speech.

Even slang has its connotative effect. The story told in John V. A. Weaver's "Concerning Pikers" has an entirely appropriate setting and the language used by the crap-shooting narrator is far better than dignified diction would have been for the humble tragedy.

## Chapter Seven

## THE TECHNICAL APPEAL

Pleasure in any art field comes, as has been said earlier in this book, from enjoyment of sensuous beauty, from active response to a connotative suggestion, and from understanding and appreciation of conventions and techniques. Each alone may give a limited pleasure, but it is in combination that they achieve the maximum effect.

In all phases of life there are conventions, most of them so common that they are accepted ordinarily without being noticed. In painting there are the conventions of framing, of representing three dimensions by two, of making the robes of the Madonna blue and red, and of using colors often for good composition rather than to reproduce reality. And in poetry there are conventions of printing each verse in a single line, begun with a capital letter, and often indented to indicate the rhyme scheme. Punctuation, a convenient convention, could be a subtle artistic means, which it sometimes is, if it were not usually determined by printer or copy editor rather than by the poet. These are more or less mechanical conventions, but they are generally accepted, and a violation usually interferes with enjoyment. Recently certain versifiers have affected a style of using no capital letters, of inserting or omitting punctuation marks for no apparent reason, and of printing with no formal indication of rhythm or meter. This obfuscation manifests exhibitionism rather than art; it interferes with the transmission of feeling and often is so offensive that it effectually destroys in a reader any desire even to find in the poem any causal emotion.

Forms that artists have found most likely to achieve the conveyance of their own feelings to others are conventions. In the long development of the arts they have come to be understood, or at least to be accepted, by those who enjoy music, painting, sculpture, aesthetic dancing, architecture, and literature. When a convention might reasonably be expected to interfere with enjoyment—like an orchestra conductor standing between the players and the audience and directing with waving arms and weaving body—it is ignored. Anyone can find numerous illustrations of conventions in the arts that are perhaps illogical but are continued because of tradition. To violate them is to risk popular offense.

Techniques are the means that have been found most likely to produce desired effects. In poetry there are the conventional techniques of using rhythm and meter, rhyme, alliteration, assonance, onomatopoeia, stanza forms, and the like. They are general in their requirements, leaving wide opportunity for variations expressing personality. In this respect they are like handwriting. Whistler and Sargent both used brushes to paint their pictures, but the former used so little pigment that it barely covers the canvas, while the latter often laid it on as if with a palette knife. The brilliant rhymed couplets of Pope are easily distinguished from the gentler ones of Goldsmith; and the cadences of Swinburne, Poe, and Lanier would never be confused by an experienced reader with those of Emily Dickinson, Amy Lowell, and Walt Whitman.

## SINCERITY

In all of the arts there are essential requirements. First of all there must be *sincerity*, or at least an apparent sincerity.

"No tears in the writer, no tears in the reader," said Robert Frost. Sincerity of feeling or of expression, however, does not necessarily result in art. A person may cry out in pain or moon in adolescent love without arousing in others a similar feeling or even sympathy. In fact, his naive expression may result in an effect quite contrary to the one intended. Audiences have laughed at Lear or at Romeo when poorly acted. The effect of sincerity is achieved by mastery of the means of expression—that is, by techniques. An obvious failure in technique—a limping line, for instance, or a strained rhyme—is likely to interfere with and even to prevent pleasure. And, at the other extreme, flaunting of skill, a sort of professional braggadocio, is also ineffective in creating sympathetic feeling, for it turns attention to the artist and his skill and away from the emotion that he presumably felt and is attempting to transmit. As Horace said, art should conceal art. Failure in mastery of techniques is more frequent than the advertising of virtuosity; but either can prevent desired results. Skill should be used for the purpose of expression, and not expression for the manifestation of skill.

The effect of sincerity is given, too, by the choice of the form used for expression and by techniques that are appropriate. A heroic subject cannot be treated in triolets, nor will an epic tolerate daintiness in form or trivialities in detail. Shakespeare's shifting from blank verse to rhyme and to prose passages is evidence of his sensitiveness to form suitable to his characters, to the situation, and to the mood that he is attempting to create. Milton used an elevated diction for expression of his lofty themes, and Adelaide Crapsey created a delicate "cinquain" form for expression in condensed diction of her feelings.

> There be
> Three silent things:
> The falling snow . . . the hour
> Before the dawn. . . . the mouth of one
> Just dead.

## UNITY

Another essential for artistic effect is *unity*. In every work of art there should be one dominant central emotion. This ideal is, of course, more easily achieved and appreciated in short compositions than in long ones. A simple picture, a brief song, an etude for the piano, a statue of a boy struggling with a goose, a lyric—all are likely to express one feeling easily apprehended.

Being short, a lyric or a sonnet is peculiarly suitable, as Edgar Allan Poe said all poetry should be, to express completely a single outburst of emotion. It makes no demand for either sustained attention or sustained feeling. It is easily grasped as a whole, and any deficiency in brevity or in length is easily detected. Consider a sonnet by John Keats.

### ON FIRST LOOKING INTO CHAPMAN'S HOMER

Much have I travell'd in the realms of gold,
    And many goodly states and kingdoms seen;
    Round many western islands have I been
Which bards in fealty to Apollo hold.
Oft of one wide expanse had I been told
    That deep-brow'd Homer ruled as his demesne:
    Yet did I never breathe its deep serene
Till I heard Chapman speak out loud and bold.
Then felt I like some watcher of the skies
    When a new planet swims into his ken;
Or like stout Cortez when with eagle eyes
    He stared at the Pacific—and all his men
Look'd at each other with a wild surmise—
    Silent, upon a peak in Darien.

On this sonnet John Middleton Murry in his *Studies in Keats* comments:

The unity of the poem lies deep and is *organic:* in the first line the last is implied, as a flower is implicit in a seed. And this perfect unity is achieved by what appears, on still closer examination, an almost miraculous subtlety. . . . Considered in its imagery alone, . . . the poem is a perfect whole—one single and complex metaphor, as intricate as it is clear. There is a real progression, as it were a crescendo, of the imagery which seems to grow out of itself. . . .

The unity of imagery and imagination is remarkable: in the octave the imagery and emotion of eager exploration; in the sestet the imagery and emotion of breathless discovery. The rhythm of the imagery precisely corresponds to, nay is indistinguishable from, the rhythm of emotion, and with a subtlety truly miraculous. . . . The silence of infinite space is first suggested, and against this silence absolute the silence of Cortez sounds like a thundercrash. . . .

The more the intricacy of the structure is realized, the more impossible it becomes to conceive that the poem was constructed deliberately, as a watch-maker constructs a chronometer. The complexity, the more closely we comprehend it, the more obviously is the complexity of an organism.

Few short poems either need or can stand such analysis as has just been given of Keats's marvelous sonnet. Most good lyrics are obviously unified in the expression of a single emotion, either simple or complex only to the extent of a fortification by contrast.

The unity is obvious in Adelaide Crapsey's poignant and compact "Dirge."

> Never the nightingale,
> Oh, my dear,
> Never again the lark
> Thou wilt hear;
> Though dusk and the morning still
> Tap at thy window sill,
> Though ever love call and call,
> Thou wilt not hear at all,
> My dear, my dear.

Simple unity is seen also in George Sterling's pictures of evening, all the details of which harmoniously contribute to the building up in the reader of the mood that possessed the poet. "Shyly the rabbit, feeding, crosses the road to home" is a poem in itself.

Far on the kelp the heron stands for a while at rest.
The lichen-colored breaker hollows a leaning breast.
Desolate, hard and tawny, the sands lie clean and wide,
Dry with the wafted sea wind, wet with the fallen tide.

Early the August sunset tinges to mauve the foam;
Shyly the rabbit, feeding, crosses the road to home.
Daylight, lingering golden, touches the tallest tree,
Ere the rain, like silver harp-strings, comes slanting in from sea.

Unity is emphasized by the form chosen by the poet for expression. The sonnet, the ode, the ballad, and other technical mediums of expression in poetry have more or less strict requirements of form which must be met or unity is impaired, if not destroyed. This result occurs, of course, only with a reader who knows the form and respects it. Such a reader appreciates the perfect satisfaction of the requirements, with no evidence of padding or suggestion of something left out because there is no room for it. The choice of a poetic form manifests the taste of an author as well as his personality.

It is easy enough to perceive the unity in a song like "Old Folks at Home," but in a composition of pure music that uses the same technical form hearers often get lost in their sensuous pleasure or in attention to contributing details. The unity of a musical canon like "Row, Row, Row the Boat" everyone can appreciate, but only an experienced and careful listener can comprehend how all the parts of a Bach fugue combine to a unified whole. Likewise the unity of most primitive paintings of the Annunciation or of the saints is obvious, but it requires a knowledge of conventions and of techniques to appreciate the unity of some of the complex compositions of Sasseta, Tintoretto, and Brueghel.

It is when artistic compositions become long and complex that there may be difficulty in focusing constantly on the central theme. The sonnet usually has two distinct parts, but together they make for one impression. Longer poems, like "L'Allegro," should make for one impression, too, however many details may be included. The poet is more likely than a reader to maintain in his mind a dominant theme. But even artists are led by temptation to introduce irrelevancies or to give such disproportionate space to a subordinate part of the composition that a reader's attention is diverted from appreciation of the unity.

The elaboration of a central theme in twelve books of "Paradise Lost" makes unity more difficult to recognize and appreciate than in the case of "They also serve who only stand and wait" in Milton's sonnet on his blindness. In fact, in some long compositions poets themselves are careless of unity, inserting passages which, though possibly good in themselves, are not essential. This violation is sometimes palliated by having one character prominent throughout, as in picaresque novels. Byron's "Childe Harold's Pilgrimage" has this kind of unity, the hero wandering through Europe and describing, occasionally but not always with brilliant success, what he saw. But practically no readers think of the poem as having real unity; they are interested in and remember only passages that are as good outside the context as in it.

In long poems it is easy to find parts which are complete in themselves. A notable illustration is the "Waterloo" stanzas xxiii–xxx from Canto Third of "Childe Harold's Pilgrimage." Of course each unit of a work of art, however small and however interwoven with the larger whole, should also have its own unity. In the Byron passage cited the unified third stanza, however justified by Byron's desire to pay tribute to the leader, could be omitted without perceptible loss.

Many excerpted passages, fairly complete units in themselves, are found in anthologies. As a matter of fact, they are usually "purple patches," which are read and remembered when the containing poem is neglected and largely forgotten. Turn the pages of anthologies and see how many selections are widely known, although readers seldom care to wade through the long poems from which they are taken. The poets, however, intended them as contributing parts of the larger unity, but they failed to sustain the level of expression that they achieved in what is still most memorable. Who recalls that it is from Goldsmith's "Deserted Village" that several old favorites ("Sweet Auburn! loveliest village of the plain," and the description of the village schoolmaster) were culled?

> A man severe he was, and stern to view;
> I knew him well, and every truant knew:
> Well had the boding tremblers learned to trace
> The day's disasters in his morning face;
> Full well they laughed, with counterfeited glee,
> At all his jokes, for many a joke had he;
> Full well the busy whisper, circling round,
> Conveyed the dismal tidings when he frowned;
> Yet he was kind, or, if severe in aught,
> The love he bore to learning was in fault.
> The village all declared how much he knew—
> 'Twas certain he could write, and cypher too;
> Lands he could measure, terms and tides presage,
> And e'en the story ran that he could gauge;
> In arguing, too, the parson owned his skill
> For, e'en though vanquished, he could argue still,
> While words of learned length and thundering sound
> Amazed the gaping rustics ranged around;
> And still they gazed, and still the wonder grew
> That one small head could carry all he knew.

Of course when we know that such passages are lifted from longer compositions we may be stimulated to search for others, to endure many lines of prosaic verse in the hope of finding gems that we might otherwise miss. And not infrequently we are rewarded, both by discovery of incorporated minor units that we treasure and by getting for known excerpts settings that give them richer meaning.

Every detail in a work of art should assuredly contribute, directly or indirectly, to the central theme. In some poems there will be an obvious central theme, with two or more major subordinate parts developing or supporting it; and each of the major subordinate parts may contain details for its own development. In Tennyson's "Bugle Song," which will be analyzed more in detail elsewhere in this book, the central theme is not given until the last stanza; earlier a setting with sensuous details and parallels of fading beauty is presented. But after the poem as a whole is understood, the unity of the contributions of the details, major and minor, is easily appreciated.

Oriental poetry, as well as Oriental painting, is content with the barest suggestion of a mood, but Western art has always felt a need of elaboration. Shelley wrote almost like an Oriental in "The Waning Moon," though with more elaboration. But Occidental readers, unaccustomed to such isolated picturing and recognizing the poem as a highly imaginative description, are likely to ask for something to justify it, to make the picture a setting for some character or situation.

> And like a dying lady, lean and pale,
> Who totters forth, wrapped in a gauzy veil,
> Out of her chamber, led by the insane
> And feeble wanderings of her fading brain,
> The moon arose up in the murky East,
> A white and shapeless mass.

## Unity by Repetition and Parallelism

Unity is often emphasized in poetry, as well as in the sister arts,* by repetition, with pleasing variation. The expression of a mood or of an idea needs to be repeated with

* The first of these forms is the characteristically musical theme and variations. As its name implies, it is based entirely on repetition with variation, and consists of a theme given out first in its simplest version (as a general rule) and then repeated with as many different treatments as the ingenuity, patience, or interest of the composer may suggest. Each variation, of course, departs from the original theme in some specific and consistent way, so that it forms an intelligible unit in itself. Thus the first may take the melody unchanged in the bass, against a running triplet-figure in the upper voice or voices; the second may take it at half-speed or in a minor key; the third may syncopate it and ornament it with brilliant runs and flourishes, etc. There is a general tendency for the later variations to depart further from the original theme than the earlier ones, for with each new variation the general idea of the theme becomes more thoroughly established in the listener's mind, and he thus becomes able to follow more radical departures from it. (Calvin S. Brown, *Music and Literature*, University of Georgia Press.)

embellishments to make a stronger impression. Note in the following poem how the form is repeated, the questions and answers being only slightly varied.

### LOVE'S WAYS

BRENDA GREEN

"Mother, how does love first come—
Quite boldly, proudly? Does a drum
Beat eagerly, as war-drums do?"
"No, dear. When all the winds are still
You lie upon a little hill
And the violets almost smother you."

"But do you always find his song
As sweet? Perhaps he stays too long
Like the slow-sinking orange sun?"
"Dear child, he seldom waits till fall.
And hills where once you heard him call
Are lonelier than oblivion."

Two other illustrations of unity achieved in part by repetition of form will be given.

### TALL CANDLES

ALICE MCALLISTER

Tonight I will light the tall candles of my dreams
With silent fingers, gently; as the flames
Burn silver I will make a dream of you.

Tall candles make more candles on my walls.
I will weave a dream in the shadow of each flame:
I will see your smile in the shadow of tall candles:
I will see your eyes. What is there more than these?

Tonight I will light the tall candles of my dreams
With longing fingers, softly, as the flames
Make glowing loveliness of still, drab things.
Tall candles make more candles. I will hear
Your voice in flames of shadows on a wall.

Tonight I will light the tall candles of my dreams
With silent fingers, gently; as the flames
Burn silver I will make a dream of you.

## INTROIT

KATHARINE TYNAN

'Twere bliss to see one lark
Soar to the azure dark,
Singing upon his high celestial road.
I have seen many hundreds soar, thank God!

To see one spring begin
In her first heavenly green
Were grace unmeet for any mortal clod.
I have seen many springs, thank God!

After the lark the swallow,
Blackbirds in hill and hollow,
Thrushes and nightingales, all roads I trod,
As though one bird were not enough, thank God!

Not one flower, but a rout
All exquisite, are out;
All white and golden every stretch of sod,
As though one flower were not enough, thank God!

Sometimes a poet apparently feels that an idea is not sufficiently expressed in a single statement and that it needs
repetition for impression on a reader. Theodosia Garrison
evidently began her poem "The Tears of Harlequin" with
a simple idea, which she expressed in the last two lines of the
first stanza. But obviously she felt that the effect would be
stronger if she repeated it with variations. If you were the
poet, what would you say in them to enforce the idea and at
the same time to preserve the unity?*

* The complete poem is quoted in Appendix E of this book. The
first stanza is as follows,

> To you he gave his laughter and his jest,
> His words that of all words were merriest,

Partly as a decoration of diction and partly as an element of form, repetition and parallelism are important in poetry. Little may be added to the idea by repetition, even by parallelism in synonyms, but the beat upon the ear dulls the critical reason and opens the way to gathering emotions. Every reader has been struck by both in the poetry of the King James Bible * and in the old ballads, and repetitive refrains at stanza ends are common in all periods of English poetry. Mrs. Browning used them frequently.

Repetition is not, as usually in prose, primarily for the purpose of emphasis. In poetry it also adds to the melody, completes the rhythm, and binds together verses and stanzas into larger unified wholes. Moreover, if the repeated words have a distinctive tone-color, as in Tennyson's "Oenone," they contribute to the suggestiveness of the music.

> O mother Ida, many fountain'd Ida,
> Dear mother Ida, harken ere I die.

The refrain in poetry is so well known that it needs no comment. But repetition is often so subtle, in exact or in varied form, that though readers may be conscious of the enhanced music that it gives, they may not note its presence.

---

> His mad, glad moments when the lights flared high
> And his wild song outshrilled the plaudit's din.
> For you that memory, but happier I—
> I, who have known the tears of Harlequin.

* To cause it to rain on the earth where no man is, on the wilderness where is no man.

. . . . .

But where shall wisdom be found? and where is the place of understanding? The depth saith, It is not in me: and the sea saith, It is not with me. It cannot be gotten for gold, neither shall silver be weighed for the price thereof. It cannot be valued with the gold of Ophir, with the precious onyx, or the sapphire. The gold and the crystal cannot equal it: and the exchange of it shall not be for jewels of fine gold. No mention shall be of coral, or of pearls: for the price of wisdom is above rubies. The topaz of Ethiopia shall not equal it, neither shall it be valued with pure gold. Whence then cometh wisdom? and where is the place of understanding?—Behold, the fear of the Lord, that is wisdom; and to depart from evil is understanding.

In "The Ancient Mariner" there is impressive repetition in many lines, exact as in

> Water, water, everywhere,
> And all the boards did shrink;
> Water, water, everywhere,
> Nor any drop to drink;

And with slight variation, as in

> I looked upon the rotting sea,
> And drew my eyes away:
> I looked upon the rotting deck,
> And there the dead men lay.

Of the two stanzas in Part IV of "The Ancient Mariner" describing the play of the water snakes, John Livingston Lowes writes: "The magical symmetry of the pair of stanzas unfolds from the initial concept of the ship's huge shadow with the inevitableness of a leaf expanding from a bud. Somehow upon the chaos of images which thronged up from their sleep, a luminous unity has been imposed."

The stanzas in Section IX of Tennyson's "In Memoriam" are bound together by the repetition of the word *calm*.

> Calm is the morn without a sound,
>   Calm as to suit a calmer grief,
>   And only thro' the faded leaf
> The chestnut pattering to the ground:
>
> Calm and deep peace on this high wold,
>   And on these dews that drench the furze,
>   And all the silvery gossamers
> That twinkle into green and gold:
>
> Calm and still light on yon great plain
>   That sweeps with all its autumn bowers,
>   And crowded farms and lessening towers,
> To mingle with the bounding main:
>
> Calm and deep peace in this wide air,
>   These leaves that redden to the fall;

And in my heart, if calm at all,
If any calm, a calm despair:

Calm on the seas, and silver sleep,
    And waves that sway themselves in rest,
    And dead calm in that noble breast
Which heaves but with the heaving deep.

Effective initial refrain, each time somewhat varied, is found in Mrs. Browning's translation of the Greek Bion's "Lament for Adonis," the first two stanzas of which are quoted:

*I mourn for Adonis—Adonis is dead!*
*Fair Adonis is dead, and the Loves are lamenting.*
Sleep, Cypris, no more on thy purple-strewed bed!
Arise, wretch, stoled in black,—beat thy breast unrelenting,
And shriek to the worlds, "Fair Adonis is dead."

*I mourn for Adonis—the loves are lamenting.*
He lies on the hills, in his beauty and death,—
The white tusk of a boar has transfixed his white thigh;
Cytherea grows mad at his thin gasping breath,
While the black blood drips down on the pale ivory
And his eye-balls lie quenched with the weight of his brows.

Repetition with pleasing effectiveness is found throughout poetry; for instances recall Lovelace's "To Althea from Prison," Suckling's "Why so pale and wan, fond lover?" Lamb's "Old Familiar Faces," Coleridge's "Christabel," Byron's "To Emma," Shelley's "When the lamp is shattered," Tennyson's "The Lady of Shalott," Whittier's "Skipper Ireson's Ride," and many of the verses of Poe and of Swinburne. Hood's "Death-Bed" ends:

Our very hopes belied our fears,
    Our fears our hopes belied—
We thought her dying when she slept,
    And sleeping when she died.

Parallelism repeats construction, and it often is found combined with repetition of words and of phrases. Poe ends "To One in Paradise" with perfect parallelism:

> And all my days are trances,
>     And all my nightly dreams
> Are where thy dark eye glances,
>     And where thy footstep gleams—
> In what ethereal dances,
>     By what eternal streams.

Lowell achieves impressiveness by parallelism in his lofty "Commemoration Ode":

> Many loved Truth. . . .
> Many in sad faith sought for her,
> Many with crossed hands sighed for her;
> But these, our brothers, fought for her,
> At life's dear peril wrought for her,
> So loved her that they died for her.

And Swinburne gives a musical illustration, heightened by alliteration in

> Spray of song that springs in April, light of love that laughs through May.

Poe uses repetition and parallelism beautifully in his "Ulalume," and "Annabel Lee."

### Unity by Contrast

Unity is also achieved by strengthening the main idea or mood by means of contrast. In music the well-known ABA form is the simplest illustration: a theme is presented and more or less developed, a contrasting theme is similarly presented and treated, and then the original, somewhat modified in the hearer's mind by what has intervened, is repeated.* In painting there are innumerable contrasts of hard strength with beauty, as in "The Rape of the Sabine Women," and Velasquez introduced dwarfs to emphasize the loveliness of the children of

---

* See in Appendix C an analysis of Chopin's "Marche Funèbre."

King Charles V. In "Musée des Beaux Arts" the poet W. H.
Auden emphasizes by contrast the tragedy of the fall into the
Icarian sea of the son of Daedalus when the heat of the sun
melted the wax with which wings were attached to his
shoulders.

> In Brueghel's *Icarus*, for instance: how everything turns away
> Quite leisurely from the disaster; the ploughman may
> Have heard the splash, the forsaken cry,
> But for him it was not an important failure; the sun shone
> As it had to on the white legs disappearing into the green
> Water; and the expensive delicate ship that must have seen
> Something amazing, a boy falling out of the sky,
> Had somewhere to get to and sailed calmly on.

The first stanza of Witter Bynner's "Tent Song" has delicate beauty of idea and form, but both are strengthened by
the contrasting second stanza, and the whole poem has a
perfect unity from the contrast.

### A TENT SONG

> Till we watch the last low star
> Let us love and let us take
> Of each other all we are.

> On some morning with that star
> One of us shall lie awake
> Lonely for the other's sake.

The same can be said for Margaret Widdemer's "The
Masters."

### THE MASTERS

> You have taught me laughter,
> Joyousness and light,
> How the day is rosy-wild,
> Star-enthrilled the night:

> Maybe God can teach me
> After you are gone

How to bear the blackened night
And the dreadful dawn.

Shelley's well-known "Ozymandias" emphasizes by contrast the futility of fame: the colossal wreck of one who was proclaimed "King of Kings" surrounded by lone and level sands. And Thomas Hood uses contrast most effectively in his sonnet "Silence."

There is a silence where hath been no sound;
There is a silence where no sound may be;
In the cold grave, under the deep, deep sea,
Or in wide desert, where no life is found,
Which hath been mute, and still must sleep profound.
No voice is hushed, no life treads silently;
But cloud, and cloudy shadows wander free,
That never spoke, over the idle ground.
But in green ruins, in the desolate walls
Of antique palaces, where man hath been,
Though the dim fox, or wild hyena, calls,
And owls, that flit continuously between,
Shriek to the echo, and the low winds moan,
There the true Silence is, self-conscious and alone.*

And Hugh M'Diarmid in a brief unrhymed poem gives an emphasis by satiric contrast that is reminiscent of the Houyhnhnms in Jonathan Swift's *Gulliver's Travels.*

## CATTLE SHOW

### HUGH M'DIARMID

I shall go among red faces and virile voices,
See stylish sheep, with fine heads and well-wooled,
And great bulls mellow to the touch,
Brood mares of marvelous approach, and geldings
With sharp and flinty bones and silken hair.

And through the enclosure draped in red and gold
I shall pass on to spheres more vivid yet

* Compare the sonnets on silence by Edgar Allan Poe and by Joseph Ellis.

> Where countesses' coque feathers gleam and glow
> And, swathed in silks, the painted ladies are
> Whose laughter plays like summer lightnings there.

Contrast is used in all of the arts not only for unity, but also for emphasis, amusement, the exciting of sympathy, and even for bringing about a feeling of self-gratulation for escape from what is presented. Beauty is increased by contrast with the ugly.

> Why entered the discorde in
> But that harmony might issue forth?

The Fool makes the mad Lear all the more tragic. And the crashing chord in Haydn's "Surprise Symphony" may have been inserted to arouse a somnolent audience, but it has amused listeners ever since by its contrast with the preceding and following beautiful music. The laboring laundress in Honoré Daumier's painting is by no means lovely, but she excites sympathy, as her strain emphasizes the comfort of our relaxation. Lucretius illustrates the last mentioned effect in his little poem expressing pleasure at looking at a shipwreck from the safety of the shore; and the marble of Laocoön and his sons in a death struggle with the strangling serpents—and no less Titian's caricature of it—would hardly please unless it suggested the safety that we enjoy. The statue is tragic, but we feel remote from death. "If ugliness is harmless," wrote Lessing, "it may be ridiculous, but when actually harmful, it is always horrible." When shown for its own sake, however effectively presented, the ugly is likely to give offense rather than pleasure. Walt Whitman not infrequently shocks a reader, rather than pleases him by such lines as:

> The malform'd limbs are tied to the surgeon's table.
> What is removed drops horribly in a pail.
>
>         . . . . .
>
> The prostitute draggles her shawl, her bonnet bobs on her tipsy
>     and pimpled neck.

## *Unity by Selection*

In building up a poem until it is long enough and strong enough to stand by itself the artist has to make nice judgments as to when he has given enough and stop before he has gone so far as to bore a reader with unnecessary repetitions. Just enough achieves success; too much means failure. Inevitably readers will differ in their judgments of sufficiency. What, if anything, is added to Charles Lamb's "Old Familiar Faces" after the first stanza? Does Matthew Arnold report the Scholar Gypsy more times than is effective? Does Katherine Dimmick send Jane to too many places, or would the contrast be even more effective if she had gone also to the Far East and to South America as well as to Europe and the tropics?

### FAR JOURNEYS

You traveled a long way, didn't you, Jane?
You rode high on the mountain tops;
You walked in silence beneath the stars;
You sipped the reddest wines in Paris;
You looked upon the face of Mona Lisa;
You heard the Valkyries in Germany;
You rode a camel over white hot sands
Toward round domes and green mirages.
You traveled a long way, didn't you, Jane,
Into the land of olives and warm nights?
You slept while guitars were strumming;
You heard the rumble of angry drums in Russia;
You lay among the throbbing scents of tropic orchids
And felt the moist earth beneath your body;
You trembled to the beat of distant tom-toms.
You traveled far, didn't you, Jane?
And here you are,
Hanging white garments on a line
In an American back yard;
And you are singing.

The same question is often raised by the poems of the masters: Do they in some instances by attempting to give just enough give too much, or, on the contrary, do they fail to give enough to achieve a satisfying unity for the reader? When they succeed, we have a poem. But it must be kept in mind that what is satisfactory for one reader may be unsatisfactory for another, and thus, at least for the time being, the verses are art to the one and not to the other. Is Shelley's "Indian Serenade" complete with the first stanza, or is there need for the second and third to complete the expression of the sentiment? What do you think the last two add?

### THE INDIAN SERENADE

I arise from dreams of thee
In the first sweet sleep of night,
When the winds are breathing low,
And the stars are shining bright.
I arise from dreams of thee,
And a spirit in my feet
Hath led me—who knows how?
To thy chamber window, Sweet.

The wandering airs they faint
On the dark, the silent stream—
The champak odors fail
Like sweet thoughts in a dream;
The nightingale's complaint,
It dies upon her heart;
As I must on thine;
Oh, beloved, as thou art!

O lift me from the grass!
I die! I faint! I fail!
Let thy love in kisses rain
On my lips and eyelids pale.
My cheek is cold and white, alas!
My heart beats loud and fast;—
Oh! press it to thine own again,
Where it will break at last.

It is interesting to examine a number of lyrics with the question in mind of the necessity of verses additional to the

one or more that present the central idea or emotion, and to
ask what the additional stanzas contribute and why you think
the poet wrote or retained them. You will find some poems
in which the unity is weakened by additions, and many others
in which a larger and more effective unity is achieved. Sometimes the additions are for the purpose of strengthening by
contrast, sometimes for interpretation. The third stanza in
Dorothy Ross's "Sham" is evidently for both purposes.

### SHAM

As a turtle hides, so hides she
Under her hard, bright shell
Of attempted sophistication.
Tall and skinny from too much dieting,
Her hair tinged red, and her lips tinged red,
She suggests a flame in its smoky casing
Rather than a young girl
In a black velvet gown.

Thickly mascaraed lashes droop
To cover eyes blue as the early dawn.
And while her soul leaps and thrills to the beauty
Of the life she is just beginning,
Her nonchalance calls forth
An uninhaled drag from her cigarette,
And a low-drawled
"Fawncy seeing you here."

So old, and yet so young;
So wise, and yet so innocent;
She trembles lest the world
See through her sham
And discover that she really cares
When stars hang low
And the moon is singing.

Ralph Hodgson's "The Bull," a memorable poem of the
tragic end of a once-powerful leader, raises the question of
the necessity of its length (30 stanzas) for presentation of the
theme. Read it carefully and see if you would omit any

stanzas to achieve a better effect, as William Butler Yeats thought he did in editing Oscar Wilde's "Ballad of Reading Gaol." *

## Unity by Coherence

In all arts there must be *coherence* to effect unity: the parts must stick together to give an impression of wholeness. Any decoration that draws attention away from the central theme, which should always be dominant, is a defect.

In the numerous paintings of the Madonna with the Christ Child there are usually balancing figures of Saints on each side, but so arranged that one's eyes are led to focus on the Mother of God and her Infant. In Leonardo's "Last Supper" the Apostles are arranged in groups of three, two to the right and two to the left of Christ, who remains the dominant figure in the coherent whole. Cohesion of parts in painting is often achieved by arranging details in a geometric pattern. The overhanging fruit in the paintings by Squarcione and his students distracts attention and adds nothing to the effect of the central figures.

To effect coherence, poetry uses the devices of stanza, of rhyme, and of thought content, and, as we have seen, it also uses the devices of repetition, of parallelism, of values emphasized by space and by tone-color, by crescendo to a climax, as in Browning's "Saul," and by resolution in a sort of summary conclusion.

An example of coherence secured by parallelism of form, by a gradual crescendo, and by increasing space given to successive stanzas is Carl Sandburg's "Cool Tombs."

> When Abraham Lincoln was shoveled into the tombs, he for-
> got the copperheads and the assassin . . . in the dust, in the
> cool tombs.

* Yeats says that he "plucked from the 'Ballad of Reading Gaol' its foreign feathers. . . . (and) plucked out even famous lines because, effective in themselves, put into the ballad they become artificial, trivial, arbitrary; a work of art can have but one subject."

And Ulysses Grant lost all thought of con men and Wall Street, cash, and collateral turned ashes . . . in the dust, in the cool tombs.

Pocahontas' body, lovely as a poplar, sweet as a red haw in November or a pawpaw in May, did she wonder? does she remember? . . . in the dust, in the cool tombs?

Take any streetful of people buying clothes and groceries, cheering a hero or throwing confetti and blowing tin horns . . . tell me if the lovers are losers . . . tell me if any got more than the lovers . . . in the dust . . . in the cool tombs.

Intentional violation of coherence may result in riotous humor, as illustrated in the following poem. The logical mind sees no connection between the details that Edward Lear has brought together with a cleverness that inevitably tickles by its very absurdities.

## INCIDENTS IN THE LIFE OF MY UNCLE ARLY

EDWARD LEAR

### I

O my ancient Uncle Arly!
Sitting on a heap of Barley
Thro' the silent hours of night,—
Close beside a leafy thicket:—
On his nose there was a Cricket,—
In his hat a Railway-Ticket
(But his shoes were far too tight).

### II

Long ago, in youth, he squander'd
All his goods away and wander'd
To the Tiniskoop-hills afar.
There in golden sunsets blazing,
Every evening found him gazing,—
Singing,— "Orb! you're quite amazing!
How I wonder what you are!"

### III

Like the ancient Medes and Persians,
Always by his own exertions

He subsisted on those hills;—
Whiles,—by teaching children spelling,—
Or at times by merely yelling,—
Or at intervals by selling
"Propter's Nicodemus Pills."

### IV

Later in his morning rambles
He perceived the moving brambles—
Something square and white disclose;—
'Twas a First-class Railway-Ticket;
But, in stooping down to pick it
Off the ground,—a pea-green Cricket
Settled on my uncle's Nose.

### V

Never—Never more,—oh! never,
Did that Cricket leave him ever,—
Dawn or evening, day or night;—
Clinging as a constant treasure,—
Chirping with a cheerious measure,—
Wholly to my uncle's pleasure
(Though his shoes were far too tight).

### VI

So for three and forty winters,
Till his shoes were worn to splinters,
All those hills he wanders o'er,—
Sometimes silent;—sometimes yelling;—
Till he came to Borley-Melling,
Near his old ancestral dwelling
(But his shoes were far too tight).

### VII

On a little heap of Barley
Died my ancient Uncle Arly,
And they buried him one night;—
Close beside the leafy thicket;—
There,—his hat and Railway-Ticket;—
There,—his ever-faithful Cricket
(But his shoes were far too tight).

## *Unity by Identification with Self*

A final characteristic to be mentioned of all the arts is that in one way or another they attempt to involve those who see, hear, or read, to induce them to identify themselves with the situation, the setting, or the mood that is expressed. Everyone is more interested in himself than in anybody else, as is evidenced by the eagerness with which one seeks first his own picture on seeing a group photograph. The more thoroughly one feels that a poem expresses what he feels, especially in language that he would like to have used, presents such a character as he aspires to be or fears that others will think he resembles, or tells a story in which he imagines himself an actor, the greater his interest and emotional response. The poet often gets this identification of self with the poem in the opening lines: "Who is at my window?" "As I lay sleeping," "Love that doth reign and live within my thought," "I can not eat but little meat," "Full many a glorious morning have I seen," "O wert thou in the cauld blast, . . . I'd shelter thee," "I am: yet what I am none cares or knows," "No coward soul is mine," and thousands more that invite the reader to adopt the expression as his own.

### CONVENTIONS

Form is important in all of the arts. In architecture, in paintings, and in all graphic productions, which remain unchanged as they are contemplated, form is the supreme, or almost the supreme, means of achieving the effect intended by the artist. A cathedral or a cottage is designed with unity, which is effected by proportion, balance, harmony of the parts, and absence of excrescences. A painting or an etching has a unity of form similarly effected, with the addition of a frame that holds all of the parts in one area. And music also has its form, which one can appreciate only if he has a memory sufficiently good to piece the evanescent parts together. Form is most potent in art when its requirements are known and respected before one considers an artifact. Many a person enjoys music sensuously because of its harmonious sounds without the greater enjoyment that would come from knowledge of the structure of such a form as a sonata and the ability to see how the parts of what is heard make a pattern.

Form may be beautiful in itself. The Rospiglioso drinking cup designed by Benvenuto Cellini has excited thousands by its sheer beauty, though it is obvious that so ornate a vessel could have no practical utility. And in the Museum of Modern Art in New York, Brancusi's "Bird in Flight" is simply a tapered piece of brass which by its static shape suggests grace of movement. Much of the "modernistic" art depends for its effect on the appeal that form alone makes.

Of course form ideally should be determined by function, as Louis Sullivan emphasized for architecture more than half a century ago: an office building should look like an office building, not like a Greek temple, and should be adapted to the uses of business. But such a building can still be pleasing and even beautiful in its form. A pitcher does not need to be ugly because it has a homely function, nor can it be entirely pleasing in form unless it holds water safely and pours it easily. However, Marianne Moore's "Ecstasy affords the occasion and expediency determines the form" is often true.

In poetry form is more important than casual readers realize. It may be so beautiful in itself that such thought-content as it may contain is entirely, or almost entirely, ignored. Adolescent readers have been known to dab their eyes and protest when after enjoying the sensuous beauty of "Tears, idle tears" they were asked some question about the meaning of the lyric; and Poe's "To Helen" will not bear a too close intellectual scrutiny. Form must be aesthetically functional, too, in that it is suitable for the expression of the thought and feeling which the poet is seeking to convey. If delicate, they may be expressed in a tercet or quatrain; if sufficiently grand, they may require an epic. A poet evidences his artistry by the selection of the vehicle for his appeal.*

* Lowell wrote that he began his "Washers of the Shroud" as a lyric,

In the development of poetry many forms have been tried, and in different cultures and times vowel quantity, parallelism, and alliteration have been the dominant elements of structure. But although modern English poetry to some extent uses all of these, it demands for its form primarily a rhythmical flow of diction. Everything else is decorative, not essential.

Rhythmical diction can ordinarily be divided into small units, called feet. And to them have been assigned technical names: iamb, trochee, dactyl, anapaest, and spondee. It is convenient to know these terms, but not essential to enjoyment. Feet are grouped into larger units, called verses, which are usually printed in separate lines; and verses are in most poems, especially if they are short, grouped into stanzas. The printing of poetry with a capital letter beginning each verse, with verses indented to indicate with which other verses their terminal words rhyme, and with spaces between stanzas is just one of our many conventions of form. Inasmuch as we are accustomed to them, they facilitate reading, and we are likely to resent their violation by innovators who have no apparent aesthetic reason for novelties in printing. If a poet uses no capital letters except at the beginning of sentences, he may have logic on his side, but he risks confusing and offending readers who respect the conventions as they have developed through several hundred years. Eccentricities of form are likely to evidence showmanship rather than art.

In English poetry the commonest small unit has been the foot composed of an unstressed and a stressed syllable, and the commonest verse consists of four or five feet.

> But change / she earth, / or change / she sky, /
> Yet will / I love / her till / I die. /

But, as can be seen in any collection of poems, artists achieve infinite variety by substituting for the iamb (an un-

---

"but it *would* be too aphoristic for that, and finally flatly refused to sing at any price. So I submitted, and took to pentameters."

accented followed by an accented syllable) trochaic feet (accented followed by an unaccented syllable) or even other combinations of stressed and unstressed syllables, by beginning or ending a verse with an extra light syllable, by shifting the caesura (metrical pause) within a line, by running the sense on from one verse to another, and by a different arrangement of the rhymes. Whatever the variations, however, early in the poem the poet adopts and sets a pattern which must persist in the ear of the reader. If the variation is purposefully made, the reason for it should be appreciated. Thought should determine form, and not form the thought. Unless a reader has the form in his mind, he is not likely to understand why it was selected or why departures are made from it.

Although it is freely adapted, the old ballads as a rule used a simple pattern of stanza, like

> There lived a wife at Usher's Well,
> And a wealthy wife was she;
> She had three stout and stalwart sons,
> And sent them o'er the sea.

In this introduction to the story there is no need to vary the pattern, for it simply states facts. But in later stanzas, especially the last, when at cockcrow the ghosts of the sons must leave, every reader will notice that the meter changes for both sense and effect.

> Fare ye well, my mother dear!
> Farewell to barn and byre!
> And fare ye well, the bonny lass
> That kindles my mother's fire!

Herrick sets the tone of his "To the Virgins to make much of Time" largely by the introductory words, "Gather ye rosebuds" and by the light syllables ending the rhymes in the second and fourth verses.

> Gather ye rosebuds while ye may,
> Old Time is still a-flying,
> And this same flower that smiles today
> Tomorrow will be dying.

And Gray adopted a longer line befitting the sentiment in his "Elegy in a Country Churchyard," with skillful use of assonance and rhyme. Note that a reader, perceiving the metrical pattern, is inclined to read "Full many a gem" as "Full menya gem," and that the second rhyming verse, being anticipated, is usually the stronger.

> Full many a gem of purest ray serene
> The dark unfathomed caves of ocean bear:
> Full many a flower is born to blush unseen,
> And waste its fragrance on the desert air.

The stanza is bound into unity not merely by the rhyme, but also by the parallelism of thought. Each verse runs smoothly to its end with no caesural pause, as suits the idea being expressed.

But notice how Browning gives an entirely different effect by his pauses and his run-on lines. Not interested here to present music, his lively mind expresses itself in the imagination that sees the meaning of the brick wall through the vines clinging to it and the meaning of the human body however it may be clothed.

> Now, what is it makes pulsate the robe?
>   Why tremble the sprays?  What life o'er-brims
> The body,—the house no eye can probe,—
>   Divined as, beneath a robe, the limbs?

In his long "In Memoriam," Tennyson makes peculiarly his own, though he did not invent it, a four-line stanza in which the first and fourth and the second and third verses rhyme. "This stanza form," wrote Professor Corson, "is admirably adapted to that sweet continuity of flow, free from abrupt checks, demanded by the spiritualized sorrow which it bears along. Alternate rhyme would have wrought an entire change in the tone of the poem." Read aloud the following stanza as it is and then again transposing, as one can do without destroying the sense, the third and fourth verses. This stanza form also permits without strain a long suspended sentence, as in Part LXXXVI, ending with the impressive single word "Peace."

> Behold, we know not anything;
>   I can but trust that good will fall
> At last—far off—at last, to all,
>   And every winter change to spring.

Fitzgerald in his "Rubaiyat of Omar Khayyam" used a free form of the quatrain that is eminently fitting to philosophic meditations on life and on the comfort of wine. The last verse in each stanza receives emphasis because of the rhyme which ties it to the first two, especially because the third verse is unrhymed.

> Myself when young did eagerly frequent
> Doctor and Saint, and heard great argument
>   About it and about: but evermore
> Came out by the same door where in I went.

In his "Palace of Art" Tennyson presents a series of pictures, each complete in a single four-line stanza and each subtly different in tone from all of the others. To indicate that each stanza is presenting a different picture, he adopted a form in which the short last verse conclusively closes the description, the ear stopping there to gather up the whole sound and sense. A normally long last line would have suggested a sweeping close inconsistent with the general repose of the poem. Two typical stanzas are quoted.

> One seemed all dark and red—a tract of sand,
>   And someone pacing there alone,
> Who paced forever in a glimmering land,
>   Lit with a low large moon.
>
> . . . . .
>
> And one, an English home,—gray twilight poured
>   On dewy pastures, dewy trees,
> Softer than sleep—all things in order stood,
>   A haunt of ancient Peace.

And in "The Daisy" Tennyson ends the unrhymed third

verse with an unaccented syllable which, by not rhyming, emphasizes the rhyme in the last verse.

> O Milan, O the chaunting quires,
> The giant windows' blazing fires,
>   The height, the space, the gloom, the glory!
> A mount of marble, a hundred spires!

A final illustration of the many that might be given of the variations poets make in the common four-verse stanza is from Emily Dickinson. It is so perfect in its form and diction that one may have even memorized it and not noticed that it has no rhyme.

> There is no frigate like a book
>   To take us lands away,
> Nor any coursers like a page
>   Of prancing poetry.

To appreciate the perfection of form that master poets use, one may try the effect of changing the order of the verses, of adding a word (however sensible it may be), of substituting a synonym, or of rearranging the order of a phrase. What a mutilation is there if we read "And waste its sweetness on the air of the desert"! And "They brought her dead warrior home" is a far cry from "Home they brought her warrior dead." It is by thus mischievously mutilating poetry that one can learn how the artist has chosen exactly the right word, placed it in exactly the right position, and associated it with other words that perfectly combine with it to convey not only the idea but also the feeling that the poet would share with the reader.

A detailed discussion of form patterns and of their variations, can be found in any book on versification or discovered by scrutiny of the poems reproduced in this book. The manifest skill and ingenuity of the poets excite the highest admiration, and conscious appreciation of it increases one's enjoyment of poetry.

## CONVENTIONS AND FREEDOM

The conventions of any art are generalized, leaving to the individual artist much freedom in detail. The conventions are continually challenged by innovators who seek effects by novel methods. Most of them fail, but when they are successful, the novelties are adopted by others and continued—until replaced by something that is more pleasing to the age. Before Beethoven, the third movement of a symphony was a minuet; but the stately dance going out of fashion, he substituted a scherzo, a lively and sometimes humorous movement. A concerto was originally played by violin and orchestra or piano; nowadays we hear in the form any solo instrument. But Antheil's adventurous combination of violin, bass drum, and piano was so offensive that no one has attempted it again. Mozart introduced bold modulations in his concertos, surprising the audiences who knew the formula that he was using, entering slowly when they expected him to enter fast, and again introducing the solo instrument where they did not expect it to enter at all. Haydn was always doing the unexpected, while at the same time observing the major conventions of form. Such ventures, as in "The Surprise Symphony," are delightful—if there is a return to the known formula.

But what was intended as humor may prove so pleasing an innovation that it is later accepted as convention. Ernest Newman said:

In "Don Quixote," Strauss, as we know from the German programme annotators to whom he confided his intentions, employed a certain sequence of harmonies to suggest, by its paradoxical modulations, the Don's wrong-headed way of looking at things. But in a dozen years or so all the paradox had gone out of the harmonies: they seem as straightforward and natural now as any dominant tonic cadence; and the result is that they make the Don not a wrong-headed gentleman, but a very respectable and indeed rather academic thinker.

Poets have also had fun in violating conventions. Don Marquis' "Sonnets to a Red-Haired Lady" and Wallace

Irwin's "Love Sonnets of a Hoodlum" are amusing because of their outrageous prostitution of a form that has from its invention been used for expressing the most serious and dignified emotions. All parody is rollicking attack on conventions of form, style, or subject matter.

For generations artists painted nature as if they had never looked on its loveliness, and it was a long process of timorous adventuring before Corot, Rousseau, Daubigny, and Constable. The human figure was for centuries presented in painting only symbolically before the odalisques gloried in it; and now "modernists" are reverting to compositions that substitute lines and colors that have no resemblance to the body, head, legs, and arms as they are generally seen.

## Conventions Change

That conventions and techniques change from age to age is obvious to anyone who reads a historical anthology of poetry, who hears music from the earliest days onward to the present,* or who turns the pages of an album of paintings. As an illustration, consider the development of the treatment of light by painters. The early Western artists were primarily draughtsmen, defining their figures with sharp lines, and adding color merely as decoration. To indicate any but an indefinite light, arriving from nowhere, encompassing all, they painted golden rays radiating from a holy figure. The later Flemings covered a background of tempera with successive layers of semitransparent oil glazes, which intensified light that seems to come from within. This method was adopted by Giorgione and Titian. Rembrandt improved the developed technique of Coravaggio, setting against strong colors strong light that sometimes originated from no perceptible source, and emphasized mass rather than outlines of his figures. ❦ Vermeer was a master above his contemporaries Pieter de Hooch and Nicholas Maes of presenting light from the out-

* Hear the phonograph records in "A Thousand Years of Music." Decca 20156–20168.

side sun playing on objects inside a room. Monet painted a light diffused at all times of day and softening every outline. Cezanne abolished light as such and modeled his forms in pure color. No artist attempted to paint beforehand like the innovators, and no artists after them failed to profit by their new techniques.

In poetry, too, conventions have changed from time to time, and in consequence techniques have also changed. Our earliest poetry was based on a formula of parallelism and alliteration in each verse, only traces of which remain. Rhyme has had its fashions, and, though not essential, still is an important element in poetry. The stanza popularized by Spenser, though used by later poets, was never popular after the sixteenth century; the Italian sonnet form was modified by Shakespeare and again by his successors; the heroic couplet of Pope and Dryden was softened by Goldsmith and then gave way to the freer verse form of Wordsworth; Keats, Shelley, and Byron created types of their own; imitation of French forms had its popularity; and today we read experiments that astonish and appall some readers but apparently please others.

As there have been fashions in poetic form, so there have been in subject matter. Though some topics are of universal and continuing interest to poets, in each period we find some that were peculiarly conventional. In the seventeenth century we find artificial and romantic imitations—poems on fairies, shepherds, idealized Dulcineas, evidencing sentiments that were expressed later in France by the paintings of Watteau and Fragonard. These poems were decorated with "conceits" of diction, which, though considered at the time graceful, if used today would seem so insincere as to be ridiculous.

> Lady, when I behold the roses sprouting,
>   Which clad in damask mantles deck the arbours,
>   And then behold your lips where sweet love harbours,
> My eyes present me with a double doubting:
> For viewing both alike, hardly my mind supposes
> Whether the roses be your lips, or your lips the roses.

I do not love thee, O my fairest,
For that richest, for that rarest
Silver pillar, which stands under
Thy proud head, that globe of wonder;
Though that neck be whiter far
Than towers of polished ivory are.

Occasionally conceits appear in contemporary verse, but the poet uses them knowing that a reader will smile, as he did, at the obvious exaggeration.

## THE UNLOVED TO HIS BELOVED

### WILLIAM ALEXANDER PERCY

Could I pluck down Aldebaran
And haze the Pleiads in your hair,
I could not add more burning to your beauty
Or lend a starrier coldness to your air.

There have been periods when religious poetry, odes to duty, sonnets on melancholy and death, and satire had in turn their conventional popularity. Then with Wordsworth * came the celebration of simple folk and of nature, preferably wild. "God made the country, and man made the town," declared Goldsmith. Even an idiot boy, a blind girl, a lowly leech-gatherer, a mouse, and the cause of pediculosis found their way into poetry. Oliver Wendell Holmes said: "The grandest objects of sense and thought are common to all climates and civilizations. The sky, the woods, the waters, the storms, life, death, love, the hope and vision of eternity,— these are images that write themselves in poetry in every soul which has anything of the divine gift." Henry Wadsworth Longfellow wrote in "The Spirit of Poetry."

Gifted bards
Have ever loved the calm and quiet shades.

* "Wordsworth effected a wholesome deliverance when he attacked the artificial diction, the personifications, the allegories, the antitheses, the barren rhymes and monotonous meters which the reigning taste had approved." —JOHN MORLEY.

For them there was an eloquent voice in all
The sylvan pomp of woods, the golden sun,
The flowers, the leaves, the river on its way,
Blue skies, and silver clouds, and gentle winds,
The swelling upland, where the sidelong sun
Aslant the wooded slope, at evening, goes,
Groves, through whose broken roof the sky looks in,
Mountain, and shattered cliff, and sunny vale,
The distant lake, fountains, and mighty trees,
In many a lazy syllable, repeating
Their old poetic legends to the wind.

In order to have appreciation of conventions and techniques, one must know what they were when the work of art
was created. It would be foolish, as well as unfair, to criticize
Chaucer, the Elizabethan lyrists, Dryden, Wordsworth,
Keats, and Browning by the same criteria, for each poet used
the techniques of his time to satisfy popular conventions.
One must not only know the conventions, but he must accept them: the diction of poetry is, of course, "unnatural,"
but in each age it is what was approved as elevated toward
an ideal expression of feeling. And for appreciation of the
skill manifested one must know the means that poets use to
effect cadence, unity, and coherence.

Sir Philip Sidney's "My true-love hath my heart" is written
in a form conventional in the sixteenth century. Note
how unity is achieved by repetition and parallelism in the
ideas and how the verses are bound together by rhymes.

My true-love hath my heart, and I have his,
By just exchange one for another given:
I hold his dear, and mine he cannot miss,
There never was a better bargain driven:
  My true-love hath my heart, and I have his.

His heart in me keeps him and me in one,
My heart in him his thought and senses guides:
He loves my heart, for once it was his own,
I cherish his because it in me bides:
  My true-love hath my heart, and I have his.

To understand conventions one should preferably know the social history of the period in which each artist worked. Then he will appreciate some of the causes of the gayety of the Jacobeans, the bright wit and the devastating cruelty of the poets after Cromwell, and the love of nature and the democratic spirit of the poets about 1800. The social history of the United States is a peculiarly revealing explanation of our own poets. Preferably also one should read the theoretical treatises on poetry, such as Wordsworth's *Preface to the Lyrical Ballads* and Edgar Allan Poe's *Philosophy of Composition*, and expositions of theories by modern scholars.

Respecting the conventions and the techniques of each period, one should also make allowances for what may today seem to be defects. The asphalt laid on gesso backgrounds used by Lorenzetti and other early Italian painters penetrated to the surface and gives now a greenish hue to what may have been lovely color. The buxom women of Rubens could not have been created in sixteenth century Italy, and Van Dyck painted his elegant cavaliers and ladies in England, not in Holland. If Mozart's music is played as he wrote it, we must recall the limitations of the orchestra of his time. And architecture was vastly handicapped until the successive invention of the pointed arch, the flying buttress, and the steel truss.

## Influence of Form and Theme

Form should always be appropriate to theme, but what is considered conventionally appropriate at one time is thought to be wholly inappropriate at another. Homer has been translated into rhymed verse, the heroic couplet, blank verse, and prose, each translator thinking that he could best present the spirit of the "Iliad" and the "Odyssey" by the form that was popular in his own day. An ode is a fit form for expression of an elevated mood of sorrow or of joy, a rondeau for a pretty conceit. Carving in granite is not suitable for presentation of a butterfly on a blossom, nor a sonata the best form for celebrating martial might. The form and the subject should be mutually worthy. It is sufficient here to say that each form must fulfill the requirements of structure, or an impression of sincerity and of unity is not achieved.

That conventions change, Margaret Widdemer has amusingly illustrated in

## DE SENECTUTE

"When you are old," said my grandmother,
   "Sometimes you eat and drink,
But mostly all that's left to do
   Is just to sit and think.
"So while you're young, my dear, and life is going on
Do gentle deeds to think about when happy youth is gone."
And she blinked her old eyes
And she told about a lover,
And his tragic surprise
When she said that all was over;
"He killed himself," said Grandma, just as pleased as she could be,
"And left a lengthy note to say 'twas all because of me."

"When you are old," . . . said my grandfather,
   "Sometimes you sit and smoke
And sometimes you can chuckle
   As you think of some old joke.
But while you are young, my child, and youth is still your own
Do noble deeds, and in your age you'll reap as you have sown."
But he looked very mellow
As he told about a deal
Which left the other fellow
Too entirely smashed to squeal;
"I got it all," said Grandad, as he wagged a happy head,
"And bought the little place, my dear, you'll have when I am
   dead."

"When you are old," . . . said my grandparents,
   And gave me counsel sage
On how to live my youth to be
   Most happy in my age,
But the things that they said and the deeds they had done
And got the biggest kick out of by no means were one—
So I'll pack my days full

With deeds of much rambunction,
And have things I can tell
When I've grown too old to function,
Because when you are old and sit drowsing in the sun
All that you are sorry for is what you have n't done!

## FORM AND PERSONALITY

The personality of an artist and the feelings that he has to express are evidenced by the form that he uses. Every poem, painting, musical composition, or piece of sculpture tells something of its creator. Michelangelo did not paint dainty miniatures, nor Wagner compose popular dance music. Pope used a crisp and pungent heroic couplet appealing primarily to the intellect, a form that would have been utterly inappropriate for the character of the sensuous Shelley or of the simple Wordsworth. The verse forms of Walt Whitman, Edgar Lee Masters, and Vachel Lindsay manifest personalities different from those of Emily Dickinson, Sara Teasdale, Edna St. Vincent Millay, and Elinor Wylie. More or less instinctively each poet, each musician, each painter, and each sculptor chooses a form of expression that his personality requires. The hearing of a bar of music distinguishes Verdi from Schönberg; a glance at a painting tells that it was done by Van Gogh and not Ingres, or by Corot and not Daubigny; and the sculpture of Epstein is a far cry from the smooth beauty of Pigalle's "Mercure."

A choice of form suitable to the personality of an artist is restricted, of course, by the conventions of the age in which he lives. The Romans, and much later the English Augustans, used verse for subjects like politics, morals, and even agriculture, which would in other times be treated in prose; vers libre was unknown when Donne, Herrick, Greene, and Lyly were composing their lyrics. But the history of literature has shown that strong personalities have broken with tradition and have either invented or made popular forms that were fit for the expression of the men that they were. Wordsworth and Whitman are eminent illustrations. And history also records failures to popularize forms that did not prove effective in arousing pleasurable emotions in readers. Whether the polyphonic prose advocated by Amy Lowell, the hard verse of the Imagists, or the novelties of present-day innovators will survive we cannot tell; the reaction of readers will determine. But one thing is certain: nothing is more likely to fail than an attempt by a poet to use a vehicle that does not express his own personality and in consequence cannot truly convey his own sincere feelings.

## Fortuitous Influence of Form

The form of verse—the stanza and the rhyme—sometimes undoubtedly leads a poet into expression that he did not intend when he began to compose. This, every amateur who has attempted to write verse will recognize as true. The only rhyme that can be found for a word that ends a satisfactory line may divert original thinking and not infrequently suggest something richer. Likewise a stanza form may necessitate omissions or additions of ideas that may not be improvements. It is impossible to illustrate this phenomenon, for we do not know what went on in a poet's mind when he was composing, but a careful reading of poems, and especially a consideration of changes made in revision, will stimulate shrewd guesses that are probably correct.

## Knowledge of Technique and Appreciation

Understanding the conventions and techniques used by an artist enables one to explain his impressions and thus get an intellectual satisfaction that supplements and supports the emotional. In a poem he can see how stanzaic structure, rhyme, and parallelism, for instance, bring about unity, and in a painting he can observe unity effected by composition. The two figures in Titian's "Noli Me Tangere," in the London National Gallery, for example, are a triangle, the high-lighted body of Christ on one side, the apex of the triangle being his head, and the other descending by the trunk of a tree, the line being carried on by the Magdalene's head and by her white clothes trailing in a graceful curve off to the right in a contrasting dark robe. The curve of the body of Christ is interrupted by the tree trunk, for balance cut across by the horizon line and by foliage, which stop the eye. The line is then continued, with less emphasis, in the slope of the hill to the right and stopped by the angularity of a group of houses. The two figures are held together by several curves continuing from one body to the other. These are a few of the technical means that the artist used to give unity to his painting. That they are effective even an amateur can appreciate.

In the field of pictorial art, one who knows even a little of the laws of composition can get a certain kind of pleasure in seeing how an artist overcame difficulties and triumphed over obstacles. It was once said that a painting could not be successful in a predominant blue or white or black: Gainsborough contradicted the statement with his "Blue Boy" and Whistler with his "Girl in White" and his "Man with a Pink Domino." The difficulty of combining into unity two human figures was perfectly overcome by Raeburn in "The Binning Children." It is a pleasure, too, to appreciate how an artist fits his picture into a space. The triangle is common, easily seen in da Vinci's "Mona Lisa" and in Le Brun's painting of herself with her daughter; Raphael fills a circle with his "Alba Madonna"; numerous artists, especially those in fifteenth century Italy, satisfied the restrictions of an arched alcove; and da Vinci in his "Last Supper" and Michelangelo in his early "Madonna, Child, St. John, and Angels" used an elongated rectangle. The amateur gets pleasure, too, by noting the devices that painters have used to prevent their pictures from running off the canvas. In Giovanni's "Flight into Egypt" the group is stopped on the left by a sturdy tree, and on the right by Joseph's upright staff.

Similarly there is pleasure in understanding how a musical composition—symphony, concerto, fugue, or simple song— is molded into unity by the repetition of announced themes, embellished and related to others that are usually in a contrasting mood and key. "The sounds have no external references to objects or ideas; what they have is the internal coherence of a kind of grammar of their own; the relations in which they are placed—in a texture of horizontal lines of sounds in sequence (melody), articulated by duration and stress (rhythm), and colored by the timbres of instruments or voices—are governed basically by this grammar, which is used in an individual style by each composer, in obedience to the laws of his own being." [1]

As he advances in his knowledge of the technique of musical composition, the student will learn from such books as Ernest Křenek's *Music Here and Now* of iteration (Arabic), free articulation (Gregorian), symmetrical scanning (Western Principle), polyphony and the idea of balance (harmony), counterpoint ("to fit the new complex of harmony into its scheme"), and contrapuntal devices (inversion, retrogression, and variation). The larger forms of music can be appreciated as coherent only if the relationship of the individual parts is recognized.

As said before, there is a certain kind of pleasure in knowing and seeing at work techniques, but fortunately all of the arts may be enjoyed sensuously and connotatively without this learning. Recognizing that the requirements of known techniques have been met—that a sonnet, for instance, comes out exactly right at the end of the fourteenth line, with no padding or strained rhymes—one gets the same sort of satisfaction as he does, of course with little consciousness, from going down familiar steps, which are in number, height, and width what he is accustomed to. A part of the gratification is a result of the recognition that he knows the required form and that he was able to see it, as "the lesser breed" could not. This gratification of personal pride is subtle, but it is also real. It was partly of technique that Ben Jonson wrote "Art hath an enemy called Ignorance."

[1] B. H. Haggin, *Music for the Man Who Enjoys Hamlet*, p. 10.

Experts get pleasure from knowledge of conventions and techniques that amateurs miss. Once I was embarrassed when a guest laughed out loud during a two-piano concert. When the number was finished and the applause had subsided, I asked, "What amused you so?" "Why," he replied, "didn't you notice that when the finale was expected the players introduced a coda?" No; I had not noticed it. I didn't know enough. Experts get pleasure from distinguishing between chest tones and head tones, and noting how a singer uses each one appropriately; they appreciate the differences in the brushwork of Correggio, Rembrandt, Monet, and Seurat; they are interested in evidences that Diserderio Settignano, Michelangelo, Rodin, and Barnard carved their masterpieces from clay models or directly from the human figure. Well and good. The amateur may or may not envy, but he need not abandon the arts because he does not know all of the techniques.

One way of learning to appreciate techniques is to try one's hand at original creation. One evening a caller was ridiculing the playing of a violin by a young man whom we knew. Bringing an instrument, I said, "See if you can draw the bow across a string smoothly." Though he protested that he had never touched a violin before, I insisted until he tried. The result brought some understanding of the difficulty, some appreciation of a simple technical requirement for playing, and an apology for criticism. Every person should at some time try to produce a tone from an oboe, to lay on paints harmoniously, to model a clay figure, and to write a sonnet. Experience will bring about understandings and appreciations of techniques that otherwise might never be suspected.

A little knowledge of techniques in the arts is not a dangerous thing; great knowledge may be. Experts tend to elevate technical matters above all else in appreciation. This is particularly true in the fields of pictorial art and of music. Critics of paintings often lose sight of a compassionate Christ in their interest in composition, and critics of music are likely to neglect the sensuous beauty while emphasizing technical details of structure or performance.

The Russian composer Aram Khachaturian, when castigated by the Central Committee of the All-Union Communist Party confessed: "The effort to master technique fully passed imperceptibly into an enthusiasm for technique. . . . Thus fascinated by technique, I arrived at formalism." Romain Rolland in one of his novels tells of a woman who "understood music, but did not love it."

This substitution of interest in means for enjoyment of the achievement is evidenced by the literature of comment—reviews in newspapers, the so-called "interpretative notes" that accompany phonograph records, and the commentaries furnished at concerts.

In program notes of any symphony concert one can easily find in what the commentators are mainly interested—the technical means used by the composer to achieve his effects. Undoubtedly the masters do achieve moving effects by the skillful use of technical means, but by having his attention focused on them and on them alone, the auditor is likely to lose what the music is attempting to convey. One might as well describe the cathedral at Chartres by calling attention to the details of its arches, buttresses, and stained-glass windows or explain poetry by pointing out the verse structure with emphasis on the rhymes, alliteration, assonance, and figures of speech. Technical details are interesting, but they are important only after there is a satisfying emotional response that evidences true appreciation.

Satiated, amused, and irritated by this substitution of understanding technical means for appreciating musical art, Ernest Boyd contributed to *Harper's Magazine* (September, 1932) his brilliant parody, "If Literary Critics Wrote Like Music Critics," from which the first and last paragraphs are quoted.

After a brief exordium, which is one of the author's most beautiful examples of synathroesmus, the theme is posited in a split infinitive, which is later repeated in its negative and affirmative forms, and in every mood and tense, until a daring zeugma introduces a brilliant brachycatalectic passage, terminating in a semicolon. The ensuing anacoluthon, which is merged, after a gradual transition, in a long parenthesis, is retrieved in antanaclasis, being finally resolved into an auxesis. A series of exquisite hendecasyllabics, enhanced at frequent intervals by hendiadys, and punctuated by the skilful interjection of four commas and six colons, brings us to the second motive, in which the author's characteristic use of the caesura is noted. The non-dominant rhymes of the virelai are transferred to the ghazel, with which the first movement reaches its triumphant close. . . .

Messrs. Jones and Brown, Inc., produced the work yesterday before an enthusiastic audience, which was again impressed by their masterly technic. They kept the deckle-edge rag paper well under control, although a certain weakness was noticeable in the joints of the brown buckram binding with bevelled edges. The foredges and margins were beautifully balanced by the gilt top, and the colophon at the conclusion of the performance brought down the house. The electrotyping and binding were worthy of the printers, whose ensemble work on the linotype has so greatly improved since last season. The passage in the second canto which Messrs. Robinson and Jones set in Caslon Old Face when the work was published in Boston two years ago is now presented in Bodoni, and yesterday's applause amply demonstrated the effectiveness of those square serifs without fillet, rendered only as Messrs. Jones and Brown know how to render them, with the slight shortening of the ascending and descending letters and the marked contrast between the light and heavy strokes. When the foreman locked the forms in the chase, every em was given its full value, and the roar of the presses thrilled every member of the audience.

Technique, to repeat, is merely the means that have been developed by long experimentation to express emotions and to arouse similar feelings in others. But sometimes artists in poetry, painting, and music are apparently interested in technique only, assuming that consumers of art will be similarly interested. Rembrandt manifests only skill in his etching "The Shell," as Velasquez did in his painting of a dead turkey, suggesting no emotion at all, and some think that Beethoven in his "Dedication of the House" was more concerned to show that he could repeat the theme more than two hundred times without monotony than he was in conveying any feeling that possessed him.

The painter Gandier-Brzeska declared, "I shall derive my emotions solely from the arrangement of surfaces, the planes, and the lines by which they are defined." He may have derived his emotions from such arrangements, but to the great majority of people who look at pictures for pleasure the surfaces, planes, and lines are mere means of achievement and have little or no significance in themselves. A critic wrote of another artist that he deprived his still life figures of all those specific characters by which we ordinarily know them and reduced them "to pure elements of space and volume . . . which are then coordinated and organized by the artist's sensual intelligence." If this results in appreciation, then a new definition of the word must be made. And its result is that "some praise the work, and some the architect."

Obsession with form, especially form that is novel, has resulted in queer inventions in modern verse. T. S. Eliot goes so far as to declare that "for many modern readers any superficial novelty of form is evidence of, or as good as, newness of sensibility; and if the sensibility is fundamentally dull and second-hand, so much the better; for there is no quicker way of catching an immediate, if transitory, popularity than to serve stale goods in new packages. One of the tests—though it be only a negative test—of anything really new and genuine, seems to be its capacity for exciting aversion among 'lovers of poetry.' " [2]

With all this, Robert Frost, who has exemplified his own theory, takes sharp issue. "Granted," he says, "that no one but a humanist cares how sound a poem is if it is only *a* sound. The sound is the gold in the ore. Then we will have the sound out alone and dispense with the inessential. We do till we make the discovery that the object in writing poetry is to make all poems sound as different as possible from each other, and the resources for that of vowels, consonants, punctuation, syntax, words, sentences, meter are not enough. We need the help of context—meaning—subject-matter.

[2] Introduction to *Selected Poems*, by Marianne Moore. Macmillan.

That is the greatest help toward variety. All that can be done
with words is soon told. So also with meters. . . . We are
back in poetry as merely one more art of having something to
say, sound or unsound. Probably better if sound, because
deeper and from wider experience." [3]

Cecil Day Lewis, a modernist himself, wrote:

> Few things can more inflame
> This far too combative heart
> Than the intellectual Quixotes of the age
> Prattling of abstract art.

This section has considered at length a third kind of appreciation, which is intellectual, in marked contrast to the first,
which is sensuous and largely unlearned. We have seen that
technique is the means that artists through the ages have developed because it helped to make effective their attempts to
express feelings and to arouse in others satisfying emotional
responses. We have considered, with no attempt to be exhaus-
tive, some of the means that poets use to achieve an effect of
sincerity, of unity, and of a harmonious, coherent composition.
There are also other effective technical devices, some of which
are considered in the discussion of poetic diction; but this
book is intended to enhance appreciation by the general
reader, not to further the education of the scholar. The professional student will easily find many books that treat in detail the techniques that poets use.

The purpose of techniques is of course to facilitate appreciative enjoyment. But as the effective use of skills is in itself
interesting—in the making of poetry as in making a touch-
down on a football field, in executing a grand *coup* in bridge,
or in juggling knives and balls on the vaudeville stage—there
is a tendency to focus attention on the skills employed and to
neglect the ends that the technician is attempting to achieve.

It is freely admitted—in fact, it is asserted—that enjoyment of poetry, as of all the other arts, is promoted by the

[3] *Complete Poems of Robert Frost.* Henry Holt, 1949.

understanding of techniques, and that the more one knows about them the more interesting they are, both in themselves and as means contributory to enjoyment. But it is maintained that understanding of them and appreciation alone of their use is not the same thing as appreciation of poetry, and that focusing on detail often, even usually, prevents the emotional response that is required. A reader should get that first. Then, to the extent that he has the interest, he may investigate and admire the means that the artist has skillfully and subtly used to convey the emotion that something beautiful or true has aroused in him. That is appreciation, too, but of a different kind. It is doubtful if anyone could ever thrill to the beauty of a cathedral if he began by a study of the ground plan, of the kind of stone used, the masonry, the buttresses, and the decorative carvings.

## Chapter Eight

## *IN CONCLUSION*

THE arts are the overtones of life. Man cannot live without
bread and meat, and he cannot live fully without the pleasure
and the stimulus that poetry, music, and pictorial art afford
to lift him from the everyday routine. Everybody enjoys art
of some kind, on high levels or low, and yet what one man
loves, another looks on with contempt.

What, then, is art? Many definitions have been proposed,
but when they are considered by one who seeks help to resolve
the conflict between his own taste and the pronouncements of
those whom he feels he ought to respect, he often goes out by
the same door where in he went. Most definitions of art
concern the means that are used rather than the effects
that are produced, but it is to produce effects that all artists
strive.

A definition of art should be so simple that it is easily understood by anyone seeking help. It should be so sound that it
is ratified by common sense. It should be so comprehensive
that it applies equally well to all media, to works ancient or
modern, to products of realists or romanticists, to the bizarre
as well as to the conventional. It should enable an individual
to retain his own independence, even though he disagrees
with those of wider experience. Such judgments he should,

of course, respectfully consider, seeking to understand what others have discovered and to appreciate it as they have done. But since the artist is appealing to him as an individual, an honest personal judgment is essential if he is to preserve his own aesthetic integrity, which is the only sound foundation for building greater culture. Not who has made a pronouncement but what is true and convincing to the individual seeking aesthetic pleasure should be the criterion of everyone who seeks to achieve more and more pleasure from the arts. If one loses confidence in his own judgments, even though they change from age to age and from mood to mood, he is on the road to pretense and dishonesty.

Such a definition—simple, sound, comprehensive, and directive to independent judgments that demand one's own respect—has been presented. Inasmuch as it applies equally to all art forms, applications have been frequently made to music and painting, although this book has been written primarily to increase understanding and enjoyment of poetry.

At first consideration the proposed definition may seem too simple. But its implications are numerous and highly important. Setting up, as it does, the criterion of the effect produced on an individual, it demands honest reaction, however it may differ from that of eminent "authorities." Using this definition, a reader realizes that a poem was written for him and that its success for him depends on what it makes him feel. To him a poem succeeds or fails regardless of how it has made others feel. He may regret that he cannot respond as others have responded, and he may hope that as he matures he will be able to respond as others have done, but at the moment he must retain respect for his own judgment, which is the only sure foundation for building a sound structure of taste. If he pretends, he is lost.

The implications of the proposed definition are important especially to a teacher. The first essential for him, of course, is a genuine love for each poem that he presents to a class; not only a love for it but also an understanding of what makes it effective. He must abandon once and forever the idea that pupils fail if they do not profess to like a poem. He must respect honesty of response from his pupils as he demands it from himself. Failure may be in the selection for study of a poem that is not appropriate to the maturity, the experiences, or the prior education of the pupils; it may result from the personality of the teacher or from his presentation; it may be inevitable in an atmosphere that is not conducive to appreciation at the time. A teacher's prime challenge is to create in his pupils (or to help them recall) the dominant emotion that the poet has felt and is trying to convey. Only after he has done this are the means that the artist has used important. Success in teaching poetry, as in teaching anything else, is best measured by pupils' desire and ability to seek independently for themselves more of the same kind.

Although this book emphasizes the response of a reader as the sole criterion of the success of a poem to him, it by no means neglects consideration of the means that the artist has used to achieve his purpose. There is a satisfaction in understanding how an artist works and the devices that make for success. These devices are of no importance in themselves, however, though they have not infrequently been emphasized by pedagogues who see only the trees and neglect the woods. Devices are important, as is pointed out, only if they lead to an appreciation of the whole, which in a successful work of art is a unity to which every detail should be an articulated contribution.

As has been indicated, art makes three appeals—the sensuous, the connotative, and the technical. Any one of these appeals may lead to a satisfying emotional response; but if all three are successful, appreciation is complete.

Response to the sensuous appeal is largely untaught, though it increases as one has experiences with the beautiful. Response to the connotative appeal, perhaps the most rewarding of the three kinds, depends on the richness of one's previous experiences and on the liveliness of his imagination in responding to the stimuli of the artist in extending what has been presented so that it becomes a personal enrichment. A reader is responsible to himself for the success of the connotative appeal. Response to the technical appeal is possible only if one knows the rules that artists have developed—some of them generally adopted, some of them popular in one age and not in another, and some so novel that they have yet to prove their value. Though musicians and painters have neglected neither of the first two appeals, they are frequently more concerned with the technical than are poets, often to the mystification of those who do not understand the conventions. The majority of readers of poetry will agree with Robert Frost that perfection in a poem is achieved when "an emotion has found its thought and the thought has found the words."

There are, of course, degrees of emotional response and also responses varying with one's maturity and one's moods. Childhood likes what to youth may seem silly; youth is enthralled by what to the adult may seem mere sentimentality. In one mood we enjoy the meditative; in another, the stirring; and in still another, the purely sensuous. But in whatever period or mood, the criterion of success is "Does the poem achieve in me a satisfying emotional response?" If it does, it is art to me. At the time, the judgment of no one else matters.

# APPENDICES

# Appendix A

# READING LYRICS

In most lyric poems there are a *setting* and a *situation*, presented in detail or implied, that demand the attention of a reader.

The *setting* is a more or less definite description of the place where the speaker is. It must, of course, be appropriate to the mood or feeling to be expressed. Sometimes it is merely harmonious with it; at other times it creates or emphasizes it. Expression of sorrow will naturally have a setting that is somber, unless for emphasis a contrast is used. Expression of joy, on the other hand, requires a setting of beauty.

Usually a setting is general, its effect being achieved by significant details that stimulate the reader's imagination or recall of similar scenes that he has experienced. Sometimes, however, the setting will be built up of carefully chosen details, which are to be assembled by the reader into a coherent picture. This latter method demands far more of a reader than is ordinarily realized by one who has developed a careless habit of doing little more than getting general impressions from descriptive poetry.

Shortcomings in observation and enjoyment are common when most people look at actual scenery or at representational paintings. Try to recall in detail a beautiful scene that has

303

pleased you, or, more exacting still, make a penciled or colored sketch of it from memory, and you will realize how inaccurate and incomplete your observation has been. A painter carefully selects the details that he will place on his canvas, rejecting the insignificant, perhaps rearranging those that give meaning and beauty, and even inventing others that will satisfy his ideal. But the great majority of those who look at a painting give a hasty general inspection, lasting perhaps less than a minute, get a vague impression, and pass on. Of course they miss the best of what the artist has seen, felt, and painstakingly attempted to share with them.*

Of course it is difficult to present in words pictorial details and then to assemble them so that a reader gets a satisfactory and pleasing whole composition, for success requires not only skill from the poet but also active cooperation from a reader. This cooperation takes time, which many readers inadequately realize is demanded, wealth of experience from which recall can be made, and an active, constructive imagination. Without these no one can read descriptive poetry with anything like the pleasure that is intended and that is possible.

The picture constructed by a reader from the details given may in some respects be different from that which the poet had in his mind's eye; in all probability it will be much different from that imagined by another reader, for everyone differs from everybody else in his past experiences and in the activity of his constructive imagination. But if the resultant setting is suitable to the feeling to be expressed, it will be an essential contribution to appreciation and enjoyment.

In "The Bugle Song" from "The Princess" Tennyson carefully builds up a setting for the poignant mood of the speaker.

> The splendour falls on castle walls
> And snowy summits old in story:
> The long light shakes across the lakes,

---

* It is just as important, and usually more difficult, to memorize great paintings as it is to "learn by heart" great music or great poems. But how wealthy is a person who carries in his memory the masterpieces of pictorial art!

And the wild cataract leaps in glory.
Blow, bugle, blow, set the wild echoes flying,
Blow, bugle; answer, echoes, dying, dying, dying.

O hark, O hear! how thin and clear,
    And thinner, clearer, farther going!
O sweet and far from cliff and scar
    The horns of Elfland faintly blowing!
Blow, let us hear the purple glens replying:
Blow, bugle; answer, echoes, dying, dying, dying.

O Love, they die in yon rich sky,
    They faint on hill or field or river:
Our echoes roll from soul to soul,
    And grow forever and forever.
Blow, bugle, blow, set the wild echoes flying,
And answer, echoes, answer, dying, dying, dying.

Read the first stanza through for the general impression.
The language is so pleasingly sonorous that you may not
realize that the poet is asking you to use the presented details
to build up a setting appropriate to the sentiment later to be
expressed. In this case the importance of the setting is para-
mount. No general impression will do. Unless a reader sees
vividly the entire pictorial setting with all the details pretty
clear, in his general pleasure in isolated details beautifully expressed, he will miss the point of the poem, certainly the contribution of the setting to it. The poet did not choose and
present these pictorial details carelessly and without definite
expectation of active cooperation from readers to realize a
setting which, though beautiful in itself, is important because
it prepares for and gives emphasis to the sentiment of the
speaker.

Having read the first stanza carefully, now answer the following questions.

"The splendour falls." The splendour of what? Obviously
it is of the sun. But is it a rising or a setting sun or a sun at
the zenith? A partial answer can be got from the third line:
"the long light" indicates that the sun is low toward the

horizon. But is it rising or setting? One is appropriate; the other is not. Only as you read further into the poem can you be sure that it is a setting sun: the colors "die in yon rich sky." What colors do you put in the heavens?

"The splendour falls on castle walls." Where is the castle? Within certain limits it does not greatly matter where you place it; but if you really see a picture, as the poet intends that you should, you will place a castle definitely *somewhere* —either to the right or left before you, high up or low on a mountain or hill, near enough for the sound of the bugle to be heard but far enough away so that the sound is faint. What sort of castle do you see? Your answer to this question will doubtless be determined by your experience: you have seen castles, or at least pictures of them; and you select or imaginatively construct one that suits what you think the atmosphere of this poem demands. Does yours have crenelated walls, pointed or square towers, a portcullis, a drawbridge over a moat? Suit yourself. You and the poet together are building up a picture that will make the poem meaningful and pleasurable.

Where are you as you build up this pictorial setting—on the shore of a lake or on an elevation above it? If the scene is clear in your mind's eye, you must be somewhere, you must have a point of view. It will help if you place yourself definitely in a position from which you can see and hear all of the details that are mentioned.

"And snowy summits old in story." Yes; there are mountains, high enough to be snow-capped. Where do you place them in your picture—on both sides of the lake, to right or left, or beyond it? If you actually see a picture, they must be definitely somewhere. And what sort of mountains are they —high and jagged or smoothly rounded? They are "old in story"; so you probably recall ballads of romance—and perhaps think of the Cheviot Hills. The Rocky Mountains will not do, for they are not yet old in romantic story.

"The long light shakes across the lakes." So there is a slight ripple that breaks up on the water the reflected splendour of the setting sun.

"And the wild cataract leaps in glory." Where in your picture do you place one or more cataracts? Perhaps more than one cataract will complicate the picture. Suit yourself. And what is the "glory" but the iridescence of the mists?

In the refrain comes an appeal to your sense of hearing. Some people have much better auditory memory and imagination than others. From your experience with bugles, what do you hear? Certainly for this poem the sound must be beautiful, gradually dying away in diminishing echoes. "Wild echoes" could come only from mountains. Note the effect of the repeated "dying." How must one read aloud these three words?

In the second stanza the appeal to the ear is continued and the diminishing of the echoes emphasized by the effective onomatopoetic words *thin*, *clear*, and *thinner*, and *clearer*. What causes the echoes? "Reverberation of sound waves from rocky cliffs" would be a good answer in a physics class, but an absurd one here. In the hills are elves who play back the bugle sounds faintly and still more faintly until they die away in the purple glens.

It is thus that the poet asks you to build up a setting in which the expression of an emotion will be right. What is the emotion or mood? To answer this question we have to read the last stanza, which gives the *situation*.

"O Love." Someone is speaking to another person. Who to whom? It betrays an inability to read poetry if the response is "Tennyson" and it begs the question to say that the lyric was sung in "The Princess." Whoever the singer, he or she is expressing a feeling to someone addressed as "Love." Is the speaker a man or a woman? Young or old? To select from the possibilities, one must consider not only what the singer says but also what he says in the situation already developed.

In the preceding stanzas the speaker has seen and heard and

been thrilled by wondrous beauty: a gorgeous sunset fading over a romantic scene and the music of a bugle dying away in the distance. Suddenly the thought comes to him that all beauty will fade and die, even the beauty of human relationship with one whom he loves dearly, one who is now by his side. Who would feel this most keenly? One answer is a young man on his honeymoon. (You may prefer a different answer, but it must be satisfactory in the setting that you have built up from the suggestions of the poet.) To the speaker the thought is shocking, even terrifying in its possibility. But instead of being depressed by it, the lover in his confidence uses it in reverse to express his assurance of the future. Read the following lines with emphasis on the italicized words.

> O Love, *they* die in yon rich sky,
>   *They* faint on hill or field or river,
> *Our* echoes roll from soul to soul,
>   And *grow* forever and forever.

The beauty of the relationship with his bride, he is confident, will continue and will increase in their unborn future.

The poem closes with the refrain,

> Blow, bugle, blow, set the wild echoes flying,
> And answer, echoes, answer, dying, dying, dying,

in which the repetition of *answer* is significant. This is not a mere technical repetition of a refrain with the same suggestion as previously. It must be read as acceptance of fading physical beauty with an almost defiant assertion of the continuance and increase of a spiritual beauty of human relationship.

A similar effect is found in Mendelssohn's popularly-called "Consolation," in his *Liede ohne Worte*, where the running chord used as an introduction concludes the music, but with the difference that its repetition is colored by the comforting body of the composition. And in Chopin's *Marche Funèbre*, Opus 35,* the beginning represents a heavy, solemn, depress-

* See Appendix C.

ing progress of a funeral cortege, but repeated in the final movement as the funeral procession passes back up the aisle of the cathedral, it is permeated and lightened by the confidence in immortality that has been expressed in the intervening "trio."

In every lyric someone is giving expression to an emotion—of sadness, grief, joy, rapture, exaltation, or what not. One does not express emotion in just any situation: sorrow is appropriate at the bier of a loved one or in recollection of grief; the thrill that comes from beauty is most convincing when in a setting of sunset or of dancing daffodils. And so the poet in his song presents, either explicitly or by suggestion, the situation in which the singer has found his emotion. "Home they brought her warrior dead," "Thy voice is heard through rolling drums," "Our enemies have fall'n, fall'n" from "The Princess," and every other moving lyric may be cited as evidence of the importance of realizing the situation in which feeling is voiced.

The singer may be the poet or he may be some other person, as in "The Bugle Song." But in any case the lyric is expressing what *you* might feel or what you would like to feel and express in the same situation. Without identifying yourself with the singer and assuming that the words are *your* expression of feeling or of mood, you will fail of appreciation.

Let us apply what has been said about setting and situation to "Ask me no more," another lyric from "The Princess."

> Ask me no more. The moon may draw the sea;
>   The cloud may stoop from heaven and take the shape,
>   With fold on fold, of mountain or of cape;
> But O too fond, when have I answered thee?
>   Ask me no more.
>
> Ask me no more. What answer should I give?
>   I love not hollow cheek or faded eye;
>   Yet, O my friend, I would not have thee die!
> Ask me no more, lest I should bid thee live;
>   Ask me no more.

Ask me no more. Thy fate and mine are sealed;
  I strove against the stream and all in vain;
  Let the great river take me to the main.
No more, dear love, for at a touch I yield;
  Ask me no more.

This lyric is like a telephone conversation of which we hear only one side, and consequently it makes unusual demands on a reader. Before the first stanza someone, obviously a lover, has said something which we can reconstruct from the reply. It is natural that one will draw his illustrations from what is seen near at hand, and so we can create a setting of a balmy evening with a moon high over a softly sounding sea and cumulus clouds over a mountain and a cape. The man must have begged the speaker to admit her love for him, arguing that just as the sea has responded to the influence of the moon and just as the clouds are determined in shape by the mountains below, the woman has responded to him. In her expressed reply she admits the influence of moon and mountain, but questions, perhaps because she is shy or coy, or perhaps because she is uncertain even of her own mind, that she has evidenced similar influence of the pleader. The final "Ask me no more" in this first stanza seems tentative rather than conclusive and discouraging.

How does the man urge his suit further? The "hollow cheek" and "faded eye" and "I would not have thee die" clearly indicate the argument that lovers have used from time immemorial. And the yielding of the lady is subtly suggested by the emphasis that should be placed on *should* in "What answer should I give?" and by prolonging the word *die*, which fills her with apprehension and a feeling of responsibility. The fourth line of the stanza is of course distinct encouragement, perhaps more than in her modesty the loved one realizes.

What the lover finally says is the most precious argument that a reader can imagine, too precious and too personal for the poet to make definite. Perhaps it is something like what Mrs. Browning expressed in her "Sonnets from the Portuguese."

If Tennyson had suggested with any definiteness the lover's last and compelling appeal, he might have diverted a reader's attention from the gradual yielding by the girl. Moreover, he would have prevented the pleasure that a reader may have in imagining the supreme appeal for surrender.

Whatever the lover says, it is effective. In maidenly modesty the loved one says "I strove against the stream and all in vain," inviting a final urge with

> Let the great river take me to the main:
> No more, dear love, for at a touch I yield.

There is no need, she says in the concluding refrain, for him to ask again.

It is really immaterial to readers whether the poet begins with a setting that is harmonious with a situation or with a situation that demands and receives a setting. If he is successful in conveying feeling, the two appeal to us as an integrated unit, not as two parts loosely joined. It is the harmony and contribution of each to the other that bring about the unified effect and the satisfying moving of our own emotions.

In some lyric poems either a setting or a situation may be minimized or entirely neglected. There are settings which in themselves and almost alone cause lyric outbursts. The situation is merely that someone viewing a scene, hearing music, reveling in odors or tastes, sensitively touching delicate things, is emotionally moved and attempts to arouse in others the same or similar feelings that were caused in him.

Of this more or less independence in lyric poetry of setting one can find illustrations in abundance. Consider Frank Dempster Sherman's "May."

> May shall make the world anew;
> Golden sun and silver dew,
> Money minted in the sky,
> Shall the earth's new garments buy.
> May shall make the orchards bloom;
> And the blossoms' fine perfume
> Shall set all the honey-bees

Murmuring among the trees.
May shall make the bud appear
Like a jewel, crystal clear,
'Mid the leaves upon the limb
Where the robin lilts his hymn.
May shall make the wild flowers tell
Where the shining snowflakes fell,
Just as if each snowflake's heart,
By some magic, secret art,
Was transmuted to a flower
In the sunlight and the shower.
Is there such another, pray,
Wonder-making month as May?

Situations, too, may be all but independent of settings. In the following narrative poem, sufficiently suffused with feeling to be classed as a lyric, Tennyson gives no definite setting, but a reader can, if he wishes, easily create one that is appropriate.

Home they brought her warrior dead:
    She nor swoon'd nor utter'd cry:
All her maidens, watching, said,
    "She must weep or she will die."

Then they praised him, soft and low,
    Call'd him worthy to be loved,
Truest friend and noblest foe;
    Yet she neither spoke nor moved.

Stole a maiden from her place,
    Lightly to the warrior stept,
Took the face-cloth from the face;
    Yet she neither moved nor wept.

Rose a nurse of ninety years,
    Set his child upon her knee—
Like summer tempest came her tears—
    "Sweet, my child, I live for thee."

## Appendix B

## READING A NARRATIVE POEM

### HOW THEY BROUGHT THE GOOD NEWS FROM GHENT TO AIX

(16—)

ROBERT BROWNING

I

I sprang to the stirrup, and Joris, and he;
I galloped, Dirck galloped, we galloped all three;
"Good speed!" cried the watch, as the gatebolts undrew;
"Speed!" echoed the wall to us galloping through;
Behind shut the postern, the lights sank to rest,
And into the midnight we galloped abreast.

II

Not a word to each other; we kept the great pace
Neck by neck, stride by stride, never changing our place;
I turned in my saddle and made its girths tight,
Then shortened each stirrup, and set the pique right,
Rebuckled the cheek-strap, chained slacker the bit,
Nor galloped less steadily Roland a whit.

III

'Twas moonset at starting; but while we drew near
Lokeren, the cocks crew and twilight dawned clear;
At Boom, a great yellow star came out to see;

313

At Duffeld, 'twas morning as plain as could be;
And from Mecheln church-steeple we heard the half-chime,
So Joris broke silence with, "Yet there is time!"

### IV

At Aershot, up leaped of a sudden the sun,
And against him the cattle stood black every one,
To stare through the mist at us galloping past,
And I saw my stout galloper Roland at last,
With resolute shoulders, each butting away
The haze, as some bluff river headland its spray:

### V

And his low head and crest, just one sharp ear bent back
For my voice, and the other pricked out on his track;
And one eye's black intelligence,—ever that glance
O'er its white edge at me, his own master, askance!
And the thick heavy spume-flakes which aye and anon
His fierce lips shook upwards in galloping on.

### VI

By Hasselt, Dirck groaned; and cried Joris, "Stay spur!
Your Roos galloped bravely, the fault's not in her,
We'll remember at Aix"—for one heard the quick wheeze
Of her chest, saw the stretched neck and staggering knees,
And sunk tail, and horrible heave of the flank,
As down on her haunches she shuddered and sank.

### VII

So, we were left galloping, Joris and I,
Past Looz and past Tongres, no cloud in the sky;
The broad sun above laughed a pitiless laugh,
'Neath our feet broke the brittle bright stubble like chaff;
Till over by Dalhem a dome-spire sprang white,
And "Gallop," gasped Joris, "for Aix is in sight!"

### VIII

"How they'll greet us!"—and all in a moment his roan
Rolled neck and croup over, lay dead as a stone;
And there was my Roland to bear the whole weight
Of the news which alone could save Aix from her fate,
With nostrils like pits full of blood to the brim,
And with circles of red for his eye-sockets' rim.

### IX

Then I cast loose my buffcoat, each holster let fall,
Shook off both my jack-boots, let go belt and all,
Stood up in the stirrup, leaned, patted his ear,
Called my Roland his pet-name, my horse without peer;
Clapped my hands, laughed and sang, any noise, bad or good,
Till at length into Aix Roland galloped and stood.

### X

And all I remember is—friends flocking round
As I sat with his head 'twixt my knees on the ground;
And no voice but was praising this Roland of mine,
As I poured down his throat our last measure of wine,
Which (the burgesses voted by common consent)
Was no more than his due who brought good news from Ghent.

## This is how one person says that he read the poem.

The title made me ask before I began reading, "How should the good news be sent?" First I thought of how it would be sent today —by radio, telephone, telegraph, airplane, or automobile. But I noticed that under the title of the poem is a date (16—), which I almost missed. Why did the poet insert it? Evidently to narrow the possibility to man or horse, or to both. Why, I then asked myself, did he not give a definite date, like 1601 or 1683? Had he done so, I should have been curious about exactly what happened then: my attention would have been diverted from any heroism in carrying the message to some historical event that is of no importance whatsoever here.

What was the good news? Never mind. It was good; it was important: the poem is to tell how it was carried.

The first stanza impressed me immediately with the urgency. The men *sprang* to their saddles and immediately *galloped* away; there is no time for description or for explanation. The urgency is emphasized also by the starting at midnight and by the "Good speed!" of the watchman. I noted how carefully the speaker "made the girths tight" and set all of his gear so that it would not fail. Later, in Stanza III, the importance of the news is stressed by "yet there is time"; when Joris went down he urged his friend on and anticipated the joy of the people at Aix; and at the arrival the burgesses voted by common consent the last measure of wine that they had.

There were three riders, for the news was too important to be entrusted to a single courier: one might fail and the message be undelivered. Why, then, were not ten sent, or a score, or a hundred? As I read on and learned that Joris and Dirck dropped out, leaving the responsibility finally on one alone, I realized that a continuance of failures would have been monotonous and in consequence artistically ineffective. Dirck's horse gave out; Joris' "Rolled neck and croup over, lay dead as a stone"; and there was only Roland to carry on. I asked myself, "Can he make it?"

After reading the entire poem, I went back and read just the parts that tell of Roland and his rider. These parts do give the story of how the good news was brought, but what a loss in effect there is! The suspense and the heroism are both diminished by the lack of contrast.

Who is the hero? Not the rider, though I gave him full credit. But the horse Roland! In a number of ways Browning focuses attention on him: it is Roland that is ridden by the teller of the story; it is "my stout galloper Roland" who with resolute shoulders butts away the haze; it was Roland who was left "to bear the whole weight of the news which alone could save Aix from her fate"; and it was Roland who galloped into Aix, was cheered, and rewarded. Altogether, Browning gives many more lines to Roland than to anything else in the poem.

Would an automobile, in which such a message might be carried today, be a hero? How, I asked myself, did Roland differ from any other possible conveyor of the man who carried the news? The poet gave the answer in "resolute shoulders" and more clearly in Stanza V:

> And his low head and crest, just one sharp ear bent back
> For my voice, and the other pricked out on his track;
> And one eye's black intelligence,—ever that glance
> O'er its white edge at me, his own master, askance!

Roland understood his responsibility; a mechanical instrument of course could not.

On reading the title of the poem my first impulse was to locate Ghent and Aix on a map and to measure the distance between them. But, I thought, the location of the towns is not important; the ride might have been made between Rome and Florence, Canterbury and London, or even Albany and New York. However, the distance *is* important; for there would be no heroism in galloping with a message, vital though it might be, three or ten miles. But suppose I found on a map that the distance is fifty or seventy or eighty-two miles between Ghent and Aix. Numbers above ten mean very little, except in a relative sense. Would there have been any significance if we had found the distance between the two towns to be 80.2 or 80.4 miles? Or even 80 or 100?

But it is important that I get an *impression* of distance, and this the poem certainly gives. How? I noted that the ride began at midnight, that after five towns had been passed the sun rose, that Roland then galloped on through four more towns before he reached Aix, probably in the late forenoon. That is distance! I tried naming in order eleven towns down the highway that runs past my home, and the last one seemed far, far away. Realizing the effect of the poet's skill in giving an *impression* of distance, I saw that there was no need to consult an atlas.

All through the poem Browning stimulated me to form vivid sense images. At the start I felt the chill of the night, and I saw a half moon hanging low in the sky. A watchman carried a lantern that cast weird shadows over the courtyard as he walked. I heard hoofs clattering over cobblestones and the squeak of withdrawn gate bolts. Having ridden horses, I could even feel between my knees Roland's moving strength as I, like the speaker, leaned to shorten the stirrups, which there had been no time for before the hurried departure.

At Lokeren I could hear the cocks crow, and at Boom the lines recalled "a great yellow star" that I had once seen just before the dawn. I heard a reminiscent church chime breaking the silence of the night. And at Aershot the poet created for me a striking picture of cattle standing black against a big rising sun and staring at us as we galloped through the mist that rose from the fields. The picture in the final stanza of the people flocking round the exhausted horse who lay with his head on his master's knees made me wish that I could paint it as Breughel might have done.

After thrilling at the story of the ride, appreciating the heroism of Roland, and enjoying the stimulated sense images, I went over the poem again to consider the skill of versification. What meter should be used to tell of a strenuous ride on horseback. I found myself recalling the rhythm of hoofbeats on a hard road that I had heard one still night: "plockety, plockety, plockety" it went, and that is just the general rhythm of the poem.*

But there is no monotony as there would be if Browning were giving an impression merely of a long uninterrupted gallop. The rhythm is varied to reflect the action, especially the failure of the

* A reader who knows music will be interested to compare the rhythm of Browning's poem, which represents a sustained gallop of horses, with that in Strauss's opera *Elektra*, when there is a mad rush of hoofs as the messenger rides away to carry to Aegisthus the news of Orestes' death.

two other horses. I noted, among other things, the strong accent on "sprang" in the first line and on "galloped" in the second; the three words "as some bluff" emphasizing the headland opposing the river; the light syllables giving the impression of the brittle stubble in Stanza VII; and the quiet return to the basic rhythm at the end.

It is in the narration of the failure of the two horses that the poet most skillfuly adapts the meter to the sense. Of Dirck's horse I read:

> For one heard the quick wheeze
> Of her chest, saw the stretched neck, and staggering knees,
> And sunk tail, and horrible heave of the flank,
> As down on her haunches she shuddered and sank.

But how differently the death of Joris' horse is told!

> And all in a moment his roan
> Rolled neck and croup over, lay dead as a stone.

Except in Alfred Noyes's "The Highwayman" I can recall no verse that so successfully as this tells of galloping horses, and I compared Browning's "Through the Metidja" and "The Last Ride Together," Scott's "Young Lochinvar Came Out of the West," Bret Harte's "Chiquita," Longfellow's "Paul Revere's Ride," Thomas Buchanan's "Sheridan's Last Ride," and Clinton Scollard's "Ride of Tench Tilghman."

Does Roland live? What happened next? No matter. The story of how the good news was brought is complete. Nothing more is desired, for the poem is a full unit; every detail contributes to the effect, and there is no excess. A good tale well told.

# Appendix C

# APPRECIATING MUSIC

### Chopin's *Marche Funèbre* (Opus 35)

THIS is a report by an amateur after hearing the music for the first time.

The mood of the music was created by the first somber chords. By the 4/4 time I knew it was a march, but a march of what kind? Certainly not of marionettes or of soldiers, human or wooden, and certainly not of joyous children. The heavy chords at once confirmed the title, a funeral march.

Then I asked myself "Whose funeral?" It could not be that of an infant or even of anyone intimately beloved, for there was no tenderness in the music, no tearing personal grief: the repeated chords suggested reverence and dignity, not poignancy. So, tentatively, I concluded that it was a funeral march for some great dignitary, a Pope or a mighty ruler, whom we might revere without personal affection.

Naturally I asked where the funeral was being held. The gloom of the music precluded the possibility that it was out-of-doors, the dignity that it was in a small chapel. So, again tentatively, I set it in a cathedral, with great space and groined arches overhead.

As the march developed a crescendo I imagined the cortege moving down the aisle to where I sat, and then the gradual diminuendo taking it to the high altar.

After a short interval something different was heard.

319

What did it signify? Physically it was a gleam of sunlight through a stained-glass window. Spiritually it was the hope of immortality expressed by the priest.

At the conclusion of what is technically called a "trio" the march was resumed and the cortege retraced its way up the aisle, the crescendo and diminuendo being repeated. But although the music was the same as in the first movement, it was different in effect, for the hope expressed in the middle section permeated the gloom and made the music solemn, but not a devastating sadness.

When I told a musical friend what the *Marche Funèbre* meant to me he said that Chopin composed it to express his emotions at the tragedy of his native land. I had to reply that this fact is interesting, but that, having no concern for Poland, I am interested in what the music means to me, what it made me feel. It is the greatness of art that its message is personal, that it can arouse in anyone emotions that are similar to, if not identical with, those that moved the artist to expression.

# Appendix D

## KEYS TO CHALLENGES

### I. Decorations of Diction, page 138.

**1**

From Elizabeth Barrett Browning, "Sonnets from the Portuguese," VIII. (1) princely; (2) purple; (3) unstained; (4) largesse; (5) ungrateful; (6) manifold; (7) render; (8) poor.

**2**

From Algernon Charles Swinburne, "The Garden of Proserpine." (1) brief; (2) forever; (3) weariest; (4) safe.

**3**

From Sidney Lanier, "The Marshes of Glynn." (1) shimmering; (2) fringe; (3) folds; (4) curl; (5) clings; (6) sweet.

### II. Onomatopoeia, pages 161–62.

| | | | |
|---|---|---|---|
| 1. drops | 3. puffs | 5. brooding | 7. fluttering |
| 2. crisping | 4. flitting | 6. whispered | 8. tumbled; oilily |

### III. Tropes, pages 236–37.

1. Than petals from blown roses on the grass.
2. Than tir'd eyelids upon tir'd eyes.      3. Than sleep.
4. As hair in leprosy.      5. As leprosy.
6. Of bugles going by.      7. As cream.
8. So the thought of you, remaining, deeply folded in my brain.

321

# Appendix E

## THE TEARS OF HARLEQUIN

### THEODOSIA GARRISON

To you he gave his laughter and his jest,
His words that of all words were merriest,
  His mad, glad moments when the lights flared high
And his wild song outshrilled the plaudits' din.
  For you the memory, but happier I—
I, who have known the tears of Harlequin.

Not mine those moments when the roses lay
Like red spilled wine on his triumphant way,
  And shouts acclaimed him through the music's beat,
Above the voice of flute and violin.
  But I have known his hour of sore defeat—
I—I have known the tears of Harlequin.

Light kisses and light words, they were not mine—
Poor perquisites of many a Columbine
  Bought with his laughter, flattered by his jest;
But when despair broke through the painted grin,
  His tortured face has fallen on my breast—
I— I who have known the tears of Harlequin.

You weep for him, who look upon him dead,
That joy and jest and merriment have fled;
  You weep for him, what time my eyes are dry,
Knowing what peace a weary soul may win
  Stifled by too much masking—even I—
I, who have known the tears of Harlequin.